DEVELOPING WEB PAGES WITH JQUERY

DON GOSSELIN

Course Technology PTR
A part of Cengage Learning

COURSE TECHNOLOGY
CENGAGE Learning·

Australia • Brazil • Japan • Korea • Mexico • Singapore • Spain • United Kingdom • United States

COURSE TECHNOLOGY
CENGAGE Learning·

Developing Web Pages with jQuery
Don Gosselin

Publisher and General Manager, Course Technology PTR:
Stacy L. Hiquet

Associate Director of Marketing:
Sarah Panella

Manager of Editorial Services:
Heather Talbot

Senior Marketing Manager:
Mark Hughes

Acquisitions Editor: Heather Hurley

Project Editor: Kezia Endsley

Technical Reviewer: David Gosselin

Copy Editor: Kezia Endsley

Interior Layout Tech: MPS Limited

Cover Designer: Mike Tanamachi

Indexer: Sharon Shock

Proofreader: Megan Belanger

For product information and technology assistance, contact us at
Cengage Learning Customer & Sales Support, 1-800-354-9706

For permission to use material from this text or product, submit all requests online at
www.cengage.com/permissions

Further permissions questions can be emailed to
permissionrequest@cengage.com

Library of Congress Control Number: 2012936597

ISBN-13: 978-1-4354-6079-9

ISBN-10: 1-4354-6079-0

Course Technology, a part of Cengage Learning

20 Channel Center Street

Boston, MA 02210

USA

Cengage Learning is a leading provider of customized learning solutions with office locations around the globe, including Singapore, the United Kingdom, Australia, Mexico, Brazil, and Japan. Locate your local office at: **international.cengage.com/region**

Cengage Learning products are represented in Canada by Nelson Education, Ltd.

For your lifelong learning solutions, visit **courseptr.com**

Visit our corporate website at **cengage.com**

Printed in the United States of America
1 2 3 4 5 6 7 14 13 12

I dedicate this book to my loving wife, Kathy, for always standing by me, in good times and bad.

ACKNOWLEDGMENTS

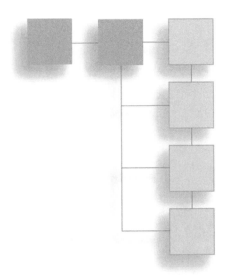

A text such as this represents the hard work of many people, not just the author. I would like to thank all the people who helped make this book a reality. First and foremost, I would like to thank Kezia Endsley, Project Editor, and Heather Hurley, Acquisitions Editor, for helping me get the job done.

Very special thanks to my brother and Technical Editor, David Gosselin, for keeping me honest, and not allowing me to write sloppy code.

On the personal side, I would like to thank my family and friends for supporting me in my career; I don't see many of you nearly as often as I'd like, but you are always in my thoughts. My most important thanks always go to my wonderful wife Kathy for her never-ending support and encouragement, and to Noah the wonder dog, my best (non-human) friend.

About the Author

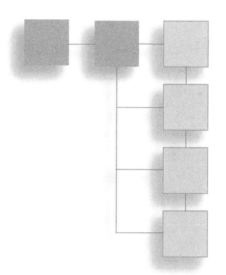

Don Gosselin is a technical communications expert with more than 25 years experience in industries that include education, finance, healthcare, information technology, insurance, and publishing. His extensive technology background includes application development, technical writing, management, training, and curriculum development. Don is also a prolific technical author, having written numerous reference works for various publishers and a dozen college-level textbooks on computer programming subjects for Course Technology/Cengage Learning/Thomson Learning.

Don's best-selling JavaScript textbook was the first textbook to be published on the JavaScript language. The book is currently in its fifth edition and continues to be the educational industry leader 12 years after its initial publication. Additionally, his textbook on PHP programming with MySQL currently holds the top sales position in academic publishing, and his textbook on ASP.NET programming with C# and SQL Server is currently in the top five best-selling sales textbooks within its class.

In addition to JavaScript, PHP, and ASP, Don has written or contributed to textbooks on Java programming with Microsoft J++, Microsoft Visual C++ 6 and .NET, web design technologies, web programming languages, and the principles of web page development with HTML, XHTML, and DHTML.

Don lives in Napa Valley and works at Oracle Corporation as a director of information development, responsible for identity management and security documentation in Oracle's Server Technologies division.

CONTENTS

INTRODUCTION

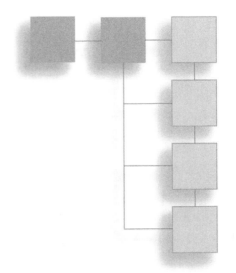

I began writing about JavaScript more than 12 years ago with the release of the first college-level textbooks on the subject, *JavaScript Introductory* and *JavaScript Comprehensive*, both published by Course Technology/Thomson Learning. JavaScript was first introduced in Navigator and was originally called LiveScript. With the release of Navigator 2.0, the name was changed to JavaScript 1.0. One of the reasons I was asked to write a textbook on JavaScript was because I had significant Java experience and had recently written a separate textbook on Java Programming with Visual J++. At the time, most people assumed that JavaScript was related to or was a simplified version of the Java programming language. However, although both languages derive from C, they are entirely different. Java is an advanced programming language that was created by Sun Microsystems and is considerably more difficult to master than JavaScript. Although Java can be used to create programs that can run from a web page, Java programs are usually external programs that execute independently of a browser. In contrast, JavaScript programs always run within a web page and control the browser.

As an object-oriented programming (OOP) language, one of the key capabilities of Java (and all other OOP languages) is to develop and use external code libraries through the use of classes and encapsulated objects. JavaScript is not a true object-oriented programming language. You can base objects in your programs on built-in JavaScript classes such as the `Array` and `Date` objects. However, you cannot create your own classes or encapsulated objects in JavaScript. For this reason, JavaScript is said to be an object-based programming language instead of an object-oriented programming language. Partly because of this limitation, until recent years no external code libraries existed that could be used to extend the JavaScript programming language. What this meant was that you were required to write all of your JavaScript solutions from scratch or dig through the many JavaScript reference sites available on the web. All of this changed with the creation of *jQuery*, which is a code library that simplifies the creation of JavaScript applications by providing access to prewritten code and examples. The jQuery library has grown so popular that over half of the 10,000 most-visited websites use jQuery, and its popularity is expected to continue growing. In fact, I firmly believe that it's only a matter of time before jQuery becomes part of the official JavaScript standard.

The Purpose of This Book

Developing Web Pages with jQuery explains how to use all major features of the jQuery library, including document traversing, event handling, animation, and the development of AJAX applications. Although you still need to understand the nuts and bolts of JavaScript in order to be successful with jQuery, what you learn in this book will significantly shorten your website development time and show you how to use the many terrific jQuery solutions with your web pages.

How This Book Is Organized

Developing Web Pages with jQuery is organized into 10 chapters that cover specific aspects of incorporating jQuery into your JavaScript programs. Chapter 1, "Getting Started with jQuery," introduces the features and benefits of jQuery, and then discusses some of the more important features of JavaScript, including how it relates to object-oriented programming. Chapter 2, "Using jQuery with JavaScript," explains how to add jQuery to your web pages and JavaScript programs, along with the basic techniques for accessing and manipulating elements and attributes on a web page. This is a critical chapter that sets the foundation for your success with jQuery. Chapter 3, "Manipulating CSS Properties with jQuery," discusses the basics of manipulating CSS with jQuery and how to dynamically position and control elements. Chapter 4, "Creating Animation and Visual Effects," introduces the basic concepts for using jQuery's animation techniques and visual effects, and Chapter 5, "Handling Events," explains how to use jQuery to handle events. Chapter 6, "Validating Forms with jQuery," shows how jQuery helps simplify form validation and manipulation by implementing various methods for use with form elements, including event registration methods and methods for validating and serializing form data. Chapter 7, "Updating Web Pages with AJAX," explains how to use jQuery to greatly simplify the incorporation of AJAX functionality into your web pages. Chapter 8, "Manipulating Web Page Content," introduces jQuery techniques for manipulating web content, including how to traverse and manipulate the elements in the XML Document Object Model (DOM). Chapter 9, "Extending jQuery with Plug-Ins," covers how to extend jQuery by using and developing plug-ins. Finally, Chapter 10, "Using the jQuery UI Library," goes a step further by explaining how to use and develop jQuery UI (user interface) plug-ins, which provide advanced animation, effects, and multimedia that JavaScript programmers can use to create web pages with dynamic and interactive functionality. In addition, you'll find three appendixes in the back of the book for your reference as you read and learn about jQuery.

THE TARGET AUDIENCE

This book is geared toward students and web professionals who have a solid understanding of how to work with JavaScript, HTML, and CSS.

SYSTEM REQUIREMENTS

To access jQuery, you can use any operating system that can run one of the following browsers that jQuery supports:

- Chrome 14.0.835
- Firefox 3.6
- Internet Explorer 6
- Opera 11
- Safari 3

To create JavaScript programs—or any type of web page—you must use a code-based HTML editor, such as Adobe Dreamweaver, or a text editor such as Notepad on Windows, GNU Emacs on UNIX/Linux, or SimpleText on the Macintosh.

Finally, you must also have a copy of the most recent jQuery source file, which you can download from http://jquery.com/download/.

CHAPTER 1

GETTING STARTED WITH jQUERY

Originally, people created web pages using *Hypertext Markup Language,* or *HTML,* which is a markup language used to create the web pages that appear on the World Wide Web. Web pages are also commonly referred to as *HTML pages* or *documents.* A *markup language* is a set of characters or symbols that defines a document's logical structure—that is, it specifies how a document should be printed or displayed. However, after the web grew beyond a small academic and scientific community, people began to recognize that greater interactivity and better visual design would make the web more useful. As commercial applications of the web grew, the demand for more interactive and visually appealing websites also grew.

A major drawback to the original version of HTML was that it could only be used to produce static documents. You can think of a static web page written in HTML as being approximately equivalent to a document created in a word-processing or desktop-publishing program; the only thing you can do with it is view it or print it. Thus, to respond to the demand for greater interactivity, an entirely new web programming language was needed. Netscape filled this need by developing JavaScript. *JavaScript* is a client-side scripting language that allows web page authors to develop interactive web pages and sites. However, JavaScript itself has a few shortcomings in that it does not include any prewritten code. To simplify the creation of web page development with JavaScript, the jQuery code library was born.

This starting chapter introduces the features and benefits of jQuery, and then discusses some of the more important features of JavaScript, including how it relates to object-oriented programming. Even if you have a solid understanding of how JavaScript and object-oriented programming work, be sure to spend a little time reviewing the sections in this chapter so that you understand the terms and technology used in this book.

WHAT IS JQUERY?

Since it was first released by Netscape in 1995, JavaScript has grown to become one of the most critical parts of web page design and authoring. This is because the JavaScript language is embedded (it "lives") within a web page's elements. In other words, the JavaScript code you write is usually placed within the elements that make up a web page. JavaScript can turn static documents into applications such as games or calculators. JavaScript code can change the contents of a web page after a browser has rendered it. It can also create visual effects such as animation, and it can control the web browser window itself. None of this was possible before the creation of JavaScript.

Originally designed for use in Navigator web browsers, JavaScript is now available in all other web browsers, including Firefox and Internet Explorer. The language is relatively easy to learn, allowing non-programmers to quickly incorporate JavaScript functionality into a web page. In fact, because it is used extensively in the countless web pages that are available on the World Wide Web, JavaScript is arguably the most widely used programming language in the world.

Caution

> Do not confuse "relatively easy to learn" with "easy to learn." Although not as involved as an advanced language such as Java or C++, JavaScript is nonetheless a programming language and much more complicated than simple HTML.

Note

> To be successful with this book, you should already have a solid knowledge of basic web development subjects including JavaScript, HTML, and CSS.

One shortcoming of JavaScript is that it is primarily a collection of programmatic functionality including functions, data types, operators, and control structures. Although JavaScript contains some simple functionality that requires no development, such as the `navigator.redirect()` function for redirecting a request to another web page, virtually no code solutions exist within the base JavaScript implementation that you can plug into your web pages. In other words, you need to write all code from scratch. For example, if you want to create animation, validate form data, manipulate page elements, or perform any other sort of interactivity, you must write the code yourself or find an example on the web that someone else wrote.

One of today's most popular solutions to this challenge was the creation of *jQuery*, which is a code library that simplifies the creation of JavaScript applications by providing access to prewritten code.

jQuery's Features and Benefits

The following sections describe some of the major JavaScript features that jQuery simplifies.

Cross-Browser Support

jQuery currently supports the following browser versions and higher:

- Chrome 14.0.835
- Firefox 3.6
- Internet Explorer 6
- Opera 11
- Safari 3

Caution

jQuery may work with older versions and other browsers such as Konqueror, although there are known problems. To be on the safe side, you should use one of the `jQuery.support` properties to ensure that the request is coming from one of the supported browsers. If not, you need to display a message warning the requestor that the browser is not supported. `jQuery.support` is described in Appendix A, "jQuery UI Reference."

CSS Manipulation

The term *Cascading Style Sheets (CSS)*, or *style sheets*, refers to a standard set by the W3C (World Wide Web Consortium) for managing web page formatting. Although the primary purpose of CSS is to format the display of a web page, you can use JavaScript and Dynamic HTML to modify CSS styles to make the document dynamic after a web browser renders the document. *Dynamic HTML (DHTML)* refers to a combination of technologies that make web pages dynamic. The term DHTML is actually a combination of JavaScript, HTML, CSS, and the Document Object Model.

Note

The *World Wide Web Consortium*, or *W3C*, was established in 1994 at MIT to oversee the development of web technology standards.

At the core of DHTML is the *Document Object Model,* or *DOM*, which represents the HTML or XML of a web page that is displayed in a browser. The Document Object Model that represents HTML content is referred to as the HTML DOM, and the Document Object Model that represents XML content is referred to as the XML DOM. Each element on a web page is represented in the DOM by its own object. The fact that each element is an object makes it possible for a Java-Script program to access individual elements on a web page and change them individually, without having to reload the page from the server. Although the individual technologies that make up DHTML have been accepted standards for some time, the implementation of DHTML has evolved slowly. One of the main delays in implementation has to do with the DOM. Earlier versions of Internet Explorer and Navigator included DOMs that were almost completely incompatible. This meant that you needed to write different JavaScript code sections for different browsers. At the time of this writing, Mozilla-based web browsers including Firefox and Internet Explorer 5.0 and higher are compatible with a standardized version of the DOM, called Level 3, which is recommended by the W3C.

Even if you write your JavaScript code so it conforms to the DOM Level 3, manipulating CSS can be tricky because you must first gain access to the styles by using the `getElementById()`, `getElementsByName()`, or `getElementsByTagName()` methods of the `Document` object. To simplify CSS manipulation, jQuery includes a number of functions that reduce the coding requirements for accessing and manipulating CSS elements.

Document Navigation and Traversal

In addition to its ability to manipulate an element's CSS styles, JavaScript can also be used to modify the elements themselves, including the displayed text, attributes, and placement of each element. You can also use JavaScript to copy, insert, and delete elements on a web page. The challenge with just using JavaScript to work with document elements is that you must use the `getElementById()`, `getElementsByName()`, or `getElementsByTagName()` methods of the `Document` object, along with some other methods and properties to manipulate document nodes. A *node* represents almost every item on a web page, including elements, text, attributes, and the entire document itself. jQuery simplifies the task of accessing and manipulating nodes with an assortment of methods that eliminate the need to call `getElementById()`, `getElementsByName()`, `getElementsByTagName()`, or any other methods and properties of the `Document` object.

Tip

For information on jQuery's document navigation and traversal techniques, see Chapter 2, "Using jQuery with JavaScript."

Event Handling

One of the primary ways in which JavaScript is executed on a web page is through events. An *event* is a specific circumstance (such as an action performed by a user, or an action performed by the browser) that is monitored by JavaScript and that your script can respond to in some way. You can use JavaScript events to allow users to interact with your web pages. The most common events are actions that users perform. For example, when a user clicks a form button, a click event is generated. You can think of an event as a trigger that fires specific JavaScript code in response to a given situation. User-generated events, however, are not the only kinds of events monitored by JavaScript. Events that are not direct results of user actions, such as the load event, are also monitored. The load event, which is triggered automatically by a web browser, occurs when a document finishes loading in a web browser.

Events are associated with HTML elements. The events that are available to an element vary. The click event, for example, is available for the `<a>` element and form controls created with the `<input>` element. In comparison, the `<body>` element does not have a click event, but it does have a load event, which occurs when a web page finishes loading, and an unload event, which occurs when a web page is unloaded.

When an event occurs, your script executes the code that responds to that particular event. Code that executes in response to a specific event is called an *event handler*. You include event handler code as an attribute of the element that initiates the event. For example, you can add to a `<button>` element a click attribute that is assigned some sort of JavaScript code, such as code that changes the color of some portion of a web page. The syntax of an event handler within an element is:

```
<element event_handler ="JavaScript code">
```

Event handler names are the same as the name of the event itself, plus a prefix of on. For example, the event handler for the click event is onclick, and the event handler for the load event is onload. The JavaScript code for an event handler, usually a function name, is contained within the quotation marks following the name of the JavaScript event handler.

jQuery simplifies the process of writing event code with prewritten methods for the most common event types. For example, the `click` event is handled in jQuery with `click()` event. The jQuery event methods primarily eliminate the requirement to include event handler code as an attribute of the element that initiates the event, although they contain other useful functionality such as the ability to execute events for specific elements on a page.

Animation and Visual Effects

By combining the `src` attribute of the `Image` object with the `setTimeout()` or `setInterval()` JavaScript methods, you can create simple animation on a web page. In this context, "animation" does not necessarily mean a complex cartoon character, but any situation in which a sequence of images changes automatically. For example, you may want to include an advertising image that changes automatically every few seconds. Or, you may want to use animation to change the ticking hands of an online analog clock (in which case each position of the clock hands would require a separate image).

With DHTML, you can use dynamic positioning to create traveling animation—that is, images that appear to travel across the screen. Typically, you would use the global `topPosition` and `leftPosition` variables to define the initial starting position of an image. Then, you would use the `setTimeout()` or `setInterval()` method to call a function that changes the position of the image, according to the specified amount of time. These same techniques can also be used for creating DHTML menus, such as expandable menus, navigation menus, and sliding menus. DHTML menus are most often used for organizing navigational links to other web pages, although they are also useful for displaying and hiding information.

jQuery simplifies animation and visual effects with methods such as `animate()`, which creates animation effects for numerous CSS properties, and the `slideUp()` and `slideToggle()` methods, which handle the sliding effects usually seen in DHTML menus. jQuery also includes other useful methods, such as `fadeIn()` and `fadeOut()`, which create a dynamic fading effect on the selected elements.

Tip

For information on jQuery's document navigation and traversal techniques, see Chapter 4, "Creating Animation and Visual Effects."

Plug-in Development

Web browsers display two basic types of media: text contained within HTML documents, and graphics such as Graphic Interchange Format (GIF) and Joint Photographic Experts Group (JPG) images. However, many other types of media are available, including word-processing documents, Adobe Acrobat files, audio, video, animation formats, and many others. To display and execute additional types of media on a web page, browsers use helper applications called *add-ons*. Add-on is a generic term; for example, some browsers support a specific type of add-on called *plug-ins*, which are external software components that display a particular type of media.

Developing add-ons with basic JavaScript is a major endeavor because you need to write the add-on according to a particular *framework*, which refers to a programming infrastructure for creating and running software components. One of the more popular frameworks is the *Netscape Plugin Application Programming Interface (NPAPI)*, which is supported by today's most popular browsers, with the exception of Internet Explorer. Although Internet Explorer supports plug-ins, it primarily uses *ActiveX controls* to execute embedded objects.

The challenge with developing plug-ins using NPAPI, ActiveX, or any other framework is that you need to understand the underlying programming technology to be successful. jQuery mitigates this problem by providing a framework that uses standard JavaScript programming techniques for developing and deploying plug-ins.

Tip

For information on developing plug-ins, see Chapter 9, "Extending jQuery with Plug-Ins."

Form Validation

Forms are one of the most common web page elements used with JavaScript. Typical forms you may encounter on the web include order forms, surveys, and applications. You use JavaScript to make sure that data was entered properly into the form fields and to perform other types of preprocessing before the data is sent to the server. Without JavaScript, the only action that a web page can take on form data is to send it to a server for processing.

JavaScript is often used with forms to validate or process form data before the data is submitted to a server-side script. For example, customers may use an online order form to order merchandise from your website. When customers click the form's Submit button, you need to make sure that their information, such as the shipping address and credit card number, is entered correctly. To use JavaScript to access form controls and verify form information, you use the Form object, which represents a form on a web page.

Using documentation navigation and traversal elements, along with some form-specific methods, jQuery simplifies the task of writing form validation code.

Tip

For information on validating forms, see Chapter 6, "Validating Forms with jQuery."

AJAX Development

Asynchronous JavaScript and XML (AJAX) refers to a combination of technologies that allows web pages displayed on a client computer to quickly interact and exchange data with a web server without reloading the entire web page. Although its name implies a combination of JavaScript and XML, AJAX primarily relies on JavaScript and HTTP requests to exchange data between a client computer and a web server. AJAX gets its name from the fact that XML is often the format used for exchanging data between a client computer and a web server (although it can also exchange data using standard text strings).

AJAX: A New Approach to Web Applications

The term AJAX was first used in an article written in 2005 by Jesse James Garrett, entitled "AJAX: A New Approach to Web Applications" (www.adaptivepath. com/publications/ essays/ archives/000385.php). The article discussed how Garrett's company, Adaptive Path, was using a combination of technologies, which they collectively referred to as AJAX, to add richness and responsiveness to web pages. Since then, AJAX has become hugely popular among JavaScript developers.

It's important to note that Garrett and Adaptive Path did not invent anything new. Rather, they improved web page interactivity by combining JavaScript, XML, XHTML, CSS, and the DOM with the key component of AJAX, the XMLHttpRequest object, which is available in modern web browsers. The XMLHttpRequest object uses HTTP to exchange data between a client computer and a web server. Unlike standard HTTP requests, which usually replace the entire page in a web browser, the XMLHttpRequest object can be used to request and receive data without reloading a web page. By combining the XMLHttpRequest object with DHTML techniques, you can update and modify individual portions of your web page with data received from a web server. The XMLHttpRequest object has been available in most modern web browsers since around 2001. However, Garrett's article was the first to clearly document the techniques for combining the XMLHttpRequest object with other techniques in order to exchange data between a client computer and a web server.

Using AJAX with JavaScript requires knowledge of both HTTP and a server-side scripting language. Most people don't realize that there is much more to HTTP than the processes of requesting and receiving a web page from a web server. HTTP client requests and server responses also include various HTTP messages, which you must manipulate with JavaScript when you use the XMLHttpRequest object.

To understand using AJAX and JavaScript requires strong knowledge of a server-side scripting language; you need to understand that the *same origin policy* restricts how JavaScript code in one window or frame accesses a web page in another window or frame on a client computer. For windows and frames to view and modify the elements and properties of documents displayed in other windows and frames, they must have the same protocol (such as HTTP) and exist on the same web server. Because JavaScript is the basis of AJAX programming, you cannot use the XMLHttpRequest object to directly access content on another domain's server; the data you request with the XMLHttpRequest object must be located on the web server where your JavaScript program is running.

In other words, you cannot directly bypass your own web server and grab data off someone else's web server. However, the same origin policy only applies to JavaScript and not to any other programs running on your web server. This means that you can use a server-side script as a proxy to access data from another domain. The term *proxy* refers to someone or something that acts or performs a request for another thing or person. The server-side proxy script can then return the data to the client computer as it is requested with the XMLHttpRequest object.

jQuery greatly simplifies the development of AJAX applications by removing the requirement to parse HTTP and for a server-side scripting language to act as a proxy for JavaScript. Essentially, the jQuery library becomes the proxy for JavaScript.

Tip

For information on validating forms, see Chapter 6, "Validating Forms with jQuery."

History of jQuery

jQuery is an open-source code library, developed under the MIT License and the GNU General Public License, Version 2, that simplifies the creation of JavaScript applications by providing access to prewritten code. *Open source* refers to software for which the source code can be freely used and modified. A draft version of the first jQuery implementation was first released in January 2006 by John Resig at a BarCamp NYC conference, with the official jQuery 1.0 version released in August 2006. Since then, numerous versions of the library have been released. At the time of this writing, the most recently available version of jQuery is 1.6.2, and is now the most popular JavaScript library in use today. According to Wikipedia as of July 2012, over half of the 10,000 most-visited websites use jQuery, and its popularity is expected to continue growing.

Note

BarCamp is an impromptu, unconventional conference where people gather in various cities around the world to discuss Internet technologies and development. You can find more information on BarCamp at www.barcamp.org.

Tip

You can find detailed information on the jQuery open-source project at www.jquery.org.

JAVASCRIPT AND OBJECT-ORIENTED PROGRAMMING

jQuery is essentially a large text file containing code that is written using custom JavaScript objects. As an open-source language, one of the primary benefits to the jQuery library is that it's extensible. In other words, you are free to modify—or improve it—as you see fit. In order to be successful with jQuery, it's helpful to understand JavaScript's approach to object-oriented programming, including how JavaScript differs from traditional object-oriented programming.

Reusing Software Objects

Libraries such as jQuery come from the concept of code reuse, which is one of the most important aspects of object-oriented programming languages such as Java or C++. *Object-oriented programming (OOP)* refers to the creation of reusable software objects that can be easily incorporated into multiple programs. The term *object* specifically refers to programming code and data that can be treated as an individual unit or component. (Objects are also called components.) The term *data* refers to information contained within variables or other types of storage structures. The procedures associated with an object are called *methods*, and the variables that are associated with an object are called *properties* or *attributes*.

Objects can range from simple controls such as a button, to entire programs such as a database application. In fact, some programs consist entirely of other objects. You'll often encounter objects that have been designed to perform a specific task. For example, in a retail sales program, you could refer to all of the code that calculates the sales total as a single object. You could then reuse that object in the same program just by typing the object name.

Popular object-oriented programming languages include C++, Java, and Visual Basic. Using any of these or other object-oriented languages, programmers can create objects themselves or use objects created by other programmers. For example, if you are creating an accounting program in Visual Basic, you can use an object named `Payroll` that was created in C++. The `Payroll` object may contain one method that calculates the amount of federal and state tax to deduct, another method that calculates the FICA amount to deduct, and so on. Properties of the `Payroll` object may include an employee's number of tax withholding allowances, federal and state tax percentages, and the cost of insurance premiums. You do not need to know how the `Payroll` object was created in C++, nor do you need to re-create it in Visual Basic. You only need to know how to access the methods and properties of the `Payroll` object from the Visual Basic program.

One way of understanding object-oriented programming is to compare it to how personal computers (PCs) are assembled. Many companies manufacturer PCs, but few build all of the components that go into a particular unit. Instead, computer manufacturers usually include components from other vendors. For example, there are many different brands of monitors, keyboards, mice, and so on. Even though different manufacturers build each of these hardware components, if they are designed for a PC, they all share common ways of attaching to the main computer. Monitors plug into standard monitor ports, keyboards plug into standard keyboard ports, mice plug into mouse ports, and so on. In fact, most of today's hardware components can plug into a Universal Serial Bus (USB) port, which is a standard interface for connecting computer hardware. Just as all hardware components can plug into the same PC, the software components of an object-oriented program can all "plug into" one application.

What Is Encapsulation?

Objects are *encapsulated*, which means that all code and required data are contained within the object itself. In most cases, an encapsulated object consists of a single computer file that contains all code and required data. Encapsulation places code inside what programmers like to call a black box; when an object is encapsulated, you cannot see "inside" it—all internal workings are hidden. The code (methods and statements) and data (variables and constants) contained in an encapsulated object are accessed through an interface. The term *interface* refers to the programmatic elements required for a source program to communicate with an object. For example, interface elements required to access a `Payroll` object might be a method named `calcNetPay()`, which calculates an employee's net pay, and properties containing the employee's name and pay rate.

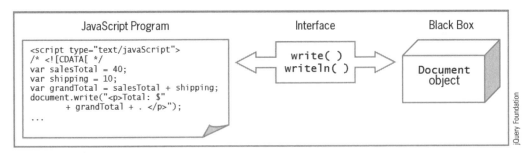

Figure 1.1
Conceptual example of the Document object black box

When you include encapsulated classes in your programs, users can see only the methods and properties of the object that you allow them to see. Essentially, the principle of *information hiding* states that any methods and properties that other programmers do not need to access or know about should be hidden. By removing the ability to see inside the black box, encapsulation reduces the complexity of the code, allowing programmers who use the code to concentrate on the task of integrating the code into their programs. Encapsulation also prevents other programmers from accidentally introducing a bug into a program, or from possibly even stealing the code and claiming it as their own.

In JavaScript, the `Document` object is encapsulated, making it a black box. The `write()` and `writeln()` methods are part of the interface that JavaScript can use to communicate with the `Document` object. Figure 1.1 illustrates the concept of a black box using JavaScript and the `Document` object.

Understanding Classes

In object-oriented programming, the code, methods, attributes, and other information that make up an object are organized into *classes*. Essentially, a class is a template, or blueprint, that serves as the basis for new objects. When you use an object in your program, you actually create an instance of the class of the object. An *instance* is an object that has been created from an existing class. When you create an object from an existing class, you are said to be *instantiating* the object.

As a conceptual example, consider an object named `BankAccount` that contains methods and properties that you might use to record transactions associated with a checking or savings account. The `BankAccount` object is created from a `BankAccount` class. To use the `BankAccount` class, you create an instance of the class. A particular instance of an object *inherits* its methods and properties from a class—that is, it takes on the characteristics of the class on which it is based. The `BankAccount` object, for instance, would inherit all of the methods and properties of the `BankAccount` class. To give another example, when you create a new word-processing document, which is a type of object, it usually inherits the properties of a template on which it is based. The template is a type of class. The document inherits characteristics of the template such as font size, line spacing, and boilerplate text. In the same manner, programs that include instances of objects inherit the object's functionality.

Because objects in the browser object model are actually part of the web browser, you do not need to instantiate them in order to use them in your programs. For example, you do not need to instantiate a `Document` object from the `Document` class in your JavaScript programs because the web browser automatically instantiates one for you. However, you do need to instantiate some objects from the built-in JavaScript classes, which you will study next.

Using Built-In JavaScript Classes

The JavaScript language includes the 11 built-in classes listed in Table 1.1. Each object contains various methods and properties for performing a particular type of task.

Table 1.1 Built-in JavaScript Classes

Class	Description
Array	Creates new array objects.
Boolean	Creates new Boolean objects.
Date	Retrieves and manipulates dates and times.
Error	Returns runtime error information.
Function	Creates new function objects.
Global	Stores global variables and contains various built-in JavaScript functions.
Math	Contains methods and properties for performing mathematical calculations.
Number	Contains methods and properties for manipulating numbers.
Object	Represents the base class for all built-in JavaScript classes; contains several of the built-in JavaScript functions.
RegExp	Contains methods and properties for finding and replacing characters in text strings.
String	Contains methods and properties for manipulating text strings.

Instantiating an Object

You can use some of the built-in JavaScript objects directly in your code, while other objects require you to instantiate a new object. The Math object is one that you can use directly in your programs without instantiating a new object. The following example shows how to use the Math object's PI (π) property in a script:

```
<script type="text/javascript">
// The following statement prints 3.141592653589793
document.write("The value of pi is " + Math.PI);
</script>
```

Unlike the Math object, an Array object requires you to instantiate a new object before you can use it. Arrays are represented in JavaScript by the Array object, which contains a constructor named Array(). A *constructor* is a special type of function that is used as the basis for creating a new object. You create new arrays in your code using the new keyword and the Array() constructor. The following statement shows an example of how to instantiate an array named deptHeads:

```
var deptHeads = new Array();
```

You may be wondering why the preceding statement instantiates the new object using the var keyword. As you should know, the var keyword is used for declaring variables. The name you use for an instantiated object is really a variable just like an integer or string variable. In fact, programmers use the terms "variable" and "object" interchangeably. The difference is that the data the variable represents happens to be an object instead of a number or string. In addition to variables, which are the values a program stores in computer memory, the JavaScript language also supports reference data types, which can contain multiple values or complex types of information, as opposed to the single values stored in primitive data types. In other words, in the same manner that you use a variable name to represent a primitive data type, such as an integer, in computer memory, you also use a variable name to represent an object. Because the objects you declare in your JavaScript program are actually a certain type of variable, you can use the var keyword to identify them as variables. You are not required to use the var keyword when declaring any variables or objects in your programs; however, it is good practice always to do so.

Note

JavaScript is not a true object-oriented programming language. You can base objects in your programs on built-in JavaScript classes such as the Array and Date objects. However, you cannot create your own classes in JavaScript. For this reason, JavaScript is said to be an object-based programming language instead of an object-oriented programming language.

Performing Garbage Collection

If you have worked with other object-oriented programming languages, you may be familiar with the term *garbage collection*, which refers to cleaning up, or reclaiming, memory that is reserved by a program. When you declare a variable or instantiate a new object, you are actually reserving computer memory for the variable or object. With some programming languages, you must write code that deletes a variable or object after you are through with it in order to free the memory for use by other parts of your program or by other programs running on your computer. With JavaScript, you do not need to worry about reclaiming memory that is reserved for your variables or objects; JavaScript knows when your program no longer needs a variable or object and automatically cleans up the memory for you.

Manipulating the Date and Time with the Date Class

You can use dates in your programs to create a calendar, calculate how long it will take to do something, and so on. For instance, a web page for a dry cleaning business may need to use the current date to calculate when a customer's dry cleaning order will be ready. The Date class contains methods and properties for manipulating the date and time. The Date class allows you to use the current date and time (or a specific date or time element, such as the current month) in your JavaScript programs. You create a Date object with one of the constructors listed in Table 1.2.

The following statement demonstrates how to create a Date object that contains the current date and time from the local computer:

```
var today = new Date();
```

The dates of the month and year in a Date object are stored using numbers that match the actual date and year. However, the days of the week and months of the

Table 1.2 Date Class Constructors

Constructor	Description
Date()	Creates a Date object that contains the current date and time from the local computer.
Date(*milliseconds*)	Creates a Date object based on the number of milliseconds that have elapsed since midnight, January 1, 1970.
Date(*date_string*)	Creates a Date object based on a string containing a date value.
Date(*year, month[, date, hours, minutes, seconds, milliseconds]*)	Creates a Date object with the date and time set according to the passed arguments; the year and month arguments are required.

year are stored in a `Date` object using numeric representations, starting with zero, similar to an array. The numbers 0 through 6 represent the days Sunday through Saturday, and the numbers 0 through 11 represent the months January through December. The following statement demonstrates how to specify a specific date with a `Date` constructor function. In this example, the date assigned to the `independenceDay` variable is July 4, 1776.

```
var independenceDay = new Date(1776, 3, 4);
```

After you create a new `Date` object, you can manipulate the date and time in the variable, using the methods of the `Date` class. Note that the date and time in a `Date` object are not updated over time like a clock. Instead, a `Date` object contains the static (unchanging) date and time as of the moment the JavaScript code instantiates the object.

Table 1.3 lists commonly used methods of the `Date` class.

Note
_____

The `Date` class does not contain any properties.

_____

Each portion of a `Date` object, such as the day, month, year, and so on, can be retrieved and modified using the `Date` object methods. For example, if you create a new `Date` object using the statement `var curDate = new Date();`, you can retrieve just the date portion stored in the `curDate` object by using the statement `curDate.getDate();`.

Tip
_____

Chapter 9, "Extending jQuery with Plug-Ins" contains a detailed example of how to use the `Date` class.

_____

Manipulating Numbers with the Number Class

The `Number` class contains methods for manipulating numbers and properties that contain static values representing some of the numeric limitations in the JavaScript language (such as the largest positive number that can be used in JavaScript). Although you can create a `Number` object using a statement similar to `var myNum = new Number();`, you are not required to do so. Instead, you can simply append the name of any `Number` class method or property to the name of an existing variable that contains a numeric value.

Table 1.3 Commonly Used Methods of the Date Class

Method	Description
getDate()	Returns the date of a Date object.
getDay()	Returns the day of a Date object.
getFullYear()	Returns the year of a Date object in four-digit format.
getHours()	Returns the hour of a Date object.
getMilliseconds()	Returns the milliseconds of a Date object.
getMinutes()	Returns the minutes of a Date object.
getMonth()	Returns the month of a Date object.
getSeconds()	Returns the seconds of a Date object.
getTime()	Returns the time of a Date object.
setDate(date)	Sets the date (1–31) of a Date object.
setFullYear(year [, month, day])	Sets the four-digit year of a Date object; optionally allows you to set the month and the day.
setHours(hours[, minutes, seconds, milliseconds)	Sets the hours (0–23) of a Date object; optionally allows you to set the minutes (0–59), seconds (0–59), and milliseconds (0–999).
setMilliseconds (milliseconds)	Sets the milliseconds (0–999) of a Date object.
setMinutes(minutes [, seconds, milliseconds])	Sets the minutes (0–59) of a Date object; optionally allows you to set seconds (0–59) and milliseconds (0–999).
setMonth(month[, date])	Sets the month (0–11) of a Date object; optionally allows you to set the date (1–31).
setSeconds(seconds [, milliseconds])	Sets the seconds (0–59) of a Date object; optionally allows you to set milliseconds (0–999).
toLocaleString()	Converts a Date object to a string, set to the current time zone.
toString()	Converts a Date object to a string.
valueOf()	Converts a Date object to a millisecond format.

Table 1.4 lists the methods of the Number class.

The primary reason for using any of the to methods listed in Table 1.4 is to convert a number to a string value with a specific number of decimal places that will be displayed to the users. If you don't need to display the number for a user, there is no

Table 1.4 Number Class Methods

Method	Description
Number()	Number object constructor.
toExponential(*decimals*)	Converts a number to a string in exponential notation using a specified number of decimal places.
toFixed(*decimals*)	Converts a number to a string with a specified number of decimal places.
toLocaleString()	Converts a number to a string that is formatted with local numeric formatting conventions.
toPrecision(*decimals*)	Converts a number to a string with a specific number of decimal places, in exponential or fixed notation.
toString(*radix*)	Converts a number to a string using a specified radix.
valueOf()	Returns the numeric value of a Number object.

need to use any of the methods. The most useful Number class method is the toFixed() method, which you can use to display a numeric value with a specified number of decimal places. For example, you may have a number in your program that represents a dollar value. However, depending on the result of a calculation or a value entered by a user, the number may contain more than the two decimal places that are acceptable in a currency value.

The following code shows a simple example of a numeric variable named salesTotal that is assigned a value of 49.95. If you apply a discount of 10% to the variable, the new number is equal to 44.995. Before displaying the value, the write() statement uses the toFixed() method to convert the value of the salesTotal variable to a string containing two decimal places.

```
var salesTotal = 49.95;
var discount = salesTotal * .1;
salesTotal -= discount; // new value is 44.955
document.write("$" + salesTotal.toFixed(2)); // displays $44.96
```

Another useful Number class method is toLocaleString(), which you can use to convert a number to a string that is formatted with local numeric formatting conventions. For example, with American numeric formatting conventions, you separate thousands with a comma. The following statements demonstrate how to convert the number 1210349 to the string $1,210,349:

```
var salesTotal = 1210349;
```

```
salesTotal = salesTotal.toLocaleString();
document.write("$" + salesTotal); // displays $1,210,349
```

Note

Firefox displays the number in the preceding code without decimal places ($1,210,349), whereas Internet Explorer displays it with decimal places ($1,210,349.00).

By default, Internet Explorer displays two decimal places for numbers that are converted with the `toLocaleString()` method, whereas Firefox displays it as a whole number. To convert a numeric value to a specified number of decimal places and to a local string is not intuitive in Firefox. First, you call the `toFixed()` method, which converts the number to a string with the specified number of decimals. Then, because it's a string, you need to convert it back to floating-point number with the `parseFloat()` function. Finally, you call the `toLocaleString()` method to convert the number to a string that is formatted with the local numeric formatting conventions. The following code converts the number 1210349.4567 to the string $1,210,349.46:

```
var salesTotal = 1210349.4567;
salesTotal = salesTotal.toFixed(2);
salesTotal = parseFloat(salesTotal);
salesTotal = salesTotal.toLocaleString();
document.write("$" + salesTotal); // displays $1,210,349.46
```

Although Internet Explorer will successfully display decimal places for numbers that are converted with the `toLocaleString()` method, you should use the `toFixed()` and `parseFloat()` methods to ensure that code that uses the `toLocaleString()` method is compatible with Internet Explorer and Firefox.

Table 1.5 lists the properties of the `Number` class. Note that there is little reason for you to use these properties. However, they are listed here for the sake of completeness.

Table 1.5 Number Class Properties

Property	Description
MAX_VALUE	The largest positive number that can be used in JavaScript.
MIN_VALUE	The smallest positive number that can be used in JavaScript.
NaN	The value NaN, which stands for "not a number".
NEGATIVE_INFINITY	The value of negative infinity.
POSITIVE_INFINITY	The value of positive infinity.

Performing Math Functions with the Math Class

Table 1.6 lists the methods of the Math class.

Unlike the Array, Date, and Number classes, the Math class does not contain a constructor. This means that you cannot instantiate a Math object using a statement such as var mathCalc = new Math(). Instead, you use the Math object and one of its methods or properties directly in your code. For example, the sqrt() method returns the square root of a number. The following code shows how to use the sqrt() method to determine the square root of 144:

```
var curNumber = 144;
squareRoot = Math.sqrt(curNumber); // returns '12'
document.write("The square root of " + curNumber + " is " + squareRoot);
```

Table 1.7 lists the properties of the Math class.

Table 1.6 Math Class Methods

Method	Description
abs(x)	Returns the absolute value of x.
acos(x)	Returns the arc cosine of x.
asin(x)	Returns the arc sine of x.
atan(x)	Returns the arc tangent of x.
atan2(x,y)	Returns the angle from the x-axis.
ceil(x)	Returns the value of x rounded to the next highest integer.
cos(x)	Returns the cosine of x.
exp(x)	Returns the exponent of x.
floor(x)	Returns the value of x rounded to the next lowest integer.
log(x)	Returns the natural logarithm of x.
max(x,y)	Returns the larger of two numbers.
min(x,y)	Returns the smaller of two numbers.
pow(x,y)	Returns the value of x raised to the y power.
random()	Returns a random number.
round(x)	Returns the value of x rounded to the nearest integer.
sin(x)	Returns the sine of x.
sqrt(x)	Returns the square root of x.
tan(x)	Returns the tangent of x.

Table 1.7 Math Class Properties

Property	Description
E	Euler's constant e, which is the base of a natural logarithm; this value is approximately 2.7182818284590452354.
LN10	The natural logarithm of 10, which is approximately 2.302585092994046.
LN2	The natural logarithm of 2, which is approximately 0.6931471805599453.
LOG10E	The base-10 logarithm of e, the base of the natural logarithms; this value is approximately 0.4342944819032518.
LOG2E	The base-2 logarithm of e, the base of the natural logarithms; this value is approximately 1.4426950408889634.
PI	A constant representing the ratio of the circumference of a circle to its diameter, which is approximately 3.1415926535897932.
SQRT1_2	The square root of 1/2, which is approximately 0.7071067811865476.
SQRT2	The square root of 2, which is approximately 1.4142135623730951.

As an example of how to use the properties of the Math object, the following code shows how to use the PI property to calculate the area of a circle based on its radius. The code also uses the round() method to round the value returned to the nearest whole number.

```
var radius = 25;
var area = Math.round(Math.PI * radius * radius); // return 1963
document.write("A circle with a radius of " + radius
   + " has an area of " + area);
```

UNDERSTANDING THE BROWSER OBJECT MODEL

The *browser object model* (BOM) (or *client-side object model*) is a hierarchy of objects, each of which provides programmatic access to a different aspect of the web browser window or the web page. You can use the methods and properties of objects in the browser object model to manipulate the window and elements displayed in a web browser. The most basic objects in the browser object model are illustrated in Figure 1.2.

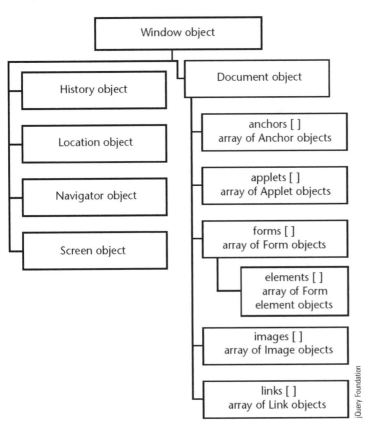

Figure 1.2
The browser object model (BOM)

Note

The browser object model is also called the JavaScript object model or the `Navigator` object model. However, other scripting technologies, such as VBScript, can also control aspects of the web browser window or web page. Therefore, the term "browser object model" or "client-side object model" is more accurate.

You do not have to create any of the objects or arrays explicitly in the browser object model; they are created automatically when a web browser opens a web page. The top-level object in the browser object model is the *Window object*, which represents a web browser window. The web browser automatically creates the `Window` object for you. The `Window` object is called the *global object* because all other objects in the browser object model are contained within it. For example, the `Window` object contains the `Document` object, just as a web browser window contains a web page document. You use the methods and properties of the `Window` object to control the web browser window, whereas you use the methods and properties of the `Document` object to control the web page.

Tip

In this book, objects in the browser object model are referred to with an initial uppercase letter (Document object). However, when you use the object name in code, you must always use a lowercase letter. For example, the following statement refers to the Document object: `document.write("Go Patriots!");`. Note the use of the lowercase d in `document`.

Working with the HTML Document Object Model

The Document object is arguably the most important object in the browser object model because it represents the web page displayed in a browser. All elements on a web page are contained within the Document object, and each element is represented in JavaScript by its own object. The Document Object Model that represents HTML content is referred to as the HTML DOM, and the Document Object Model that represents XML content is referred to as the XML DOM. So which should you use? The W3C formally recommends using the XML DOM instead of the HTML DOM. Nonetheless, it's easier to use the HTML DOM, so the majority of this book focuses on HTML DOM techniques. Keep in mind, however, that you must use the XML DOM when using some advanced JavaScript techniques, such as AJAX, which is discussed in Chapter 7, and manipulating web page content with jQuery, which is covered in Chapter 6.

Tip

For a complete listing of objects in the HTML DOM, see the W3Schools' HTML DOM reference at http://w3schools.com/htmldom/dom_reference.asp.

Next, you will spend a little time studying more of the Document object's properties and methods.

HTML DOM Document Object Methods

The Document object contains several methods for dynamically generating web pages and manipulating elements. Table 1.8 lists the methods of the Document object that are specified in the WC3 DOM.

HTML DOM Document Object Properties

The HTML DOM Document object contains various properties used for manipulating web page objects. Table 1.9 lists the properties of the Document object that are specified in the WC3 DOM.

The only property you can dynamically change after a web page is rendered is the title property, which allows you to change the title of the document that is

Table 1.8 HTML DOM Document Object Methods

Method	Description
close()	Closes a new document that was created with the open() method.
getElementById(ID)	Returns the element represented by ID.
getElementsByName(name)	Returns a collection of elements represented by name.
getElementsByTagName (tag name)	Returns a collection of elements represented by tag name.
open()	Opens a new document in a window or frame.
write(text)	Writes new text to a document.
writeln(text)	Writes new text to a document, followed by a line break.

Table 1.9 HTML DOM Document Object Properties

Property	Description
anchors[]	Returns an array of the document's anchor elements.
Body	Returns the document's <body> or <frameset> element.
Cookie	Returns the current document's cookie string, which contains small pieces of information about a user that are stored by a web server in text files on the user's computer.
Domain	Returns the domain name of the server where the current document is located.
forms[]	Returns an array of the document's forms.
images[]	Returns an array of the document's images.
links[]	Returns an array of a document's links.
Referrer	Returns the Uniform Resource Locator (URL) of the document that provided a link to the current document.
Title	Returns or sets the title of the document as specified by the <title> element in the document <head> section.
URL	Returns the URL of the current document.

specified by the `<title>` element in the document `<head>` section. For example, you can use the following statement to change the text displayed in the title bar after the web page is rendered:

```
document.title = "Pete's Pizzeria Home Page";
```

Opening and Closing the Document Object

Although the `Document` object's `write()`and `writeln()` methods are part of the DOM, they cannot be used to change the content after a web page has been rendered. You can write code that executes the `write()` and `writeln()` methods in the current document after it is rendered, but they replace the content that is currently displayed in the web browser window.

You can, however, use the *open() method* to create a new document in a window or frame and then use the `write()` and `writeln()` methods to add content to the new document. The *close() method* notifies the web browser that you are finished writing to the window or frame and that the document should be displayed. Although later versions of Internet Explorer and Netscape do not require you to use the `open()` and `close()` methods with the `write()` and `writeln()` methods, some older browsers do not display any content in the window until you execute the `close()` method. In addition, some browsers, including Firefox, do not stop the spinning icon in the browser's upper-right corner that indicates a document is loading until the `close()` method executes. Because Firefox is the most widely used browser, you should always use the `open()` and `close()` methods when dynamically creating document content.

You should always use the `open()` and `close()` methods when you want to use the `write()` and `writeln()` methods to update the text displayed in an existing window or frame. Specifically, if you do not use the `close()` method to notify the web browser that you are finished writing to the window or frame, any new calls to the `write()` and `writeln()` methods are appended to the existing text that is currently displayed in the window or frame.

Referencing JavaScript Objects

Some of the objects in the browser object model represent arrays. In Figure 1.2, those objects that are arrays are followed by brackets, such as `forms[]` and `images[]`. The arrays contain objects created from the corresponding elements on a web page. For example, the `images[]` array contains `Image` objects that represent all the `<img>` elements on a web page. `Image` objects for each `<img>` element are assigned to the elements of the `images[]` array in the order that they appear on the web page. The first `Image` object is represented by `images[0]`, the second `Image` object is represented by `images[1]`, and so on.

You can use JavaScript to reference any element on a web page by using periods to append the element's name to the name of any elements in which it is nested, starting with the `Document` object. For elements that are represented by arrays, you can reference the object through the array instead of with the element name. Consider an `Image` object, which contains a `src` property that contains the URL assigned to an `<img>` element's `src` attribute. Assuming that the image is assigned a name of `companyLogo`, you use the following code to display the image's URL in an alert dialog box:

```
<img src="company_logo.gif" name="companyLogo" height="100" width="200"
    onclick="window.alert ('This image is located at the following URL: '↵
        (+ document.companyLogo.src);" alt="Image of a company logo." />
```

Instead of referencing the image by name, you can access it through the `images[]` array. The following `<img>` element includes an `onclick` event handler that uses the `Document` object to display the image's URL in an alert dialog box. The code assumes the image is the first image on the page by referencing the first element (0) in the `images[]` array.

```
<img src="company_logo.gif" height="100" width="200"
    onclick="window.alert ('This image is located at the following URL: '↵
        (+ document.images[0].src);" alt="Image of a company logo." />
```

Manipulating the Browser with the Window Object

The `Window` object includes several properties that contain information about the web browser window. For instance, the `status` property contains information displayed in a web browser's status bar. Also contained in the `Window` object are various methods that allow you to manipulate the web browser window itself. You have already used some methods of the `Window` object, including the `window.alert()`, `window.confirm()`, and `window.prompt()` methods, which all display dialog boxes. Table 1.10 lists the `Window` object properties, and Table 1.11 lists the `Window` object methods.

Note

Some web browsers, including Internet Explorer, have custom properties and methods for the `Window` object. This book describes only the properties and methods that are common to browser objects in all current web browsers.

Table 1.10 Window Object Properties

Property	Description
Closed	Returns a Boolean value that indicates whether a window has been closed.
defaultStatus	Sets the default text that is written to the status bar.
Document	Returns a reference to the Document object.
History	Returns a reference to the History object.
Location	Returns a reference to the Location object.
Name	Returns the name of the window.
Opener	Refers to the window that opened the current window.
Parent	Refer to a frame within the same frameset.
Self	Returns a self-reference to the Window object; identical to the window property.
Status	Specifies temporary text that is written to the status bar.
Top	Returns the topmost Window object.
Window	Returns a self-reference to the Window object; identical to the self property.

Opening a Window

Most web browsers allow you to open new web browser windows in addition to the web browser window or windows that may already be open. There are several reasons why you may need to open a new web browser window. You may want to launch a new web page in a separate window, allowing users to continue viewing the current page in the current window. Or, you may want to use an additional window to display information such as a picture or an order form.

Whenever a new web browser window is opened, a new Window object is created to represent the new window. You can have as many web browser windows open as your system will support, each displaying a different web page. For example, you can have one web browser window display Microsoft's website, another web browser window display Firefox's website, and so on.

To open new windows, you use the open() method of the Window object. The syntax for the open() method is as follows:

```
window.open(url, name, options, replace);
```

Table 1.11   Window Object Methods

Method	Description
`alert()`	Displays a simple message dialog box with an OK button.
`blur()`	Removes focus from a window.
`clearInterval()`	Cancels an interval that was set with `setInterval()`.
`clearTimeout()`	Cancels a timeout that was set with `setTimeout()`.
`close()`	Closes a web browser window.
`confirm()`	Displays a confirmation dialog box with the OK and Cancel buttons.
`focus()`	Makes a `Window` object the active window.
`moveBy()`	Moves the window relative to the current position.
`moveTo()`	Moves the window to an absolute position.
`open()`	Opens a new web browser window.
`print()`	Prints the document displayed in the current window.
`prompt()`	Displays a dialog box prompting a user to enter information.
`resizeBy()`	Resizes a window by a specified amount.
`resizeTo()`	Resizes a window to a specified size.
`scrollBy()`	Scrolls the window by a specified amount.
`scrollTo()`	Scrolls the window to a specified position.
`setInterval()`	Repeatedly executes a function after a specified number of milliseconds have elapsed.
`setTimeout()`	Executes a function once after a specified number of milliseconds have elapsed.

Table 1.12 lists the arguments of the `window.open()` method.

You can include all or none of the `window.open()` method arguments. The statement `window.open("http://www.wikipedia.org");` opens the Wikipedia home page in a new web browser window. If you exclude the URL argument, a blank web page opens.

Table 1.12   Arguments of the Window Object's open() Method

Argument	Description
URL	Represents the web address or filename to be opened.
Name	Assigns a value to the name property of the new Window object.
Options	Represents a string that allows you to customize the new web browser window's appearance.
Replace	A Boolean value that determines whether the URL should create a new entry in the web browser's history list or replace the entry.

Caution

If a user clicks a link or a button, you can use an event handler to call the window.open() method, and the window will open successfully. However, if you include JavaScript code in a web page that opens a new window without a request from the user, the pop-up blocker feature that is available in most current web browsers will prevent the window from opening.

When you open a new web browser window, you can customize its appearance by using the options argument of the window.open() method. Table 1.13 lists some common options that you can use with the window.open() method.

Table 1.13   Common Options of the Window Object's open() Method

Name	Description
height	Sets the window's height.
left	Sets the horizontal coordinate of the left of the window, in pixels.
location	Includes the URL Location text box.
menubar	Includes the menu bar.
resizable	Determines whether the new window can be resized.
scrollbars	Includes scroll bars.
status	Includes the status bar.
toolbar	Includes the Standard toolbar.
top	Sets the vertical coordinate of the top of the window, in pixels.
width	Sets the window's width.

All the options listed in Table 1.13, with the exception of the `width` and `height` options, are set using values of `yes` or `no`, or 1 for yes and 0 for no. To include the status bar, the options string should read `"status=yes"`. You set the `width` and `height` options using integers representing pixels. For example, to create a new window that is 200 pixels high by 300 pixels wide, the string should read `"height=200,width=300"`. When including multiple items in the options string, you must separate the items by commas. If you exclude the options string of the `window.open()` method, all the standard options are included in the new web browser window. However, if you include the options string, you must include all the components you want to create for the new window; that is, the new window is created with only the components you explicitly specify.

The `name` argument of the `window.open()` method specifies the name of the window where the URL should open. If the `name` argument is already in use by another web browser window, JavaScript changes focus to the existing web browser window instead of creating a new window. A `Window` object's `name` property can be used only to specify a target window with a link and cannot be used in JavaScript code. If you want to control the new window by using JavaScript code located within the web browser in which it was *created*, you must assign the new `Window` object created with the `window.open()` method to a variable. You can use any of the properties and methods of the `Window` object with a variable that represents a `Window` object.

Closing a Window

The `close()` method, which closes a web browser window, is the method you will probably use the most with variables representing other `Window` objects. To close a web browser window represented by the `OpenWin` variable, you use the statement `OpenWin.close();`. To close the current window, you use the statement `window.close()` or `self.close()`.

Caution

It is not necessary to include the `Window` object when using the `open()` and `close()` methods of the `Window` object. However, the `Document` object also contains methods named `open()` and `close()`, which are used for opening and closing web pages. Therefore, the `Window` object is usually included with the `open()` and `close()` methods, in order to distinguish between the `Window` object and the `Document` object.

Working with the History, Location, Navigator, and Screen Objects

In this section, you learn how to work with the History, Location, and Navigator, and Screen objects.

The History Object

The History object maintains an internal list (known as a history list) of all the documents that have been opened during the current web browser session. Each web browser window contains its own internal History object. You cannot view the URLs contained in the history list, but you can write a script that uses the history list to navigate to web pages that have been opened during a web browser session.

An important security feature associated with the History object is that it will not actually display the URLs contained in the history list. This is important because individual user information in a web browser, such as the types of websites a user likes to visit, is private. Preventing others from viewing the URLs in a History list is an essential security feature because it keeps people's likes and interests (as evidenced by the types of websites a person visits) confidential.

The History object includes three methods, listed in Table 1.14.

When you use a method or property of the History object, you must include a reference to the History object itself. For example, the back() and forward() methods allow a script to move backward or forward in a web browser's history. To use the back() method, you must use the following: history.back().

The go() method is used for navigating to a specific web page that has been previously visited. The argument of the go() method is an integer that indicates how many pages in the history list, forward or backward, you want to navigate. For example, history.go(-2); opens the web page that is two pages back in the history list; the statement history.go(3); opens the web page that is three pages forward in

Table 1.14 Methods of the History Object

Method	Description
back()	Produces the same result as clicking a web browser's Back button.
forward()	Produces the same result as clicking a web browser's Forward button.
go()	Opens a specific document in the history list.

the history list. The statement `history.go(-1);` is equivalent to using the `back()` method, and the statement `history.go(1);` is equivalent to using the `forward()` method.

The `History` object contains a single property, the `length` property, which contains the specific number of documents that have been opened during the current browser session. To use the `length` property, you use the syntax `history.length;`. The `length` property does not contain the URLs of the documents themselves, only an integer representing how many documents have been opened. The following code uses an alert dialog box to display the number of web pages that have been visited during a web browser session:

```
window.alert("You have visited " + history.length + " web pages.");
```

The `History` object is included in this chapter in order to introduce you to all of the major objects in the browser object model. However, you should avoid using the `History` object to navigate to web pages that have been opened during a web browser session. Instead, you should use the full URL with the `href` property of the `Location` object, as explained in the next section.

The Location Object

When you want to allow users to open one web page from within another web page, you usually create a hypertext link with the `<a>` element. You can also use JavaScript code and the `Location` object to open web pages. The `Location` object allows you to change to a new web page from within JavaScript code. One reason you may want to change web pages with JavaScript code is to redirect your website visitors to a different or updated URL. The `Location` object contains several properties and methods for working with the URL of the document currently open in a web browser window. When you use a method or property of the `Location` object, you must include a reference to the `Location` object itself. For example, to use the `href` property, you must write `location.href = URL;`. Table 1.15 lists the `Location` object's properties, and Table 1.16 lists the `Location` object's methods.

The properties of the `Location` object allow you to modify individual portions of a URL. When you modify any properties of the `Location` object, you generate a new URL, and the web browser automatically attempts to open that new URL. Instead of modifying individual portions of a URL, it is usually easier to change the `href` property, which represents the entire URL. For example, the statement `location.href = "http://www.google.com";` opens the Google home page.

The `assign()` method of the `Location` object performs the same action as changing the `href` property: It loads a new web page. The statement `location.assign`

Table 1.15 Properties of the Location Object

Properties	Description
hash	A URL's anchor.
host	The host and domain name (or IP address) of a network host.
hostname	A combination of the URL's host name and port sections.
href	The full URL address.
pathname	The URL's path.
port	The URL's port.
protocol	The URL's protocol.
search	A URL's search or query portion.

Table 1.16 Methods of the Location Object

Method	Description
assign()	Loads a new web page.
reload()	Causes the page that currently appears in the web browser to open again.
replace()	Replaces the currently loaded URL with a different one.

("http://www.google.com"); is equivalent to the statement location.href = "http://www.google.com";.

The reload() method of the Location object is equivalent to the Reload button in Firefox or the Refresh button in Internet Explorer. It causes the page that currently appears in the web browser to open again. You can use the reload() button without any arguments, as in location.reload();, or you can include a Boolean argument of true or false. Including an argument of true forces the current web page to reload from the server where it is located, even if no changes have been made to it. For example, the statement location.reload(true); forces the current page to reload. If you include an argument of false, or do not include any argument at all, the web page reloads only if it has changed.

The replace() method of the Location object is used to replace the currently loaded URL with a different one. This method works somewhat differently from loading a new document by changing the href property. The replace() method actually overwrites one document with another and replaces the old URL entry in the web browser's history list. In contrast, the href property opens a different document and adds it to the history list.

Tip

You can use this.location to retrieve the URL of the current web page.

The Navigator Object

The Navigator object is used to obtain information about the current web browser. It gets its name from Netscape Navigator, but is also supported by Firefox, Internet Explorer, and other current browsers. Some web browsers, including Internet Explorer, contain unique methods and properties of the Navigator object that cannot be used with other browsers. Table 1.17 lists properties of the Navigator object that are supported by most current web browsers, including Firefox and Internet Explorer.

The Screen Object

Computer displays can vary widely, depending on the type and size of the monitor, the type of installed graphics card, and the screen resolution and color depth selected by the user. For example, some notebook computers have small screens with limited resolution, whereas some desktop systems can have large monitors with very high resolution. The wide range of possible display settings makes it challenging to

Table 1.17 Properties of the Navigator Object

Properties	Description
appCodeName	The web browser code name.
appName	The web browser name.
appVersion	The web browser version.
platform	The operating system in use on the client computer.
userAgent	The string stored in the HTTP user-agent request header, which contains information about the browser, the platform name, and compatibility.

determine the size and positioning of windows generated by JavaScript. The `Screen` object is used to obtain information about the display screen's size, resolution, and color depth. Table 1.18 lists the properties of the `Screen` object that are supported by most current web browsers.

The `colorDepth` and `pixelDepth` properties are most useful in determining the color resolution that the display supports. For example, if the `colorDepth` property returns a value of 32, which indicates high color resolution, you can use JavaScript to display a high-color image. However, if the `colorDepth` property returns a value of 16, which indicates medium color resolution, you may want to use JavaScript to display a lower-color image. The following code illustrates how to use the `colorDepth` property to determine which version of an image to display:

```
if (screen.colorDepth >= 32)
   document.write("<img href='companyLogo_highres.jpg' />");
else if (screen.colorDepth >= 16)
   document.write("<img href='companyLogo_mediumres.jpg' />");
else
   document.write("<img href='companyLogo_lowres.jpg' />");
```

The remaining `Screen` object properties determine the size of the display area. For example, on a computer with a screen resolution of 1280 by 768, the following statements print "Your screen resolution is 1280 by 768".

Table 1.18 Properties of the Screen Object

Properties	Description
availHeight	Returns the height of the display screen, not including operating system features such as the Windows taskbar.
availWidth	Returns the width of the display screen, not including operating system features such as the Windows taskbar.
colorDepth	Returns the display screen's bit depth if a color palette is in use; if a color palette is not in use, returns the value of the pixelDepth property.
height	Returns the height of the display screen.
pixelDepth	Returns the display screen's color resolution in bits per pixel.
width	Returns the width of the display screen.

```
var screenWidth = screen.width;
var screenHeight = screen.height;
document.write("<p>Your screen resolution is " + screenWidth
   + " by " + screenHeight + ".</p>");
```

One of the more common uses of the Screen object properties is to center a web browser window in the middle of the display area. For windows generated with the window.open() method, you can center a window when it first displays by assigning values to the left and top options of the options argument. To center a window horizontally, subtract the width of the window from the screen width, divide the remainder by two, and assign the result to the left option.

Similarly, to center a window vertically, subtract the height of the window from the screen height, divide the remainder by two, and assign the result to the top option. The following code demonstrates how to create a new window and center it in the middle of the display area:

```
var winWidth=300;
var winHeight=200;
var leftPosition = (screen.width-winWidth)/2;
var topPosition = (screen.height-winHeight)/2;
var optionString = "width=" + winWidth + ",height=" + winHeight + ",left="
   + leftPosition + ",top=" + topPosition;
OpenWin = window.open("", "CtrlWindow", optionString);
```

Note

> Remember that the statements for opening a new window must be called from an event handler or a web browser's pop-up blocker will prevent the window from opening.

Summary

In this chapter, you learned about jQuery's features and benefits, and also about the critical object-oriented programming capabilities in JavaScript. In Chapter 2, you will jump right in and learn how to add jQuery to your JavaScript programs, and how to access web page elements with jQuery.

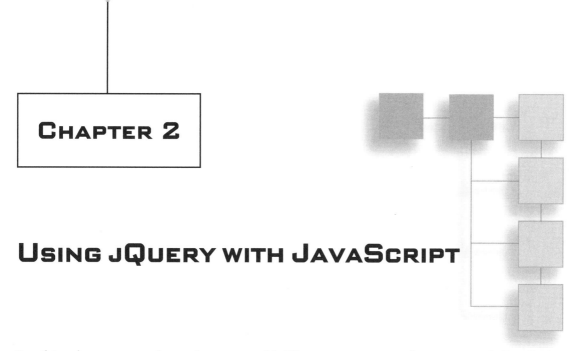

CHAPTER 2

USING JQUERY WITH JAVASCRIPT

In this chapter you learn how to add jQuery to your web pages and JavaScript programs, along with the basic techniques for accessing and manipulating elements and attributes on a web page. This is a critical chapter that sets the foundation for your success with jQuery, so be sure you understand the concepts here before moving on to Chapter 3.

ADDING JQUERY TO YOUR WEB PAGES

JavaScript is often incorporated directly into a web page. However, you can also save JavaScript code in an external file called a *JavaScript source file*. You can then write a statement in the document that executes (or calls) the code saved in the source file. When a browser encounters a line calling a JavaScript source file, it looks in the Java-Script source file and executes it.

A JavaScript source file is usually designated by the file extension .js and contains only JavaScript statements, although it can legally have any extension that you like. It does not contain a `<script>` element. Instead, the `<script>` element is located within the document that calls the source file.

To access the JavaScript code that is saved in an external file, you use the `src` attribute of the `<script>` element. You assign to the `src` attribute the URL of a Java-Script source file. For example, to call a JavaScript source file named scripts.js, you would include the following code in a document:

```
<script type="text/javascript" src="scripts.js">
</script>
```

jQuery is essentially a large text JavaScript source file containing code that is written using custom JavaScript objects. To use jQuery with your JavaScript applications, you first need to download the jQuery text file from `docs.jquery.com/Downloading_jQuery`. Currently released versions of jQuery are available in the following formats:

■ **Compressed (jquery-*version*.min.js)**—The best choice for production environments.

■ **Uncompressed (jquery-*version*.js)**—Downloads slower than the compressed versions, but is the best choice for application development.

After you download the jQuery source file, you can access the library as an external file using code similar to the following (which assumes an uncompressed jQuery source file):

```
<script type="text/javascript" src="jquery-version.js">
</script>
```

Caution

This book assumes that the jQuery library source file is located in the same directory as your web pages. Your best bet is to create a directory for the jQuery library source file that you can reference from your web pages.

Part of the purpose of the last section was to understand that the jQuery library was written using object-oriented programming techniques. After you download the jQuery library, open the file in a text editor. If you examine the file, you will see that it uses many of the techniques discussed in the last section. Figure 2.1 shows a portion of the jQuery source file that uses the `prototype` property.

Including references to the jQuery library source file assumes that the file is located on the server from which your web pages are hosted. However, in addition to referencing the jQuery library from your server, you can also reference it from several commercial sites on the *Content Delivery Networks* or *Content Distribution (CDN)* networks from several large commercial websites, including these:

■ **jQuery**—code.jquery.com/jquery-1.6.2.min.js

■ **Google Ajax API**—ajax.googleapis.com/ajax/libs/jquery/1.6.2/jquery.min.js

■ **Microsoft**—ajax.aspnetcdn.com/ajax/jQuery/jquery-1.6.2.min.js

```
function returnTrue() {
        return true;
}

// jQuery.Event is based on DOM3 Events as specified by the ECMAScript Language Binding
// http://www.w3.org/TR/2003/WD-DOM-Level-3-Events-20030331/ecma-script-binding.html
jQuery.Event.prototype = {
        preventDefault: function() {
                this.isDefaultPrevented = returnTrue;

                var e = this.originalEvent;
                if ( !e ) {
                        return;
                }

                // if preventDefault exists run it on the original event
                if ( e.preventDefault ) {
                        e.preventDefault();
```

jQuery Foundation

Figure 2.1
jQuery source file

You can access a referenced jQuery host using code similar to the following (which assumes access to the jQuery referenced host):

```
<script type="text/javascript" src="http://code.jquery.com/
   jquery-version.js ">
</script>
```

So which should you use—a reference to jQuery on your local server or a hosted reference? If you can be sure that your jQuery web pages will always be 100% compatible with the most current version of jQuery, you can safely reference the hosted versions. However, most web developers prefer to have more control over the code that controls their web pages. A best practice is to always reference a local copy of the jQuery source file on your local server, although that decision is entirely dependent on the needs of your websites and organization.

ACCESSING ELEMENTS AND ATTRIBUTES WITH JAVASCRIPT

Almost every jQuery script begins by selecting one or more *nodes* from the DOM. Almost everything on a web page can be referred to as a node, including elements, the text within an element, attributes, comments, and even the entire document itself. After you select some nodes, you can then perform some sort of action on them using jQuery methods. Before reading about jQuery node selection techniques, it helps to understand how you can select nodes with basic JavaScript.

One of the simplest node selection methods is to access HTML elements as properties of the Document object.

For example, the statement `document.forms[0].email.value` returns the value in a text box named `"email"` from the first form in a document. Although this technique works well, it has its limitations because you can only access anchor, form, image, and link elements. But what if you want to access a paragraph (`<p>`) or table (`<table>`) element? To access any element in a document with JavaScript—and modify it dynamically—you must use one of the following methods of the `Document` object: `getElementsByName()`,`getElementsByTagName()`, or `getElementById()`.

Accessing Elements by Name

The `getElementsByName()` method returns an array of elements with a `name` attribute that matches a specified value. You append the `getElementsByName()` method to the `Document` object and pass to it a single argument representing the `name` attribute of the elements you want to retrieve. For example, consider the following form, which creates four check boxes. The `name` attribute of each check box is assigned a value of committees.

```
<form action="FormProcessor.html" method="get"
enctype="application/x-www-form-urlencoded" onsubmit="return submitForm()">
<h3>Which committees would you like to serve on? </h3>
<p><input type="checkbox" name="committees" value="program_dev" />
Program Development <br />
<input type="checkbox" name="committees" value="fundraising" />
   Fundraising<br />
<input type="checkbox" name="committees" value="pub_relations" />
Public Relations<br />
<input type="checkbox" name="committees" value="education" />Education</p>
<p><input type="submit" /></p>
</form>
```

Now, consider the following event handler function. In this version, the function uses the `getElementsByName()` method to return an array of elements that represent the check boxes with the `name` attribute of committees.

```
function submitForm() {
   var committeesSelected = false;
   var selectedCommittees = document.getElementsByName("committees");
   for (var i=0; i<selectedCommittees.length; ++i) {
      if (selectedCommittees[i].checked == true) {
         committeesSelected = true;
         break;
      }
   }
   if (committeesSelected == false) {
```

```
      window.alert("You must select at least one committee.");
      return committeesSelected;
   }
   else
      return committeesSelected;
}
```

Keep in mind that the getElementsByName() method always returns an array, even if there is only one element in the document with a matching name attribute. This means that even if the document only contains a single element with the specified name, you must refer to it in your JavaScript code by using the first index (0) of the returned array. For example, suppose that you have a form with a text box whose name attribute is assigned a value of "email" and it is the only element in the document with that value assigned to its name attribute. The following statement demonstrates how to create an array consisting of a single element with a value of "email" assigned to its name attribute, and then display its value in an alert dialog box:

```
var email = document.getElementsByName("email");
window.alert(email[0].value);
```

With methods like the getElementsByName() method, which always return an array, you can also append the index number of the element you want to access to the statement containing the method, as follows:

```
window.alert(document.getElementsByName("email")[0].value);
```

Accessing Elements by Tag Name

The getElementsByTagName() method is similar to the getElementsByName() method, except that, instead of returning an array of elements with a name attribute that matches a specified value, it returns an array of elements that match a specified tag name. You append the getElementsByTagName() method to the Document object and pass to it a single argument representing the name of the elements you want to retrieve. As an example, the following statement returns an array of all the paragraph (<p>) tags in a document:

```
var docParagraphs = document.getElementsByTagName("p");
```

Caution

Be sure not to include the tag name's brackets (such as <p>) in the argument you pass to the getElementsByTagName() method. The chevrons (< >) that surround element names are primarily included to notify the browser that their contents contain an element, so they are not necessary when using a method such as getElementsByTagName().

Consider the following modified version of the form containing the committee check boxes. This version contains radio buttons that allow users to select "Yes" if they want to serve on a committee or "No" if they don't. Clicking one of the radio buttons calls a function named `enableCommittees()` and passes to it a Boolean value of either `true` (to disable the committee check boxes) or `false` (to enable them).

```
<form action="FormProcessor.html" method="get"
enctype="application/x-www-form-urlencoded" onsubmit="return submitForm()">
<p>Would you like to serve on a committee?</p>
<p><input type="radio" name="committeeInvolvement"
    checked="checked" onclick="enableCommittees(false)" /> Yes
<input type="radio" name="committeeInvolvement"
onclick="enableCommittees(true)" /> No</p>
<p>Which committees would you like to serve on? </p>
<p><input type="checkbox" name="committees" value="program_dev" />
Program Development<br />
<input type="checkbox" name="committees" value="fundraising" />
    Fundraising<br />
<input type="checkbox" name="committees" value="pub_relations" />
Public Relations <br />
<input type="checkbox" name="committees"value="education" />Education</p>
</form>
```

The following `enableCommittees()` function demonstrates how to use the `getElementsByTagName()` method. The function's first statement uses the `getElementsByTagName()` method to return an array of all the `<input>` elements in the document, which is then assigned to a variable named `committeeBoxes[]`. Then, the `for` loop iterates through each of the elements in the `committeeBoxes[]` array and checks the value of each `Input` object's `type` property. If the `type` property is equal to "checkbox," the element is enabled or disabled by assigning the value of the `boolValue` variable to the `disabled` property of the `Input` object.

```
function enableCommittees(boolValue) {
    var committeeBoxes = document.getElementsByTagName("input");
    for (var i=0; i<committeeBoxes.length;
        ++i) {
        if (committeeBoxes[i].type == "checkbox")
            committeeBoxes[i].disabled = boolValue;
    }
}
```

The `getElementsByTagName()` method works the same way as the `getElementsByName()` method in that it always returns an array, even if there is only one element in the document that matches the specified tag name. For example, with a document that contains a single form that is submitted with the POST method, the following `document.write()` statement refers to the first element in the array returned from a `getElementsByTagName()` method that is passed a value of "form." The statement prints, "The form will be submitted with the POST method."

```
document.write("<p>The form will be submitted with the "
  + document.getElementsByTagName("form")[0].method + " method.</p>");
```

Accessing Elements by ID

The `getElementsByName()` and `getElementsByTagName()` methods are extremely useful if you need to work with collections of elements that have the same name attribute or are of the same type. However, if you are only interested in accessing a single element, you should use the `getElementById()` method, which returns the first element in a document with a matching `id` attribute. You append the `getElementById()` method to the `Document` object and pass to it a single argument representing the ID of the element you want to retrieve. For example, consider again a document that contains a single form that is submitted with the POST method and that is also assigned a value of `customerInfo` to its `id` attribute. The following `document.write()` statement uses the `getElementById()` method to access the form and its `method` attribute:

```
document.write("<p>The form will be submitted with the "
  + document.getElementById("customerInfo").method + " method.</p>");
```

As another example, the following statement uses the `getElementById()` method to retrieve the value entered into a text box that is assigned an `id` attribute of `"email"`:

```
window.alert("You entered the following email address: "
  + document.getElementById("email").value);
```

Be sure to notice that the `getElementById()` method does not refer to an array because it only returns a single element instead of an array, as do the `getElementsByName()` and `getElementsByTagName()` methods. If your document contains multiple elements with the same `id` attribute, the `getElementById()` method only returns the first matching element.

Caution
A common mistake when using the `getElementById()` method is to capitalize the last d, as in `getElementByID()`, which causes an error because JavaScript is case sensitive. The correct syntax is `getElementById()`, with a lowercase d.

WORKING WITH jQUERY SELECTORS

The key to success with jQuery is to thoroughly understand how to access web page elements with *selectors*. jQuery includes two basic types of selectors. The first selector type simply selects any elements or attributes you specify; you must then use other jQuery methods to modify the selected objects. The second type of selectors refers to jQuery methods that perform actions on the selected elements. You can think of the first type of selectors as being similar to the getElementById(), getElementsByName(), or getElementsByTagName() methods of the Document object; once you gain access to an element using one of these methods, you must use other JavaScript techniques to manipulate it. For example, the jQuery id selector selects the element that matches a specified ID. If you want to do anything else with the selected element, such as change text color or position, you must write additional code using jQuery. The second type of jQuery selectors can both access and modify an element with the same statement.

When using JavaScript to manipulate the elements on a web page, you primarily access and modify the properties of element styles or objects such as the Document object. Traditional object-oriented programming languages such as Java and C++ use methods, called *accessor methods*, in a similar way to retrieve or modify the value of object properties. Because accessor methods often begin with the words *get* or *set*, they are also referred to as "get" or "set" methods. *Get methods* retrieve property values while *set methods* modify property values. For example, if you write a class named Payroll that includes a private data member containing the current state income-tax rate, you could write an accessor method named getStateTaxRate() that allows clients to retrieve the variable's value. Similarly, you could write a setStateTaxRate() function that performs various types of validation on the data passed from the client (such as making sure the value is not null, is not greater than 100%, and so on) prior to assigning a value to the private state tax rate data member.

Unlike traditional object-oriented programming languages, the jQuery library includes single methods that act as both get and set methods. In other words, you don't need to call separate methods to retrieve or modify a property. For example, the jQuery css() method is used for both getting and setting element style information. In comparison, with a language such as Java, you probably need to call a getCSS() method to retrieve CSS properties and a setCSS() method modify CSS properties.

You will learn more about how to use the two basic types of jQuery selectors throughout this section.

Note

The terms accessor, get, and set methods are not contextually accurate when it comes to jQuery development, considering there are no actual get or set methods in the jQuery library. However, most other texts on jQuery—including the source documentation on `docs.jquery.com`—use these terms consistently, so you need to understand their meaning.

Understanding Selector Syntax

Selector syntax can range from very simple statements that return single elements to fairly complicated statements that select and filter numerous elements according to their type, attributes, CSS classes and styles, and other aspects. This section discusses the basics of how to use selector syntax, although you will see numerous more complicated examples throughout this book.

Table 2.1 lists the jQuery basic selectors.

jQuery uses a single method, `jQuery()`, to select web page elements and to provide access to the jQuery library. For example, the following statement uses the All selector to select all of the elements on a web page:

```
jQuery("*")
```

You can also use a special alias, `$()`, in place of the `jQuery()` method, as follows:

```
$("*")
```

Because of its brevity, most jQuery programmers prefer to use the `$()` alias, which is the convention followed throughout this book.

Table 2.1   jQuery Basic Selectors

Selector	Selects
All ("*")	All elements.
Class (".*class*")	All elements that use a specified CSS `class`.
Element ("*element*")	All elements that match the specified element name.
ID ("#*id*")	The first element that matches the specified `id` attribute.
Multiple ("*selector1, selector2, ...*")	All elements that match the results of one or more specified selectors.

Although you can execute jQuery code by just using jQuery() or $(), you should always place your jQuery statements inside a document.ready() method. This method ensures that the DOM is fully loaded before executing any jQuery statements. You pass to the document.ready() method an anonymous function, in which you place your jQuery statements. Here is the syntax for using the document.ready() method:

```
$(document).ready(function() {
 // jQuery statements
});
```

jQuery does not include a selector that is equivalent to the getElementsByName() method, although it does include two selectors that are equivalent to the getElementById() and $("element") and getElementsByTagName() methods: $("#id").

As with the getElementsByTagName() method, the $("element") selector returns an array of elements with a name attribute that matches a specified value. Like the getElementsByName() method, the $("element") selector always returns an array, even if there is only one element in the document with a matching name attribute. To access an array of elements, you use a statement and syntax similar to $("p"), which returns an array of the document's paragraph elements.

Note

You do not need to append any jQuery selectors, such as the $("element") selector, to the Document object, as you do with the getElementById(), getElementsByName(), or getElementsByTagName()methods.

Unlike the getElementsByName() method, you cannot use JavaScript looping structures or array syntax to refer to the individual elements in a jQuery array. Instead, you must use the jQuery each() method or another jQuery utility function. The each() utility function iterates through a jQuery array in order to get and set element values. The basic each() utility syntax is:

```
$("element").each(function() {
  statement(s);
});
```

The following example demonstrates how to use the $("element") selector to select an unordered list containing fruit names. The example uses the $("element") selector to return an array of the <li> items in the document body, and then uses the each() and text() methods to print the text contained within each <li> tag pair.

```
<head>
<script type="text/javascript" src="jquery-1.7.2.js"></script>
<script type="text/javascript">
/* <![CDATA[ */
$(document).ready(function(){
   $("li").each(function() {
     window.alert($(this).text());
   });
});
/* ]]> */
</script>
</head>
<body>
<ul>
<li>Apples</li>
<li>Peaches</li>
<li>Pears</li>
<li>Oranges</li>
</ul>
</body>
```

Note

The text() function is a jQuery accessor method used to get and set the text displayed within an element tag pair.

The following statement uses the $("#id") selector to retrieve the value entered into a text box that is assigned an id attribute of "email":

```
window.alert("You entered the following email address: "
   + $("#customerEmail").attr("value"));
```

The preceding statement also uses the attr() accessor method.

When you append the attr() method to a selector and pass to it a single string argument containing an attribute name, the attr() method returns the value assigned to the specified element attribute for the first matching element in the returned set. If you pass two string arguments to the attr() method, the contents of the second argument are assigned as the value of the attribute specified in the first argument for all matching elements in the returned set. The following statement uses

the $("*") selector with the attr() and each() methods to select all check box
<input> buttons contained on a page:

```
$(document).ready(function(){
  $("*").each(function(){
    ($(this).attr("checked", "checked"));
  });
});
```

Caution

As with the getElementById() method, the $("#id") selector does not refer to an array. If your document contains multiple elements with the same id attribute, the $("#id") selector returns only the first matching element.

Tip

To access an element by its ID, be sure to precede the value assigned to the id attribute with a # sign. If you don't, jQuery will attempt to return an array of elements that match the value passed to the jQuery function, which will normally result in an empty array, unless you pass an existing HTML element name.

The final basic jQuery selector is the $("selector1, selector2, …") selector, which returns an array of specified, multiple selectors. You can use the $("#id"), $("element"), and other selectors to return an array of matching elements. The following code demonstrates how to access the text of the <li> elements along with the text of two <p> elements using their id attributes:

```
<head>
<script type="text/javascript" src="jquery-1.7.2.js"></script>
<script type="text/javascript">
/* <![CDATA[ */
$(document).ready(function(){
  $("li, #plums, #lemons").each(function() {
    window.alert($(this).text());
  });
});
/* ]]> */
</script>
</head>
<body>
<ul>
```

```
<li>Apples</li>
<li>Peaches</li>
<li>Pears</li>
<li>Oranges</li>
</ul>
<p id="plums">Plums</p>
<p id="lemons">Lemons</p>
</body>
```

Selecting Elements According to Hierarchy

If you need to access an element and you know its ID, the JavaScript `getElementsByTagName()` method is the easiest to use.

However, some elements may not have IDs, especially dynamic web pages with the ability to add and remove elements. For example, you may have a web page that dynamically adds new `<option>` elements to a `<selection>` list based on user input. Or, you may need to access child elements that are contained within a parent element, and you do not know their ID values. For cases like these, you use a *hierarchical selector*, which allows you to select one or more elements according to their relationship with other elements. Table 2.2 lists the jQuery hierarchical selectors.

As an example of how to use the hierarchical selectors, consider the following modified version of the fruit script. This version uses the Child (`"parent > child"`)

Table 2.2   jQuery Hierarchical Selectors

Selector	Selects
Child (`"parent > child"`)	All specified child elements of a specified parent element.
Descendant (`"ancestor descendant"`)	All specified descendant elements of a specified ancestor.
Next Adjacent (`"prev + next"`)	All specified sibling elements that immediately follow a specified previous sibling element.
Next Siblings (`"prev ~ siblings"`)	All specified sibling elements that follow the specified element, regardless of hierarchy.

selector to access the child `<li>` elements contained within the parent `<ul>` element:

```
<script type="text/javascript">
/* <![CDATA[ */
$(document).ready(function(){
   $("ul > li").each(function() {
     window.alert($(this).text());
});
```

As another example of how to use the hierarchical selectors, the following version of the fruit script uses the Descendant (`"ancestor descendant"`) selector to access the child `<li>` elements contained within the parent `<ul>` element:

```
$(document).ready(function(){
   $("ul li").each(function() {
     window.alert($(this).text());
});
/* ]]> */
</script>
```

Note

The difference between the `Child` (`"parent > child"`) and `Descendant` (`"ancestor descendant"`) selectors is that the `Child` (`"parent > child"`) only selects all specified elements that are contained directly beneath another element, whereas the `Descendant` (`"ancestor descendant"`) selector selects all matching specified elements beneath another element, even if the descendant elements are contained within other elements. For example, if you simply want to access all `<li>` elements contained with a `<ul>` element, you use the `Child` (`"parent > child"`) selector. However, if you want to select all of a form's `<input>` elements, regardless of whether they are contained within other elements such as a `<p>` element, you use the `Descendant` (`"ancestor descendant"`).

Filtering Selected Elements

Accessing web page elements with jQuery is fairly straightforward, but in order to narrow the set of returned elements, you must use a *filter*. The basic and hierarchical jQuery filters are listed in Table 2.3.

As an example of how to user the filters, consider the `:first` filter, which restricts the returned element set to the first specified element. The following statement demonstrates how to access the value assigned to the first `<li>` element in a script using the Descendant (`"ancestor descendant"`) selector:

```
$(document).ready(function(){
   window.alert($("ul li:first").text());
});
```

Table 2.3   jQuery Basic and Hierarchical Filters

Selector	Selects
:animated	All elements that are processing an animation when the selector is executed.
:contains()	All elements that contain the specified text.
:empty	All elements that contain no text or other elements.
:even	All even elements.
:first	The first element.
:first-child	The first child element.
:gt()	All elements greater than a specified index.
:header	All heading-level elements, `<h1>` through `<h6>`.
:hidden	All hidden elements
:last	The last element.
:last-child	The last child element.
:lt()	All elements less than a specified index.
:nth-child()	All elements that are the *n*th child of a specified selector.
:odd	All odd elements.
:only-child	All odd child elements.
:parent	All elements that are the parent of a specified element.
:visible	All visible elements.

Other filters return more complex results, such as the :header filter, which selects all heading elements, `<h1>` through `<h6>`, that the web page contains.

The following code uses the :header filter and the .css() method to change all headings to blue after the page finishes loading. Figure 2.2 shows the output in a web browser.

```
<head>
<script type="text/javascript" src="jquery-1.7.2.js">
</script>
<script type="text/javascript">
/* <![CDATA[ */
$(document).ready(function(){
   $(":header").css({ color:'blue' });
```

```
});
/* ]]> */
</script>
</head>
<body>
<h1>San Francisco Bay Area</h1>
<h2>Hiking Destinations</h2>
<h3>Fort Funston</h3>
<p>Distance: 1.5 Miles<br />
Elev. (low/high): 0/183 ft.<br />
Difficulty: Easy</p>
<h3>Rodeo Beach</h3>
<p>Distance: 4.3 Miles<br />
Elev. (low/high): 20/850 ft.<br />
Difficulty: Easy</p>
<h3>Mission Peak</h3>
<p>Distance: 5.6 Miles<br />
Elev. (low/high): 425/2453 ft.<br />
Difficulty: Moderate</p>
</body>
```

Figure 2.2
Output of a script that uses the :header filter

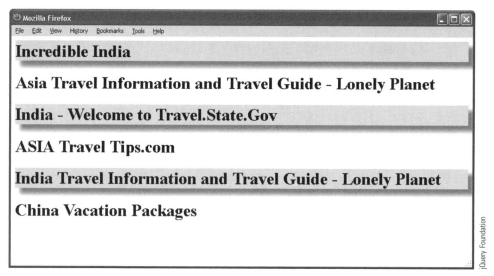

Figure 2.3
Output of a script that uses the :contains filter

Tip

Remember that you can use the $("*element*") selector to select specific heading elements, such as the <h1> element.

Notice that some of the filters in Table 2.3 accept arguments within parentheses, the same as functions or methods. For example, the :contains() filter selects all elements that contain the specified text, as demonstrated in the following statement, which selects all heading elements containing the text "India," and then highlights the elements in yellow and adds a shadow box around them. Figure 2.3 shows the output in a web browser.

```
<head>
<script type="text/javascript" src="jquery-1.7.2.js">
</script>
<script type="text/javascript">
/* <![CDATA[ */
$(document).ready(function(){
  $(":header:contains('India')").css({
    backgroundColor:'yellow',
    boxShadow: '10px 10px 5px #888888' });
});
/* ]]> */
</script>
</head>
```

```
<body>
<h1>Incredible India</h1>
<h1>Asia Travel Information and Travel Guide - Lonely Planet</h1>
<h1>India - Welcome to Travel.State.Gov</h1>
<h1>ASIA Travel Tips.com</h1>
<h1>India Travel Information and Travel Guide - Lonely Planet</h1>
<h1>China Vacation Packages</h1>
</body>
```

Note

The `.css()` method is discussed in Chapter 3.

Using Selectors with Form Elements

The selector filters you will probably use most are form filters, which allow you to select specific form elements. Table 2.4 describes the jQuery form filters.

Table 2.4   jQuery Form Filters

Filter	Returns
:button	All `<button>` elements.
:checkbox	All `<input>` elements with a `type` attribute of "checkbox".
:checked	All checked input fields.
:disabled	All disabled input fields.
:enabled	All enabled input fields.
:file	All `<file>` elements.
:focus	The element with the current focus.
:image	All `<image>` elements.
:input	All `<input>` elements
:password	All `<input>` elements with a `type` attribute of "password".
:radio	All `<input>` elements with a `type` attribute of "radio".
:reset	All `<reset>` elements.
:selected	All selected elements.
:submit	All `<submit>` elements.
:text	All `<input>` elements with a `type` attribute of "text".

The following example is a modified version of the committees web page from the beginning of this chapter. This version uses jQuery syntax to capture the `click` event and change the `disabled` attribute of the check boxes. Notice that the `click` event handler and the `.each()` function use jQuery form filters to access the radio and check box fields.

```
$(document).ready(function(){
  $("input:radio").click(function(){
    $("input:checkbox").each(function(){
      if ($(this).attr("disabled") == "disabled")
          $(this).attr("disabled", false);
    else
          $(this).attr("disabled", "disabled");
    });
  });
});
```

As mentioned earlier in this section, jQuery does not include a selector that is equivalent to the `getElementsByName()` method. In fact, it's considered poor programming form to rely on values assigned to the `name` attribute when writing JavaScript applications.

However, the `name` attribute is important, especially when it comes to working with forms. For example, the `<input>`, `<textarea>`, and `<select>` elements can include `name` and `value` attributes. The `name` attribute defines a name for an element, and the `value` attribute defines a default value. When you submit a form to a web server, the form data is submitted in *name=value pairs*, based on the `name` and `value` attributes of each element. Consider the following element, which creates a text `<input>` field:

```
<input type="text" name="company_info" value="Gosselin Aviation" />
```

For the preceding element, a name=value pair of `"company_info=Gosselin Aviation"` is sent to the web server (unless the user types something else into the field). If you intend to have your script submit forms to a web server, you must include a `name` attribute for each `<input>`, `<textarea>`, and `<select>` element.

Another important use of the `name` attribute with forms is that it is used to define groups of radio buttons and check boxes. When multiple form elements share the same name, JavaScript creates an array out of the elements using the shared name. Radio buttons, for instance, share the same name so that a single name=value pair can be submitted to a server-side script. When you have an array that is created from a group of buttons that share the same name, you can use the `checked` property to determine which element in a group is selected. The `checked` property returns a value of `true` if a check box or radio button is selected, and a value of `false` if it is not.

When you have an array that is created from a group of buttons that share the same name, you can use the checked property to determine which element in a group is selected. The checked property returns a value of true if a check box or radio button is selected, and a value of false if it is not. For example, if you have a group of radio buttons named maritalStatus, you can use an onsubmit event handler similar to the following to determine if one of the radio buttons in the group is selected:

```
<head>
<script type="text/javascript">
/* <![CDATA[ */
function submitForm() {
    var maritalStatusSelected = false;
    for (var i=0; i<5; ++i) {
        if (document.forms[0].maritalStatus[i].checked == true) {
            maritalStatusSelected = true;
            break;
        }
    }
    if (maritalStatusSelected == false) {
        window.alert("You must select your marital status.");
        return false;
    }
    else
        return true;
}
/* ]]> */
</script>
</head>
<body>
<form action="FormProcessor.html" method="get"
enctype="application/x-www-form-urlencoded" onsubmit="submitForm()">
<p>What is your current marital status?<br />
<input type="radio" name="maritalStatus"
    value="single" />Single<br />
<input type="radio" name="maritalStatus"
    value="married" />Married<br />
<input type="radio" name="maritalStatus"
    value="divorced" />Divorced<br />
<input type="radio" name="maritalStatus"
    value="separated" />Separated<br />
<input type="radio" name="maritalStatus"
    value="widowed" />Widowed</p>
<p><input type="submit" /></p>
</form>
</body>
```

To create the same programmatic functionality with jQuery, you need to use the `input:checked` filter, as follows. Notice that the code calls the submit event handler of the `Form` element and that it uses the standard JavaScript array `length` property to determine the number of returned elements. If there is at least one returned element, that means one of the radio buttons is selected.

```
$(document).ready(function(){
  $("form").submit(function(){
    if ($("input:checked").length > 0)
        return true;
    else {
        window.alert("You must select your marital status.");
        return false;
    }
  });
});
```

MANIPULATING HTML ATTRIBUTES

Up to this point you have only seen selectors and filters that return entire sets of elements. This section discusses selectors and methods that you can use to access and manipulate elements according to their attributes.

Selecting Attributes

Table 2.5 describes the jQuery selectors that allow you to access elements by their attributes.

You can use the attribute selectors in two ways: either by calling the selector directly or appending it to an element name with a colon. For example, the most basic of the selectors listed in Table 2.5 is the [name] selector, which returns all elements that include the specified attribute, regardless of the attributes assigned value. The statement $("[value]") returns all elements that include a value attribute. In comparison, the following example demonstrates how to use the [name] selector to return the value attribute of all text <input> elements.

```
<head>
<script type="text/javascript" src="jquery-1.7.2.js">
</script>
<script type="text/javascript">
/* <![CDATA[ */
$(document).ready(function(){
```

```
    $("input:submit").click(function(){
      $("input:text[value]").each(function(){
        window.alert($(this).attr("value"));
      });
    });
  });
});
/* ]]> */
</script>
</head>
<body>
<h1>Forestville Funding</h1><hr />
<h2>Online Banking Registration</h2>
<form action="" method="get" enctype="application/x-www-form-urlencoded">
<p><strong>First Name</strong><br />
<input type="text" name="firstName" id="firstName" value="First Name" /></p>
<p><strong>Last Name</strong><br />
<input type="text" name="lastName" id="lastName" value="Last Name" /></p>
<p><strong>Account Number</strong><br />
<input type="text" name="acctnum" id="acctNum" value="Account Number" /></p>
<p><input type="submit" value="Register" /></p>
</form>
</body>
```

Accessing and Modifying Attributes

Earlier in this chapter, you saw the basic syntax for working with the attr()
method. Table 2.6 lists the additional jQuery attribute methods.

The .html() method is essentially jQuery's version of JavaScript's *innerHTML
property*, which sets and retrieves the contents of a specified element. The
innerHTML property was originally introduced by Microsoft into Internet Explorer
browsers, but has been adopted by most current web browsers. The W3C has not
officially approved the innerHTML property as part of the DOM, but probably will
at some point due to the method's popularity and versatility. In comparison to the
document.write() and document.writeln() methods, which cannot be used
to change content after a web page has been rendered, the innerHTML property
allows you to retrieve and modify the contents of almost any element without having
to reload the entire web page. In fact, many JavaScript programmers view the
innerHTML property as a replacement for the document.write() and
document.writeln() methods.

Although the innerHTML property is popular with many JavaScript programmers, it
also has its detractors. To learn about the arguments against using the innerHTML

Table 2.5 jQuery Attribute Selectors

Selector	Selects
Attribute Contains Prefix [*name*|="*value*"]	Elements with the specified attribute and value or with a value that begins with the specified value followed by a hyphen (-).
Attribute Contains [*name**="*value*"]	Elements with the specified attribute with a value containing the specified string.
Attribute Contains Word [*name*~="*value*"]	Elements with the specified attribute with a value containing the specified word.
Attribute Ends With [*name*$="*value*"]	Elements with the specified attribute with a value ending with the specified string.
Attribute Equals [*name*="*value*"]	Elements with the specified attribute name and value.
Attribute Not Equal [*name*!="*value*"]	Elements that either do not include the specified attribute or that include the specified attribute with a value that does not match the specified string.
Attribute Starts With [*name*^="*value*"]	Elements with the specified attribute with a value beginning with the specified string.
Has Attribute [*name*]	Elements that include the specified attribute regardless of the assigned value.
Multiple Attribute [*name*="*value*"] [*name2*="*value2*"]	Elements that match all of the specified attribute names and values.

property, along with some alternative solutions, search the web for "alternatives to innerHTML". The alternative solutions to the innerHTML property primarily use some fairly complex techniques involving the XML DOM. Yet, it's important to point out that one of the greatest benefits of JavaScript is its simplicity and ease of use, and using the XML DOM to manipulate web pages is anything but simple. In this author's opinion, any techniques that continue to make JavaScript easier to understand and use, such as the innerHTML property, should be embraced in favor of more complex solutions.

Table 2.6   jQuery Attribute Methods

Method	Description
`.attr()`	Gets the attribute value from the first element in a set of matching elements or sets the attribute value for all matching elements.
`.html()`	Gets the content from the first element in a set of matching elements or sets the content for all matching elements.
`.removeAttr()`	Removes a specified attribute from a set of matching elements.
`.val()`	Gets the attribute value from the first input field in a set of matching elements or sets the attribute value for all matching input fields.

To use the `innerHTML` property, you append it to an object representing the element whose value you want to retrieve or modify. As an example, the following paragraph element contains an anchor element that displays the text "How's this for a deal?". An `onmouseover` event uses the `innerHTML` property and a `this` reference to change the contents of the anchor element to "Order now and receive 20% off!". Then, an `onmouseout` event uses the `innerHTML` property and a `this` reference to change the contents of the anchor element back to "How\'s this for a deal?".

```
<p><a href="sales.html" id="salesLink"
onmouseover="this.innerHTML='Order now and receive 20% off!'"
onmouseout="this.innerHTML='How\'s this for a deal?'">
   How's this for a deal?</a></p>
```

The following code demonstrates how to use jQuery syntax and the `html()` method to perform the same functionality as the preceding example.

```
<head>
<script type="text/javascript" src="jquery-1.7.2.js"></script>
<script type="text/javascript">
/* <![CDATA[ */
$(document).ready(function(){
   $("#salesLink").mouseover(function() {
     $(this).html("Order now and receive 20% off!");
   });
   $("#salesLink").mouseout(function() {
     $(this).html("How\'s this for a deal?");
   });
});
/* ]]> */
```

```
</script>
</head>
<body>
<p><a href="sales.html" id="salesLink">How's this for a deal?</a></p>
</body>
```

Note

> The JavaScript innerHTML property version of the code is actually simpler than the jQuery html()
> method. However, you must use the html() method in order to gain access to an element's content
> with jQuery.

As its name implies, the removeAttr() method removes a specified attribute from a set of matching elements. To use the removeAttr() method, append it to a selector and pass to it a string containing the name of the attribute you want to use. The following example is a modified version of the committees web page. This version uses the removeAttr() method to remove the disabled attribute instead of assigning it a value of false with the attr() method.

```
$(document).ready(function(){
  $("input:radio").click(function(){
    $("input:checkbox").each(function(){
      if ($(this).attr("disabled") == "disabled")
        $(this).removeAttr("disabled");
      else
        $(this).attr("disabled", "disabled");
      });
  });
});
```

The final jQuery attribute method you will learn about in this chapter is the val() method, which returns the value from the first input field in a set of matching elements or sets the attribute value for all matching input fields. For example, consider the following statement from earlier that uses the attr() method to retrieve the value assigned to a text box with an id value of customerEmail:

```
window.alert("You entered the following email address: "
  + $("#customerEmail").attr("value"));
```

Instead of using the attr() method, you can more easily use the val() method, as follows:

```
window.alert("You entered the following email address: "
  + $("#customerEmail").val());
```

The following example demonstrates a modified version of the JavaScript code for the online banking registration form you saw earlier. This version uses the `val()` method to determine whether the value entered into each text field is the same as the default value, meaning that the user did not enter a unique value into the field. If the values are the same, the script replaces the contents of each field with `"REQUIRED VALUE"`.

```
var badReqField = false;
$(document).ready(function(){
   $("input:submit").click(function(){
      $("input:text").each(function(){
         if ($(this).val() == $(this)[0].defaultValue) {
            $(this).val("REQUIRED VALUE");
            badReqField = true;
         }
      });
      if (badReqField == true)
          return false;
      else
          return true;
   });
});
```

Notice that the `if` statement uses `$(this)[0].defaultValue` to refer to the default value of the current element. The `defaultValue` property is an internal JavaScript property that returns the value assigned to a form element's value attribute. Note that the default value is not the same as the value currently entered into the form field, which is accessed using `$(this).val()`. Also notice that the `$(this)` reference is followed by `[0]`, which refers to the first dimension in an array. The `$(this)` reference essentially returns an array consisting of a single element. In order to access the JavaScript properties of this single element, you must use array notation and refer to the first element in the array, represented by the 0 index.

SUMMARY

In this chapter you learned how to add jQuery to your web pages and JavaScript programs. Most importantly, you learned about the critical techniques for accessing the elements on a web page. The next chapter expands on these techniques. You'll learn how to use jQuery and CSS to manipulate web page content.

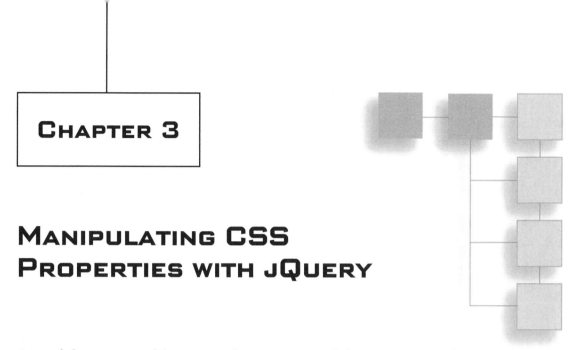

CHAPTER 3

MANIPULATING CSS PROPERTIES WITH JQUERY

One of the most useful aspects of jQuery is its ability to access and manipulate CSS properties after a web page has been rendered. This chapter discusses the basics of manipulating CSS with jQuery and how to dynamically position and control elements.

ACCESSING CSS PROPERTIES

To refer to a CSS style in JavaScript, you use the this reference and the style property in an event handler within the element itself. You use the style property to modify an element's CSS properties with JavaScript. In order to refer to a style with the this reference, you use a period to append the style property to it, followed by another period and a CSS property. CSS properties without hyphens are referred to in JavaScript with all lowercase letters. However, when you refer to a CSS property containing a hyphen in JavaScript code, you remove the hyphen, convert the first word to lowercase, and convert the first letter of subsequent words to uppercase. For example, the text-decoration property is referred to as textDecoration, font-family is referred to as fontFamily, font-size is referred to as fontSize, and so on. In the following code the onmouseover event underlines the link when the mouse passes over it while the onmouseout event removes the link when the mouse passes off of it:

```
<p><a id="sox" href="redsox.html"
  onmouseover="this.style.textDecoration='underline';"
  onmouseout="this.style.textDecoration='none';"
  style="text-decoration: none"
  >Red Sox Fan Club</a></p>
```

Using jQuery to Access CSS Properties

When working with jQuery, you use the `.css()` accessor method to access and modify CSS properties. In its simplest form, you append the `.css()` method to a selector and pass to it a single argument containing the name of the CSS property you want to access. For example, the statement `$("h1").css("fontSize")` returns the font size of the first `<h1>` element found in a document. The second form of the `.css()` method changes the value of the specified property for all matching elements to the value of a second argument that you pass to the `.css()` method. To change the text color of all paragraph elements in a document to blue, you use a statement similar to `$("p").css("color", "blue")`.

The following example demonstrates the jQuery version of the code that changes the `text-decoration` property:

```
<head>
<script type="text/javascript" src="jquery-1.7.21.7.2.js">
</script>
<script type="text/javascript">
/* <![CDATA[ */
$(document).ready(function(){
   $("#sox").mouseover(function(){
     $(this).css("textDecoration", "underline");
   });
   $("#sox").mouseout(function(){
     $(this).css("textDecoration", "none");
   });
});
/* ]]> */
</script>
</head>
<body>
<p><a id="sox" href="redsox.html" style="text-decoration: none">
Red Sox Fan Club</a></p>
</body>
```

To change multiple properties, pass *property:value* pairs, separated by commas, to the `.css()` method. The next example shows how to use `onmouseover` and `onmouseout` event handlers to give users the option of changing the text to make it easier to read. Specifically, it allows users to change the text color and weight of a line simply by passing the mouse pointer over it. Moving the mouse pointer away from the line returns it to its original text color and weight. Figure 3.1 shows the document in a web browser when the mouse pointer passes over the third line. Notice that the jQuery statements use the Descendant (`"ancestor descendant"`)

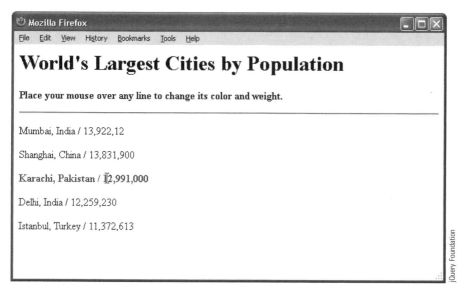

Figure 3.1
Web page that uses the jQuery .css() method

selector to gain access to the paragraphs contained within a `<div>` element with an ID of `"cities"`.

```
<head>
<script type="text/javascript" src="jquery-1.7.21.7.2.js">
</script>
<script type="text/javascript">
/* <![CDATA[ */
$(document).ready(function(){
  $("#cities p").mouseover(function(){
    $(this).css({"color":"blue", fontWeight:"bold"});
  });
  $("#cities p").mouseout(function(){
    $(this).css({"color": "black", fontWeight:"normal"});
  });
});
/* ]]> */
</script>
</head>
<body>
<h1>World's Largest Cities by Population</h1>
<p><strong>Place your mouse over any line to change its
  color and weight.</strong></p><hr />
<div id="cities">
```

```
<p>Mumbai, India / 13,922,12</p>
<p>Shanghai, China / 13,831,900</p>
<p>Karachi, Pakistan / 12,991,000</p>
<p>Delhi, India / 12,259,230</p>
<p>Istanbul, Turkey / 11,372,613</p>
</div>
</body>
```

Referring to CSS Properties with jQuery

The code in this section used JavaScript syntax to access each CSS property. For example, the preceding code uses `fontWeight` instead of the `font-weight` syntax that is used in standard CSS. However, jQuery allows you to use CSS syntax to refer to properties, provided you enclose them in quotations. With the preceding code, you could also use `$(this).css({"color":"blue",` `"fontweight":"bold"});` to refer to the `font-weight` CSS property. Whichever syntax you choose, be sure to use it consistently for best practice purposes.

An important issue to point out when it comes to using JavaScript syntax is to reference CSS properties. You are not actually required to enclose within parentheses a property name that uses JavaScript syntax, although you can. For example, both `$(this).css(fontWeight, "bold"});` and `$(this).css("fontWeight", "bold"});` will function correctly. However, at the time of this writing, jQuery does not appear to support JavaScript syntax for certain CSS properties that are not enclosed within parentheses. For example, `$(".danger").css(fontSize, "32pt");` does not currently function although `$(".danger").css("fontSize", "32pt");` works fine. To be on the safe side, always enclose the property names you pass to the `.css()` method within quotations.

Using jQuery with CSS Classes

If you're not familiar with them, *class selectors* allow you to create different groups of styles. You create a class selector within a `<style>` element by appending a class name to a selector with a period. You then assign the class name to the standard class attribute of elements in the document that you want to format with the class's style definitions.

The following code defines a class selector named `danger` that formats paragraph text as red and bold. The class selector is applied to two of the paragraphs in the document body.

```
...
<style type="text/css">
h1 {color: navy; font-size: 1.5em;
   font-family: Arial }
h2 { color: navy; font-size: 1em;
   font-family: Arial }
body {color: blue; font-family: Arial;
   font-size: 10pt; font-weight: normal }
```

```
p.danger { color: red; font-weight: bold }
</style>
</head>
<body>
<h1>Coast City Kites</h1>
<h2>Safety Tips</h2>
<p>Never fly over people.</p>
<p>Never fly near trees or buildings.</p>
<p>Never fly near the airport.</p>
<p class="danger">Never fly in rain or thunderstorms.</p>
<p>Never fly near busy streets or roadways.</p>
<p class="danger">Never fly near power lines.</p>
</body>
```

When you create a class selector by appending a class name to a selector with a period, you can only use that class selector with the element for which it was created. For instance, you can only use the `danger` class selector in the preceding example with `<p>` elements.

You can also create a generic class selector that is not associated with any particular element. You create a generic class selector to use with any element by defining a class name preceded by a period, but without appending it to an element. The following code shows an example of the danger class `selector`, but this time it is not appended to the `<p>` selector. Notice that in the document body, the `danger` class selector is now applied to two different elements: `<p>` and `<strong>`. Figure 3.2 shows the document in a web browser.

```
...
<style type="text/css">
...
.danger { color: red; font-weight: bold }
</style>
</head>
<body>
<h1>Coast City Kites</h1>
<h2>Safety Tips</h2>
<p>Never fly over <strong class="danger">people</strong>.<p>
<p>Never fly near <strong class="danger">trees</strong>
or <strong class="danger">buildings</strong>.</p>
<p>Never fly near the <strong class="danger">airport</strong>.</p>
<p class="danger">Never fly in rain or thunderstorms.</p>
<p>Never fly near busy <strong class="danger">streets
</strong> or <strong class="danger">roadways</strong>.</p>
<p class="danger">Never fly near power lines.</p>
</body>
```

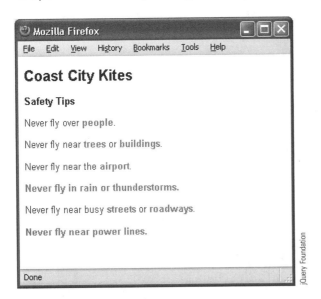

Figure 3.2
Web page formatting with a class selector

With jQuery, you use the Class (".*class*") selector to gain access to elements that use a particular class. With the preceding example, the statement $(".danger").css("fontSize", "32pt"); changes the font size of the two paragraphs that are assigned the danger class to 32 points. For example, if you add the following jQuery section to the preceding document, the two paragraphs will display as shown in Figure 3.2 as soon as the page finishes loading:

```
$(document).ready(function(){
   $(".danger").css(fontSize, "32pt");
});
```

In addition to the Class (".class") selector, you can also use the CSS methods listed in Table 3.1 to manipulate CSS classes with jQuery.

Note

The jQuery CSS methods do not actually create or delete CSS classes. Rather, they add and remove existing CSS classes to and from specified elements.

The following example demonstrates how to use the .addClass() and .removeClass() methods. The example includes a table and two buttons. The first button uses the .addClass() method to add gray stripes to every other row in the table to make it easier to read while the second button uses the

Table 3.1   jQuery CSS Methods

Method	Description
.addClass()	Adds a specified class to a set of matching elements.
.hasClass()	Determines whether a specified class is assigned to a set of matching elements.
.removeClass()	Removes a specified class from a set of matching elements.
.toggleClass()	Adds or removes a specified class from a set of matching elements.

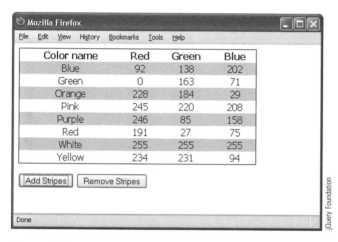

Figure 3.3
Table formatted with the .addClass() and .removeClass() methods

.removeClass() method to remove the stripes. Notice that the selectors use the :odd filter with the <tr> element to select every other row in the table. Figure 3.3 shows the output with the gray stripes.

```
<head>
<script type="text/javascript" src="jquery-1.7.2.js">
</script>
<script type="text/javascript">
/* <![CDATA[ */
$(document).ready(function(){
  $("#addStripes").click(function(){
    $("tr:odd").each(function() {
      $(this).addClass("stripes");
    });
  });
```

```
    $("#removeStripes").click(function(){
        $("tr:odd").each(function() {
            $(this).removeClass("stripes");
        });
    });
});
/* ]]> */
</script>
<style type="text/css">
body { font-family: tahoma, arial; }
table {width: 40%; border: 1px solid black; border-collapse:collapse; }
td { text-align: center; }
.stripes { background-color: #D3D3D3; }
</style>
</head>
<body>
<table>
<tr>
<th>Color name</th><th>Red</th><th>Green</th><th>Blue</th>
</tr>
<tr><td>Blue</td><td>92</td><td>138</td><td>202</td></tr>
<tr><td>Green</td><td>0</td><td>163</td><td>71</td></tr>
<tr><td>Orange</td><td>228</td><td>184</td><td>29</td></tr>
<tr><td>Pink</td><td>245</td><td>220</td><td>208</td></tr>
<tr><td>Purple</td><td>246</td><td>85</td><td>158</td></tr>
<tr><td>Red</td><td>191</td><td>27</td><td>75</td></tr>
<tr><td>White</td><td>255</td><td>255</td><td>255</td></tr>
<tr><td>Yellow</td><td>234</td><td>231</td><td>94</td>
</tr>
</table>
<p><input id="addStripes" type="button" value="Add Stripes" />
     <input id="removeStripes" type="button"
    value="Remove Stripes" /></p>
</body>
```

The preceding code uses two functions to add and remove the stripes from the table. You can use the .hasClass() method to consolidate the two functions into a single function. The following code includes a single function with an if...else statement that uses the .hasClass() method to determine whether the stripes class is assigned to any of the <tr> elements. If so, the .removeClass() method in the if clause removes the stripes class from the <tr> elements. If the stripes class is not assigned to any of the <tr> elements, the .addClass() method in the else clause adds them to the odd rows.

```
...
$(document).ready(function(){
  $("#updateClass").click(function(){
    if ($("tr").hasClass("stripes")) {
      $("tr").each(function() {
        $(this).removeClass("stripes");
      });
      $("#updateClass").attr("value", "Add Stripes");
    }
    else {
      $("tr:odd").each(function() {
        $(this).addClass("stripes");
      });
      $("#updateClass").attr("value", "Remove Stripes");
    }
  });
});
...
<p><input id="updateClass" type="button" value="Add Stripes" /></p>
...
```

The page also now includes a single button with an ID of updateClass and a value of "Add Stripes". Notice that the if…else statement in the preceding code uses the attr() accessor method to change the value of the button to either "Add Stripes" or "Remove Stripes", depending on whether the stripes class is assigned to the <tr> elements.

The final jQuery CSS method is .toggleClass(), which adds or removes a specified class from a set of matching elements. The basic syntax is to pass to the .toggleClass() method a string argument representing the name of the class you want to use. The following example is a simplified version of the stripes class code that uses the .toggleClass() method:

```
$(document).ready(function(){
  $("#updateClass").click(function(){
    $("tr:odd").each(function() {
      $(this).toggleClass("stripes");
    });
    if ($("#updateClass").attr("value") == "Add Stripes")
      $("#updateClass").attr("value", "Remove Stripes");
    else
      $("#updateClass").attr("value", "Add Stripes");
  });
});
```

Tip

You can apply multiple CSS classes with the `toggleClass()` method by separating them with spaces in the text argument.

MANIPULATING ELEMENT SIZE AND POSITION

Although the primary purpose of CSS is to format the display of a web page, you can use JavaScript to modify CSS styles and make the document dynamic after a web browser renders it. As you probably know, a major drawback to the original version of HTML was that it could only be used to produce static documents. One important aspect of DHTML is to use CSS to position elements on a web page. Actually, there is no way to reposition an element on a web page unless you use *CSS positioning* to lay out web elements. Table 3.2 lists common CSS positioning properties.

The most critical CSS positioning property is the `position` property, which determines the type of positioning applied to an element. Table 3.3 lists the values that can be assigned to the `position` property.

Table 3.2 CSS Positioning Properties

Property	Description
`clip`	Determines the region of an element that is displayed.
`display`	Specifies whether to display an element.
`height, width`	Determines an element's height and width.
`top, left`	Determines the position of an element's upper-left corner in relation to the upper-left corner of the document window.
`overflow`	Determines how to handle an image that is bigger than its assigned space.
`position`	Specifies the type of CSS positioning.
`bottom, right`	Determines the position of an element's lower-right corner in relation to the lower-right corner of the document window.
`visibility`	Specifies whether an element is visible.
`z-index`	Determines the order in which dynamically positioned elements are layered.

Table 3.3 CSS Positioning Values	
Positioning Type	**Description**
absolute	Positions an element in a specific location on a web page.
fixed	Positions an element in relation to the browser window.
relative	Positions an element in relation to other elements on a web page.
static	Positions an element according to the normal flow of other elements and text on a web page; elements that include this positioning type cannot be moved with CSS positioning.

Caution

A value of static essentially means that you cannot use CSS positioning with an element. To use CSS positioning, you must use one of the other three values listed in Table 3.3.

Dynamic Positioning with JavaScript

The easiest way to dynamically position an element with CSS is to use the left and top properties. The left property specifies an element's horizontal distance from the upper-left corner of the window, and the top property specifies an element's vertical distance from the upper-left corner of the window. Both property values are assigned in pixels. For example, the following code dynamically positions three images of a bird on a web page.

Figure 3.4 shows how the images appear in a web browser.

```
<p>
   <img src="up.gif"
     style="position: absolute; left: 40px; top: 200px"
     alt="Image of a bird"
     height="218px" width="200px" />
</p>
<p>
   <img src="down.gif"
     style="position: absolute; left: 250px; top: 80px"
     alt="Image of a bird"
     height="218px" width="200px" />
</p>
<p>
   <img src="up.gif"
```

```
        style="position: absolute; left: 480px; top: 10px"
        alt="Image of a bird"
        height="218px" width="200px" />
</p>
```

To modify elements after a web page renders, you must gain access to one or more elements by using a method such as getElementById(). Then, you can use the CSS positioning properties to manipulate the element. The following code shows a modified version of the three birds web page. This version contains a single bird image with an ID of birdID along with a button labeled "Flap." Clicking the Flap button executes the flyBird() event handler function, which changes the style elements of the image. Each time you click the Flap button, the CSS values assigned to the left, top, width, and height properties change to make it appear as if the bird is "flying" across the screen. The JavaScript code uses an if...else statement along with a counter variable named position to track and update the currently displayed image.

Figure 3.4
Dynamically positioned images

```
...
<script type="text/javascript">
/* <![CDATA[ */
   var position = 1;
   function flyBird() {
      var bird = document.getElementById("birdID");
      if (position == 1) {
         bird.src = "down.jpg";
         bird.style.left = "75px";
         bird.style.top = "225px";
         bird.style.width = "225px";
         bird.style.height = "143px";
         position = 2;
      }
      else if (position == 2) {
         bird.src = "up.jpg";
         bird.style.left = "300px";
         bird.style.top = "110px";
         bird.style.width = "126px";
         bird.style.height = "250px";
         position = 3;
      }
      else if (position == 3) {
         bird.src = "down.jpg";
         bird.style.left = "350px";
         bird.style.top = "50px";
         bird.style.width = "225px";
         bird.style.height = "143px";
         position = 4;
      }
      else {
         bird.src = "up.jpg";
         bird.style.left = "50px";
         bird.style.top = "300px";
         bird.style.width = "126px";
         bird.style.height = "250px";
         position = 1;
      }
   }
/* ]]> */
</script>
</head>
<body>
<form action="">
```

```
<input id="flyBird" type="button" value="Flap" onclick="flyBird()" />
</form>
<p><img id="birdID" src="up.jpg"
style="position: absolute; left: 40px; top: 300px" alt="Image of a bird"
height="250" width="126" /></p>
</body>
```

Notice in the preceding code that the first statement in the if and else if clauses does not reference the style property. Instead, it refers directly to the Image object to change the currently displayed image. An Image object represents an image created using the <img> element. You need to use an Image object if you want to dynamically change an image that is displayed on a web page. The Image object contains various properties that you can use to manipulate your objects, the most important of which is the src property, which allows JavaScript to dynamically change an image. Changing the value assigned to the src property changes the src attribute associated with an <img> element, which dynamically changes an image displayed on a web page.

Dynamic Positioning with jQuery

The techniques for dynamic positioning with jQuery do not differ all that greatly from JavaScript. Instead of changing an image with the src property of the Image element, you use the .attr() method, and to change most CSS properties, you use the .css() method. jQuery also includes the positioning methods listed in Table 3.4.

Half of the methods listed in Table 3.4 only return the assigned values for specific properties, so they are primarily useful for querying CSS property values. For example, the .innerHeight() method returns the height, including padding but not border, of the first element in a set of matching elements, but does not allow you to change any settings. The other methods listed in the table perform duties that are similar to the CSS positioning properties described in the last section. For example, the jQuery .height() and .width() methods correspond to the CSS height and width positioning properties, and allow you to get or set an element's height and width, respectively. The difference between the CSS property and the jQuery method versions is that the CSS property version returns a value with the unit of measure appended to the value, such as 200px. The jQuery methods return the value minus the unit of measure, such as 200, which allows you to use the returns values in a mathematical formula without having to first use a string method to strip the unit of measure (such as "px") from the value.

The following code contains a jQuery version of the flying bird web page. This version is similar to the JavaScript version, except that it uses the .attr() method to

Table 3.4 jQuery Positioning Methods

Method	Description
`.height()`	Returns the height of the first element in a set of matching elements or sets the height for all matching elements.
`.innerHeight()`	Returns the height, including padding but not border, of the first element in a set of matching elements.
`.innerWidth()`	Returns the width, including padding but not border, of the first element in a set of matching elements.
`.offset()`	Returns the coordinates of the first element in a set of matching elements or sets the coordinates for all matching elements.
`.outerHeight()`	Returns the height, including padding, border, and optional margin, of the first element in a set of matching elements.
`.outerWidth()`	Returns the width, including padding, border, and optional margin, of the first element in a set of matching elements.
`.position()`	Returns an object containing an object's top and left properties.
`.scrollLeft()`	Returns the horizontal position of the scrollbar of the first element in a set of matching elements or sets the horizontal position of the scrollbar for all matching elements.
`.scrollTop()`	Returns the vertical position of the scrollbar of the first element in a set of matching elements or sets the vertical position of the scrollbar for all matching elements.
`.width()`	Returns the width of the first element in a set of matching elements or sets the width for all matching elements.

change the currently displayed image and the `.css()` method to change the `left` and `top` properties. It also uses the jQuery `.width()` and `.height()` methods to change the size of the displayed image.

```
<head>
<script type="text/javascript" src="jquery-1.7.2.js">
</script>
<script type="text/javascript">
/* <![CDATA[ */
var position = 1;
$(document).ready(function(){
  $("#flyBird").click(function(){
    var birdElement = $("#birdID");
    if (position == 1) {
      birdElement.attr("src", "down.jpg");
```

```
              birdElement.css("left", "75px");
              birdElement.css("top", "225px");
              birdElement.width("225px");
              birdElement.height("143px");
                  position = 2;
          }
        else if (position == 2) {
              birdElement.attr("src", "up.jpg");
              birdElement.css("left", "300px");
              birdElement.css("top", "110px");
              birdElement.width("126px");
              birdElement.height("250px");
                  position = 3;
          }
        else if (position == 3) {
              birdElement.attr("src", "down.jpg");
              birdElement.css("left", "350px");
              birdElement.css("top", "50px");
              birdElement.width("225px");
              birdElement.height("143px");
                  position = 4;
          }
        else {
              birdElement.attr("src", "up.jpg");
              birdElement.css("left", "50px");
              birdElement.css("top", "300px");
              birdElement.width("126px");
              birdElement.height("250px");
                  position = 1;
          }
      });
  });
  /* ]]> */
  </script>
  </head>
  <body>
  <form action="">
  <input id="flyBird" type="button" value="Flap" />
  </form>
      <p>
        <img id="birdID" src="up.jpg"
            style="position: absolute; left: 40px; top: 300px"
            alt="Image of a bird" height="250" width="126" />
      </p>
  </body>
```

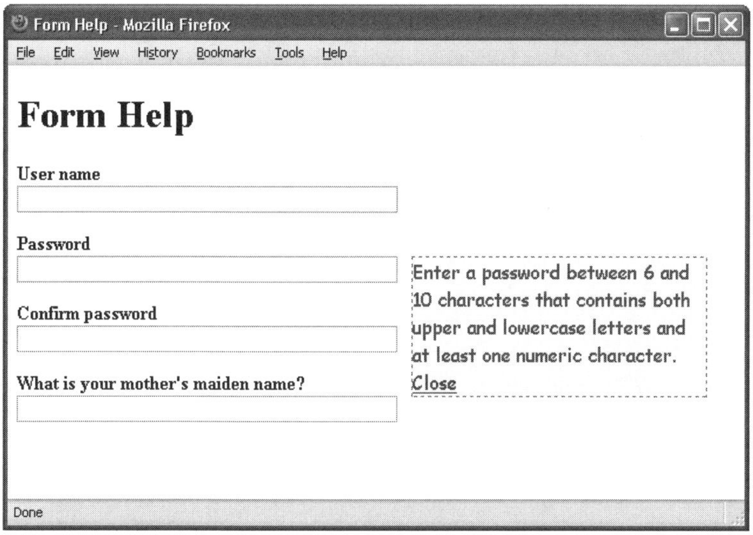

Figure 3.5
Form Help web page

One drawback to creating dynamic web pages with CSS is that you can only use CSS positioning to set and return the position of elements that include properties such as the `position`, `left`, and `top` properties. To find the position of an element that does not include CSS positioning properties, you can use the HTML DOM `offsetLeft` and `offsetTop` properties. Similarly, you can use the `offsetWidth` and `offsetHeight` properties to return the size of an element on a web page. The `offsetLeft`, `offsetTop`, `offsetWidth`, and `offsetHeight` properties are available to most current web browsers.

The following example demonstrates how to use the standard JavaScript CSS `offsetTop` and `offsetWidth` properties to display context-sensitive help for the fields on a form. The project also uses the CSS `cursor` property to dynamically change the cursor to a help cursor when the mouse pointer passes over a form element that contains context-sensitive help. Figure 3.5 shows the page after clicking the Password text box.

```
<head>
  <title>Form Help</title>
  <meta http-equiv="content-type" content="text/html; charset=utf-8" />
  <script type="text/javascript">
  /* <![CDATA[ */
  function showHelp(elementId) {
    var curElement = document.getElementById(elementId);
    var helpElement = document.getElementById("box");
```

```
        switch (elementId) {
          case "username":
            helpElement.innerHTML = "Enter a unique user name that is
                between 5 and 12 characters.";
            break;
          case "password":
            helpElement.innerHTML = "Enter a password between 6 and 10
                characters that contains both upper and lowercase letters
                and at least one numeric character. ";
            break;
          case "password_confirm":
            helpElement.innerHTML = "Confirm your selected password. ";
            break;
          case "challenge":
            helpElement.innerHTML = "Enter your mother's maiden name.
                This value will be used to confirm your identity in the
                event that you forget your password. ";
            break;
        }
      helpElement.innerHTML += "<a href=''
        onclick=\"document.getElementById('box')
        .style.visibility='hidden';return false;\">Close</a>";
      document.getElementById("box").style.visibility = "visible";
      document.getElementById("box").style.left = curElement.offsetWidth
        + 20 + "px";
      document.getElementById("box").style.top = curElement.offsetTop + "px";
    }
    /* ]]> */
    </script>
</head>
<body>
<h1>Form Help</h1>
<form action="" method="get"
enctype="application/x-www-form-urlencoded">
<p><strong>User name</strong><br />
<input type="text" id="username" size="50"
  onmouseover="this.style.cursor='help'"
  onclick="showHelp(this.id)" /></p>
<p><strong>Password</strong><br />
<input type="password" id="password" size="50"
  onmouseover="this.style.cursor='help'"
  onclick="showHelp(this.id)" /></p>
<p><strong>Confirm password</strong><br />
```

```
<input type="password" id="password_confirm" size="50"
   onmouseover="this.style.cursor='help'"
   onclick="showHelp(this.id)" /></p>
<p><strong>What is your mother's maiden name?</strong><br />
<input type="password" id="challenge" size="50"
   onmouseover="this.style.cursor='help'"
   onclick="showHelp(this.id)" /></p>
</form>
<div id="box" style="position: absolute; visibility: hidden;
   width: 250px; background-color:#FFFFC0;
   font-family:Comic Sans MS; color: #A00000;
   border:1px dashed #D00000"></div>
</body>
```

In comparison to the JavaScript HTML DOM *offset* properties, jQuery includes two methods, .offset() and .position(),which set and return the two most important CSS positioning properties: top and left. The difference between these two methods is that .offset() returns the current position relative to the document while the .position() method returns the current position relative to the offset parent. For example, consider the following <div> element. For the <img> element, the .position() method returns values of 200 and 40 for the top and left properties because those are the values relative to the <div> offset parent. The .offset() method returns values of 300 and 140 for the top and left properties because it takes into account positioning values assigned to the <div> element.

```
<div style="position: absolute; left: 100px; top: 100px ">
<p><img src="up.gif" style="position: absolute; top: 200px; left: 40px"
   alt="Image of a bird" height="218px" width="200px" />
</p>
</div>
```

The following example shows a jQuery version of the Form Help web page. This version includes jQuery versions of both the mouseover and click events.

```
<head>
<script type="text/javascript" src="jquery-1.7.2.js">
</script>
<script type="text/javascript">
/* <![CDATA[ */
$(document).ready(function(){
   $("input").mouseover(function() {
      var elementId = $(this).attr('id');
         $("#" + elementId).css("cursor", "help");
   });
```

```
$("input").click(function() {
   var elementId = $(this).attr('id');
   var helpBox = $("#box");
      switch (elementId) {
         case "username":
            helpBox.html("Enter a unique user name that is
               between 5 and 12 characters.");
            break;
         case "password":
            helpBox.html("Enter a password between 6 and 10
               characters that contains both upper and
               lowercase letters and at least one numeric
               character.");
            break;
         case "password_confirm":
            helpBox.html("Confirm your selected password.");
            break;
         case "challenge":
            helpBox.html("Enter your mother's maiden name.
               This value will be used to confirm your identity
               in the event that you forget your password.");
            break;
      }
      helpBox.css("visibility", "visible");
      helpOffset = $("#" + elementId).offset();
      helpBox.css("left", $("#" + elementId).width() + 20);
      helpBox.css("top", helpOffset.top);
   });
});
/* ]]> */
</script>
</head>
<body>
<h1>Form Help</h1>
<div>
<form action="" method="get"
enctype="application/x-www-form-urlencoded">
<p><strong>User name</strong><br />
<input type="text" id="username" size="50" /></p>
<p><strong>Password</strong><br />
<input type="password" id="password" size="50" /></p>
<p><strong>Confirm password</strong><br />
<input type="password" id="password_confirm" size="50" /></p>
<p><strong>What is your mother's maiden name?</strong><br />
```

```
<input type="password" id="challenge" size="50" /></p>
</form>
</div>
<div id="box" style="position: absolute; visibility: hidden;
   width: 250px; background-color:#FFFFC0;
   font-family:Comic Sans MS; color: #A00000;
   border:1px dashed #D00000"></div>
</body>
```

SUMMARY

This chapter introduced the very basics of using jQuery to manipulate CSS properties. The next chapter continues the discussion of how to manipulate CSS properties by explaining how to create animation and visual effects.

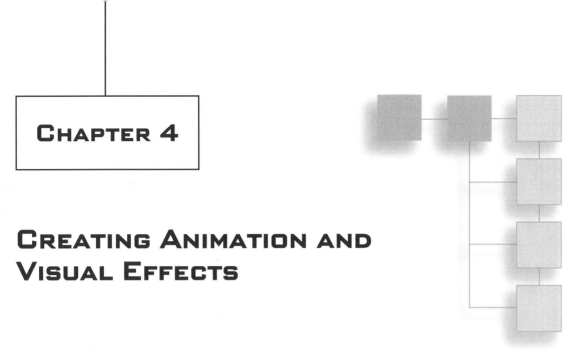

CHAPTER 4

CREATING ANIMATION AND VISUAL EFFECTS

Today, more and more businesses want their websites to include formatting and images that can be updated without requiring the users to reload a web page from the server. They also want to use animation and interactive web pages in innovative ways to attract and retain visitors and to make their websites effective and easy to navigate. You cannot create these kinds of effects with standard HTML; instead, you need to use DHTML or jQuery.

ANIMATING WEB PAGE ELEMENTS

As you have probably realized by now, web pages are much more useful when they are dynamic. In Internet terminology, the word *dynamic* means several things. Primarily, it refers to web pages that respond to user requests through buttons or other kinds of controls. Among other things, a dynamic web page can allow users to change the document background color, submit a form, process a query, and participate in an online game or quiz. The term *dynamic* also refers to various effects, such as animation, that appear automatically in a web browser. In this section, you learn about basic techniques for animating web page elements.

Working with Timeouts and Intervals

As you develop web pages, you may need to have some JavaScript code execute repeatedly, without user intervention. Alternately, you might want to create animation or allow for some kind of repetitive task that executes automatically. For example, you might want to include an advertising image that changes automatically every few seconds. Or, you might want to use animation to change the ticking hands of an online analog clock (in which case each position of the clock hands would require a separate image).

You use the Window object's timeout and interval methods to create code that executes automatically. The *setTimeout() method* is used in JavaScript to execute code after a specific amount of time has elapsed. Code executed with the setTimeout() method executes only once. The syntax for the setTimeout() method is var variable = setTimeout("code", milliseconds);. This statement declares that the variable will refer to the setTimeout() method. The code argument must be enclosed in double or single quotation marks and can be a single JavaScript statement, a series of JavaScript statements, or a function call. The amount of time the web browser should wait before executing the code argument of the setTimeout() method is expressed in milliseconds.

Note

A millisecond is one-thousandth of a second; there are 1,000 milliseconds in a second. For example, five seconds is equal to 5,000 milliseconds.

The *clearTimeout() method* is used to cancel a setTimeout() method before its code executes. The clearTimeout() method receives a single argument, which is the variable that represents a setTimeout() method call. The variable that represents a setTimeout() method call must be declared as a global variable.

The script section in the following code contains a setTimeout() method and a clearTimeout() method call. The setTimeout() method is set to execute after 10,000 milliseconds (10 seconds) have elapsed. If a user clicks the OK button, the buttonPressed() function calls the clearTimeout() method.

```
<head>
<script type="text/javascript">
/* <![CDATA[ */
var buttonNotPressed = setTimeout(
    "window.alert ('You must press the OK button to continue!')", 10000);
function buttonPressed() {
    clearTimeout(buttonNotPressed);
    window.alert("The setTimeout() method was cancelled!");
}
/* ]]> */
</script>
</head>
<body>
<form action="">
```

```
<input type="button" value=" OK "
  onclick="buttonPressed();" />
</form>
</body>
</html>
```

Two other JavaScript methods that create code and execute automatically are `setInterval()` and `clearInterval()`. The *setInterval() method* is similar to the `setTimeout()` method, except that it repeatedly executes the same code after being called only once. The *clearInterval() method* is used to clear a `setInterval()` method call in the same fashion that the `clearTimeout()` method clears a `setTimeout()` method call. The `setInterval()` and `clearInterval()` methods are most often used for starting animation code that executes repeatedly. The syntax for the `setInterval()` method is the same as the syntax for the `setTimeout()` method: `var variable = setInterval("code", milliseconds);`. As with the `clearTimeout()` method, the `clearInterval()` method receives a single argument, which is the global variable that represents a `setInterval()` method call.

By combining the `src` attribute of the `Image` object with the `setTimeout()` or `setInterval()` methods, you can create simple animation on a web page. The following code uses the `setInterval()` method to automatically swap the motorcycle images shown in Figure 4.1 every couple of seconds.

Figure 4.1
Banner images animated with the setInterval() method

```
<head>
<script type="text/javascript">
/* <![CDATA[ */
var curBanner="cycle1";
function changeBanner() {
    if (curBanner == "cycle2") {
        document.images[0].src = "v500tec.gif";
        curBanner = "cycle1";
    }
    else  {
        document.images[0].src = "showroom.gif";
        curBanner = "cycle2";
    }
}
/* ]]> */
</script>
</head>
<body onload="var begin=setInterval('changeBanner()', 2000);">
<p><img src="v500tec.gif" height="90px" width="700px"
alt="Banner images" /></p>
</body>
```

The simple stationary animations you have seen so far were created by swapping the image files assigned to an <img> element's src attribute. With DHTML, you can use dynamic positioning to create traveling animation—that is, images that appear to travel across the screen, as described in the following section.

Using Simple Animation with jQuery

One of the most basic of the jQuery visual effect methods is the .animate() method. How this method works is by incrementing or decrementing CSS properties that accept numeric values according to a specified duration. You can use the .animate() method to animate the following CSS properties:

backgroundPosition	font	marginLeft
borderBottomWidth	fontSize	marginRight
borderLeftWidth	height	marginTop
borderRightWidth	Left	maxHeight
borderSpacing	letterSpacing	maxWidth
borderTopWidth	lineHeight	minHeight
borderWidth	margin	minWidth
bottom	marginBottom	outlineWidth

padding	paddingTop	width
paddingBottom	right	wordSpacing
paddingLeft	textIndent	
paddingRight	top	

Caution

Keep in mind that you can use the `.animate()` method with the preceding CSS properties only because they accept numeric values. The `.animate()` method does not work with CSS properties that accept text values, such as `fontFamily`.

Tip

Notice that the CSS properties listed in the preceding table use JavaScript syntax instead of CSS syntax, such as `fontSize` instead of `font-size`. Unlike the jQuery `.css()` property, which allows you to use either JavaScript or jQuery CSS property syntax, you must use JavaScript syntax with the `.animate()` method.

The basic syntax for the `.animate()` method is as follows:

```
(selector).animate({properties}, duration, easing, complete)
```

The *properties* portion of the method contains the list of styles, separated by commas, that you want to change for the selected element. Be sure to notice that the styles are contained within a pair of braces { }. The following code demonstrates how to update multiple styles for a text string. Figure 4.2 shows the starting page.

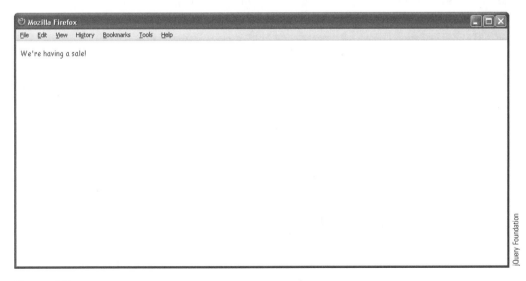

Figure 4.2
Starting size and position of page animated with .animate()

Figure 4.3
Ending size and position of page animated with .animate()

If you run the code in a browser, the text string will appear to grow and move to the size and shape shown in Figure 4.3.

```
<head>
<script type="text/javascript" src="jquery-1.7.2.js"></script>
<script type="text/javascript">
/* <![CDATA[ */
$(document).ready(function(){
    $("#sale").animate({fontSize:"48pt", marginLeft: "100pt",
    marginTop: "100pt"});
});
/* ]]> */
</script>
</head>
<body>
<p id="sale" style="font-family: Comic Sans MS; font-size: 10pt">
We're having a sale!</p>
</body>
```

The *duration* portion of the .animate() method determines the speed in which the style properties change from their starting to their final values. This is essentially the same as the second argument you pass to the JavaScript setInterval() method to control the speed of an animation. You can apply a specified number of milliseconds to the speed portion of the .animate() method or one of three values: slow, normal, and fast. A value of slow represents 200 milliseconds, a value of normal represents 400 milliseconds, and a value of fast represents 600 milliseconds. The default value is normal, or 400 milliseconds.

The *easing* portion of the .animate() method is not so easy to understand. There are two built-in easing values: "linear" and "swing". The linear easing value essentially applies the same change intervals to the affected CSS properties, depending on the value assigned to the speed portion of the method. For example, if you use the .animate() method to change the marginLeft property of an element from 0 to 100, with a speed value of 500 and linear easing, jQuery will change the element's left margin every 1/2 second. You can compare linear easing to a train traveling between two stations at the exact same speed without stopping at either station, with each click of a mile representing an update to the element values. In comparison, the swing easing value starts the animation slowly, speeds up, and then slows down to "ease" the elements into their final position. The swing easing value is more comparable to an airplane, which starts out slowly on the runway, takes off and achieves fast speed, and then slows down when it lands and "eases" into the terminal. In other words, the swing easing value is similar to a child's swing set, which slows down at each end of the swing arc, and significantly speeds up during the progression between each end of the arc. Swing is the default easing value and is usually sufficient for most animations.

Tip

Many more types of easing functions are available as jQuery plug-ins. Refer to Chapter 9, "Extending jQuery with Plug-Ins," for more information on using and developing jQuery plug-ins.

The last argument passed to the .animate() method is *complete*, which refers to a callback function that is called when the animation completes. Callback functions are further described in the next section.

The following code demonstrates how to create traveling animation with an animated GIF image of a butterfly. The butterfly travels from the lower-left side of the screen, over the paragraph, to the upper-right corner. The global topPosition and leftPosition variables define the initial starting position of the image. The $(document).ready() method calls a JavaScript function named flyButterfly(). The first statement in the flyButterfly() function uses the .css() method to display the butterfly image, which is initially hidden. The second and third statements modify the values assigned to the topPosition and leftPosition variables, which the function uses to dynamically position the butterfly image.

The if statement then calculates the current location of the butterfly. If it's within 200 pixels of the right edge of the window, the image's position is reset to its starting

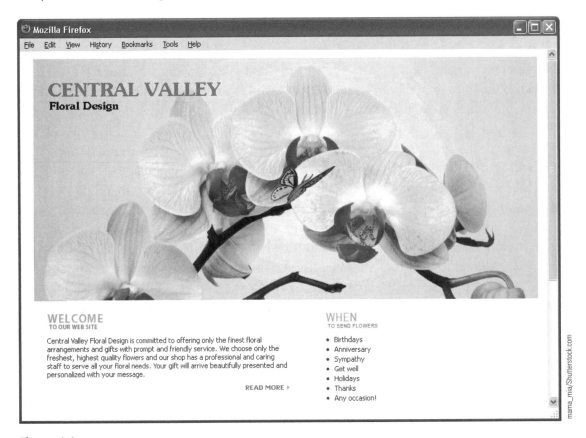

Figure 4.4
Butterfly animation web page

values and then hidden with the `.css()` method. Hiding the image is necessary in this case because if you reset the image's position and it is still visible, it will appear to "zip" across the screen to the starting point. The `.animate()` method then changes the `left` and `top` CSS properties, and then calls the `flyButterfly` function to repeat the method and continue the animation. Figure 4.4 shows how the web page appears in a browser.

```
<head>
<link href="css.css" type="text/css" rel="stylesheet" />
<script type="text/javascript" src="jquery-1.7.2.js"></script>
<script type="text/javascript">
/* <![CDATA[ */
var topPosition = 250;
var leftPosition = -100;
$(document).ready(function() { flyButterfly(); });
   function flyButterfly() {
      $("#butterfly").attr("display", "block");
```

```
            topPosition -= 2;
            leftPosition += 10;
            if (leftPosition >= window.innerWidth - 200) {
                topPosition = 250;
                leftPosition = -100;
            $("#butterfly").attr("display", "hide");
            }
            $("#butterfly").animate( {
                left: leftPosition, top: topPosition
            },  100, "linear", flyButterfly);
    }
/* ]]> */
</script>
</head>
<body>
    <p>
        <img src="butterfly.gif" id="butterfly"
            style="position: absolute; left: -100px; top: 250px;
            display: "none" alt="Image of a butterfly"
            height="120" width="150" />
    </p>
...
```

Understanding Callback Functions

In the previous section, you saw how to use a callback function with the
.animate() method to call the flyButterfly function to continue the animation.
Another important aspect of callback functions is that they ensure an animation
completes before executing subsequent lines of code. Like most programming languages, JavaScript executes code statements line-by-line, in the order that they appear
in a script section or function. However, animations such as those created with the
.animate() method usually execute according to the *duration* portion of the
.animate() method. By default, JavaScript will not wait for the animation (or any
functionality) to complete before executing the next statement in the queue. This can
cause problems if you need to execute JavaScript code after an animation sequence
completes.

For example, the following code uses an .animate() statement with the CSS
fontsize property to grow the text "Memorial Day Sale!", contained within a
<p> element with an ID of ad, from 1em to 3em. The second statement uses the
setInterval() method with the .toggleClass() method and CSS visibility
property to show and hide the text, simulating a blinking effect.

```
<style type="text/css">
.blink { visibility: hidden }
</style>
<script type="text/javascript">
/* <![CDATA[ */
$(document).ready(function(){
   $("#ad").animate({fontSize: "3em"}, 2000, "linear");
   setInterval("$('#ad').toggleClass('blink')", 500);
/* ]]> */
</script>
</head>
<body>
<p id="ad" style="text-align: center; margin-top: 175px;
font-family: Arial, sans-serif;font-weight: bold;font-size: 1em">
Memorial Day Sale!</p>
</body>
```

The problem with the preceding code is that the `setInterval()` method will begin executing before the `.animate()` method finishes, causing the text to both grow in size and blink at the same time. Although this result may be desirable in some cases, if you want the blinking effect to run after the `.animate()` method grows the text, you need to call the `setInterval()` method from a callback function, as follows:

```
$(document).ready(function(){
   $("#ad").animate({fontSize: "3em"}, 2000, "linear", function() {
     blinkText = setInterval("$('#ad').toggleClass('blink')", 500);
   });
});
```

The following example presents a simple splash advertisement that displays the animated `"Memorial Day Sale!"` text for 15 seconds before hiding the `<div>` element, represented by an ID of `splash`, that contains it. Visitors can either view the page for 15 seconds or click the Skip Advertisement link, represented by an ID of `a1`, in the upper-right corner.

The first four statements in the `document.ready()` method dynamically position the `<div>` element in the center of the document, according to the dimensions of the user's browser. The next two statements use a `setInterval()` method to dynamically change the value next to the Skip Advertisement link, which represents the number of seconds remaining for the advertisement and is contained within a `<span>` element with an ID of `sp1`. Notice that instead of calling a separate function, the new `setInterval()` method uses an anonymous function to count down and display the number of remaining seconds.

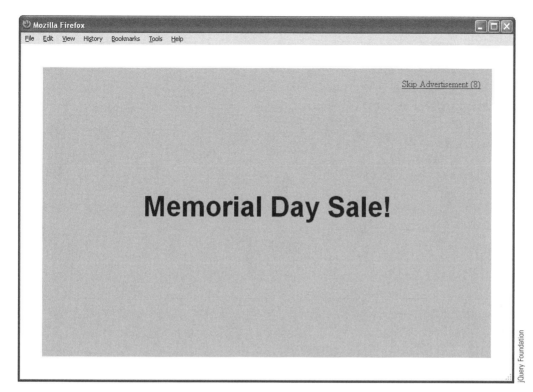

Figure 4.5
Splash advertisement

The `if` statement within the anonymous function contains a conditional expression that determines when a counter variable named `secondsLeft` is equal to 1, at which point the `if` statement calls the `.click()` method for the `anchor` element. The statements within the `.click()` method clear the two `setInterval()` methods, hide the `<div>` element, and return a value of `false` to prevent the link from attempting to jump to another page. Figure 4.5 shows how the page appears in a web browser.

```
<head>
<script type="text/javascript" src="jquery-1.7.2.js"></script>
<style type="text/css">
.blink { visibility: hidden }
</style>
<script type="text/javascript">
/* <![CDATA[ */
var countSeconds;
var blinkText;
$(document).ready(function(){
```

```
    var splashElement = $("#splash");
    splashElement.css("position","absolute");
    splashElement.css("top", (($(window).height()
        - splashElement.outerHeight()) / 2)
        + $(window).scrollTop() + "px");
    splashElement.css("left", (($(window).width()
        - splashElement.outerWidth()) / 2)
        + $(window).scrollLeft() + "px");
    var secondsLeft = 15;
    countSeconds = setInterval(function(){
        if (secondsLeft == 1)
            $("#a1").click();
        $("#s1").html(-secondsLeft);
    }, 1000);
    $("#ad").animate({fontSize: "3em"}, 2000, "linear", function() {
        blinkText = setInterval("$('#ad').toggleClass('blink')", 500);
    });
    $("#a1").click(function(){
        clearInterval(blinkText);
        $("#splash").css("visibility", "hidden");
        return false;
    });
});
/* ]]> */
</script>
</head>
<body>
<div id="splash" style="background-color: #99CCCC; height:500; width:800">
<p style="text-align: right; padding-right: 20px">
<a id="a1" href="">Skip Advertisement (<span id="s1">15</span>)</a></p>
<p id="ad" style="text-align: center; margin-top: 175px;
font-family: Arial, sans-serif; font-weight: bold; font-size: 1em">
Memorial Day Sale!</p>
</div>
</body>
```

CREATING DHTML MENUS

Creating menus is one of the more popular uses of DHTML. DHTML menus are most often used for organizing navigational links to other web pages, although they are also useful for displaying and hiding information. This section discusses basic expandable and navigation menus and the next section explains how to create sliding menus.

Building an Expandable Menu

The CSS display property specifies whether to display an element on a web page.

You can use the display property to simulate expandable and collapsible menus on a web page. You typically use the display property with a block-level element, which gives a web page its structure. Most web browsers render block-level elements so that they appear on their own line. Block-level elements can contain other block-level elements or inline elements. The <div>, <p>, and heading elements (<h1>, <h2>, and so on) are examples of common block-level elements. Inline elements, or text-level elements, describe the text that appears on a web page. Unlike block-level elements, inline elements do not appear on their own lines; instead, they appear within the line of the block-level element that contains them. Examples of inline elements include the <b> (bold) and
 (line break) elements. By placing elements and text within a <div> element, you can use the display property to simulate expandable and collapsible menus.

If you assign a block-level element's display property a value of none, the associated element is not displayed. In fact, the web page does not even allocate space for the element on the page. However, if you assign a value of block to a block-level element's display property, the web page is reformatted to allocate sufficient space for the element and its contents, which are then displayed.

The following code shows a web page that displays Hall of Fame players for the National Football League. The style section defines a class selector named collapsed for the <div> element. The collapsed class selector includes the display property, which turns off the display of each <div> element when the web page is first rendered. This example uses two functions in the jQuery section for the mouseover and mouseout event handlers. Notice how the single statements within each function identify the <div> element to expand or collapse. Each statement uses $("#" + $(this).attr('id') to identify the calling paragraph, and then appends " + div" to create a Next Adjacent ("*prev + next*") hierarchical selector. The .css() methods appended to each hierarchical selector then use the display property to either display or hide the <div> element. Figure 4.6 shows the document in a web browser when the mouse pointer passes over the Cleveland Browns link.

```
<head>
<style type="text/css">
  div.collapsed
  {
    display: none;
  }
```

```
</style>
<script type="text/javascript" src="jquery-1.7.2.js"></script>
<script type="text/javascript">
/* <![CDATA[ */
$(document).ready(function(){
  $("p").mouseover(function() {
    $("#" + $(this).attr("id") + " + div").css("display", "block");
  });
  $("p").mouseout(function() {
    $("#" + $(this).attr("id") + " + div").css("display", "none");
  });
});
/* ]]> */
</script>
</head>
<body>
  <h1>
    National Football League</h1>
  <h2>
    Hall of Fame Players</h2>
  <p id="billsMenu"><a href="">
    Buffalo Bills</a></p>
  <div id="bills" class="collapsed">
    <p>Joe DeLamielleure '03, Jim Kelly '02, Marv Levy '01 (coach),
    James Lofton '03, Billy Shaw '99, Thurman Thomas '07</p>
  </div>
  <p id="brownsMenu"><a href="">
    Cleveland Browns</a></p>
  <div id="browns" class="collapsed">
    <p>Doug Atkins '82, Jim Brown '71, Paul Brown '67 (coach/owner),
    Willie Davis '81, Len Dawson '87, Joe DeLamielleure '03, Len Ford '76,
    Frank Gatski '85, Otto Graham '65, Lou Groza '74, Gene Hickerson '07,
    Henry Jordan '95, Leroy Kelly '94, Dante Lavelli '75,
    Mike McCormack '84, Tommy McDonald '98, Bobby Mitchell '83,
    Marion Motley '68, Ozzie Newsome '99, Paul Warfield '83,
    Bill Willis '77</p>
  </div>
</body>
```

jQuery includes two methods, .show() and .hide(), that simplify displaying and hiding elements. To use either method, append it to the selector that you

Figure 4.6
Web page with expandable menus

want to show or hide, as the following jQuery code for the Hall of Fame players demonstrates:

```
$(document).ready(function(){
  $("p").mouseover(function() {
    $("#" + $(this).attr('id') + " + div").show();
  });
  $("p").mouseout(function() {
    $("#" + $(this).attr('id') + " + div").hide();
  });
});
/* ]]> */
```

Constructing Navigation Menus

You are probably already familiar with drop-down menus, or pull-down menus, which are similar to the menus you find in a Windows application. Menus can greatly improve the design of your web page, and they help visitors navigate through your website. Figure 4.7 shows a navigation menu that helps visitors to eBay's website locate specific shopping categories.

Although you can create a navigation menu in several ways, the easiest way is to use a table to contain your menu items. First, you create a master table whose purpose is to contain nested tables for each individual menu. The following code shows the beginnings of a table that will create a navigation menu for an electronics store. Figure 4.8 shows the document in a web browser.

Figure 4.7
Navigation menu on eBay

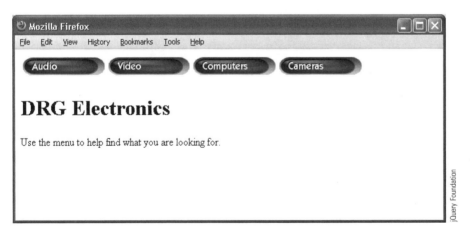

Figure 4.8
Document with a top navigation menu

```
<table>
   <tr align="left">
      <td>
         <a href="">
         <img src="button1up.png" id="b1"
            border="0" vspace="1"
            hspace="1" />
         </a></td>
      <td>
         <a href="">
         <img src="button2up.png" id="b2"
            border="0" vspace="1"
            hspace="1" /></a>
      </td>
      <td>
         <a href="">
         <img src="button3up.png" id="b3"
            border="0" vspace="1"
            hspace="1" /></a>
      </td>
      <td>
         <a href="">
         <img src="button4up.png" id="b4"
            border="0" vspace="1"
            hspace="1" /></a>
      </td>
   </tr>
</table>
<h1>
   DRG Electronics</h1>
<p>
   Use the menu to help find what you
   are looking for.</p>
```

You nest the contents of a navigation menu within the same cell as the top navigation menu heading. The following code shows a <div> element in which the Audio
menu items are nested within the same cell as the Audio menu:

```
<td
   onmouseover="document.getElementById(
   ('b1').src='button1over.png'"
   onmouseout="document.getElementById(
   ('b1').src='button1up.png'"><a href=""><br />
   <img src="button1up.png" id="b1" border="0"
      vspace="1" hspace="1" /></a>
   <div class="dropmenu">
```

```
     <ul>
        <li><a href="audiosys.html">
           Audio Systems</a></li>
        <li><a href="audioplayers.html">
           iPods and MP3 Players</a></li>
        <li><a href="headphones.html">
           Headphones</a></li>
     </ul>
   </div>
</td>
```

To show and hide each menu, you use the `display` property, as shown in the following version of the table elements for the Audio menu. This time, the `<div>` element containing the menu includes a `style` property that hides the element and sets its position to absolute. In the following code, the `mouseover` and `mouseout` event handlers in the jQuery section use the `.show()` and `.hide()` methods to handle the display of the menu. Note that the `mouseover` and `mouseout` event handlers also include statements that modify the menu buttons. Therefore, when the mouse passes over each image, it is replaced with a more vivid one and then changes back to the original image when the mouse pointer is removed. Figure 4.9 shows the web page in a browser with the mouse pointer over the Audio menu.

```
<head>
   <link rel="stylesheet" type="text/css" href="menustyle.css" />
<script type="text/javascript" src="jquery-1.7.2.js"></script>
<script type="text/javascript">
/* <![CDATA[ */
$(document).ready(function(){
   $("tr").mouseover(function(){
      $("#audio").show();
      $("#b1").attr("src", "button1over.png");
   });
   $("tr").mouseout(function(){
      $("#audio").hide();
      $("#b1").attr("src", "button1up.png");
   });
});
/* ]]> */
</script>
</head>
<body>
<table>
   <tr align="left">
      <td>
         <a href="">
```

```
<img src="button1up.png" id="b1"
  border="0" vspace="1"
  hspace="1" />
</a>
<div id="audio" class="dropmenu"
style="display:none; position:absolute">
<ul>
  <li><a href="audiosys.html">Audio Systems</a></li>
  <li><a href="audioplayers.html">iPods and MP3 Players</a></li>
  <li><a href="headphones.html">Headphones</a></li>
</ul>
</div>
</td>
```

In addition to the .show() and .hide() methods, which simplify displaying and hiding elements, jQuery includes a related method named .toggle(). When used without any arguments, the .toggle() method simply toggles between displaying and hiding the specified elements, as shown with the following version of the jQuery code for the Audio menu:

```
$(document).ready(function(){
  $("#b1").mouseover(function(){
    $("#audio").toggle();
    $(this).attr("src", "button1over.png");
  });
  $("#b1").mouseout(function(){
    $("#audio").toggle();
    $(this).attr("src", "button1up.png");
  });
});
```

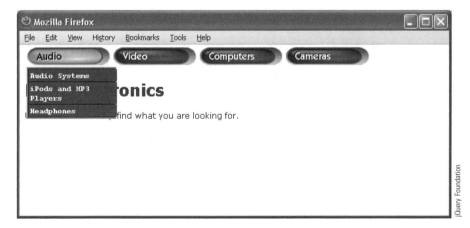

Figure 4.9
Audio navigation menu

USING SLIDING FUNCTIONALITY

Sliding refers to an animation technique that causes elements to appear to slide open or closed. As their name implies, *sliding menus* are menus that appear to slide open and closed. To create a simple sliding menu, you can use the .show(), .hide(), and .toggle() methods to perform simple animation by passing to them the same *speed*, *duration*, and *complete* arguments that the .animate() method accepts. By default, these methods show and hide selected elements immediately. However, you can assign to each method the same speed values that you assign to the .animation() method: "slow" (200 milliseconds), "normal" (400 milliseconds), "fast" (600 milliseconds), or any number representing milliseconds. For example, the .toggle() methods from the Audio menu you saw in the preceding code show and hide the menu immediately. By adding a speed argument to the .toggle() method, you can turn the menu into a sliding menu, which appears to slide open and closed when the mouse passes over it. The following version of the jQuery code creates a sliding menu by passing a speed argument of "slow" to the .toggle() methods:

```
<head>
   <link rel="stylesheet" type="text/css" href="menustyle.css" />
<script type="text/javascript" src="jquery-1.7.2.js"></script>
<script type="text/javascript">
/* <![CDATA[ */
$(document).ready(function(){
   $("tr").mouseover(function(){
      $("#audio").show();
      $("#b1").attr("src", "button1over.png");
   });
   $("tr").mouseout(function(){
      $("#audio").hide();
      $("#b1").attr("src", "button1up.png");
   });
});
/* ]]> */
</script>
</head>
<body>
<table>
   <tr align="left">
      <td>
         <a href="">
         <img src="button1up.png" id="b1"
```

```
              border="0" vspace="1"
              hspace="1" />
       </a>
       <div id="audio" class="dropmenu"
       style="display:none; position:absolute">
       <ul>
          <li><a href="audiosys.html">Audio Systems</a></li>
          <li><a href="audioplayers.html">iPods and MP3 Players</a></li>
          <li><a href="headphones.html">Headphones</a></li>
       </ul>
       </div>
```

```
$(document).ready(function(){
   $("#b1").mouseover(function(){
      $(this).attr("src", "button1over.png");
      $("#audio").toggle("slow");
   });
   $("#b1").mouseout(function(){
      $(this).attr("src", "button1up.png");
      $("#audio").toggle("slow");
   });
});
```

jQuery includes three additional methods for creating sliding functionality: .slideDown(), .slideUp(), and .slideToggle(). These methods are almost identical to the .show(), .hide(), and .toggle() methods. The difference between these two sets of methods is that the .show(), .hide(), and .toggle() methods show and hide elements immediately by default, whereas the .slideDown(), .slideUp(), and .slideToggle() methods show and hide selected elements using a speed of 400 milliseconds by default. The following shows an example of the Audio menu code using the .slideToggle() method:

```
$(document).ready(function(){

   $("#b1").mouseover(function(){
      $(this).attr("src", "button1over.png");
      $("#audio").slideToggle();
   });
   $("#b1").mouseout(function(){
      $(this).attr("src", "button1up.png");
      $("#audio").slideToggle();
   });
});
```

USING FADING TECHNIQUES

Fading refers to an animation technique that causes the opacity of elements to fade in or out. jQuery includes four basic methods to handle fading: .fadeIn(), .fadeOut(), .fadeTo(), and .fadeToggle(). The .fadeIn(), .fadeOut(), and .fadeToggle() methods are very similar in form to the .slideDown(), .slideUp(), and .slideToggle() methods, except that they change the opacity instead of the position of selected elements. With the exception of the .fadeTo() method, all of the fading methods accept the same *duration*, *easing*, and *complete* arguments that the .animate() and sliding methods accept.

At the beginning of this chapter, you saw how to use the basic JavaScript setTimeout() and setInterval() methods in order to help you understand the challenges involved with using basic JavaScript to handle animation. Consider the following version of the motorcycles banner website you saw at the beginning of this chapter. Instead of simply swapping the images out for each iteration of the function, each image gradually fades in and out before changing. In the changeBanner() function, the .fadeIn() method first fades the currently displayed image and the final statement uses the .fadeOut() method to show the new version.

```
<head>
<script type="text/javascript" src="jquery-1.7.2.js"></script>
<script type="text/javascript">
/* <![CDATA[ */
$(document).ready(function() { changeBanner(); });
   function changeBanner() {
      var bannerVar = $("#banner");
      bannerVar.fadeIn(2000);
      if (bannerVar.attr("src") == "showroom.jpg")
         bannerVar.attr("src", "v500tec.jpg");
      else
         bannerVar.attr("src", "showroom.jpg");
      bannerVar.fadeOut(2000, changeBanner);
}
/* ]]> */
</script>
</head>
<body>
<p><img id="banner" src="showroom.jpg" height="90px" width="700px"
alt="Banner images" /></p>
</body>
```

The final jQuery fading method is `.fadeTo()`, which changes the opacity of selected elements to a specified value. The `.fadeTo()` method requires two arguments—*duration* and *opacity*—and also supports an optional callback argument. The *duration* argument specifies how long the animation should last, in milliseconds. The *opacity* argument determines the final opacity of the selected elements. You can assign a value from 0.0 to 1.0 to the `opacity` argument; the lower the value the more transparent the element becomes. A value of 0.0 makes the element completely transparent, whereas a value of 1.0 makes the element completely opaque.

The following page demonstrates how to use the `.fadeTo()` method. The page includes an image of the Golden Gate bridge. When you place your mouse over the image, a text box fades in and displays some information about the bridge, and then fades out when you move your mouse off of the image. The `<div>` element containing the text is initially assigned an opacity value of 0.0, making the element completely transparent. A `.hover()` method in the `document.ready()` method uses the `.fadeTo()` method to change the opacity of the `<div>` element to a value of 0.7 when the mouse is placed over it. The `.fadeTo()` method's callback argument then calls another `.fadeTo()` method to reset the element's opacity back to 0.0 when the mouse moves off the element. Figure 4.10 shows the image with the mouse off of it and Figure 4.11 shows the image with the mouse placed over it.

Figure 4.10
Web page with a <div> element's opacity set to 0.0

Figure 4.11
Web page with a <div> element's opacity set to 0.7

```
<head>
<script type="text/javascript" src="jquery-1.7.2.js"></script>
<script type="text/javascript">
$(document).ready(function(){
   $("#imageDiv").hover(function(){
      $("#messageBox").fadeTo(500, 0.7);
   },function(){
      $("#messageBox").fadeTo(500, 0);
   });
});
</script>
<style>
div.imageDivStyle {
   position: relative;
   width: 423px;
   height: auto
}
div.messageBoxStyle{
   opacity: 0.0;
   width: 403px;
   position: absolute;
   bottom: 0px;
   left: 0px;
   background-color: black;
   font-family: tahoma;
```

```
        font-size: 14px;
        color: white;
        padding: 10px
    }
    </style>
    </head>
    <body>
        <div id="imageDiv" class="imageDivStyle">
            <img src="ggbridge.jpg" width="423px" height="270px"
                alt="Photo of the Golden Gate Bridge" />
            <div id="messageBox" class="messageBoxStyle">
                The Golden Gate Bridge spans the opening of San Francisco Bay
                into the Pacific Ocean. Construction began in January, 1933
                and the bridge was finished in April, 1937, at a cost of $35
                million. The bridge celebrated its 75th anniversary in 2012.</div>
        </div>
    </body>
```

UNDERSTANDING JQUERY QUEUE FUNCTIONS

Earlier in this chapter, you learned how to use callback functions to schedule an animation to run when the current animation finishes. You can also use the queue methods listed in Table 4.1 to control when animations execute in jQuery.

jQuery has a built-in effects queue named `fx` and effect methods such as `.animate()`, `.fadeIn()`, and `.fadeOut()` are automatically added to this queue and executed in consecutive order. For example, with the splash page, the following methods are executed on the text in the order in which they are encountered. In other words, each method will wait its turn before running. After the font size is

Table 4.1   jQuery Queue Methods

Method	Description
`.clearQueue()`	Clears all remaining functions in the effects queue.
`.delay()`	Delays the execution of queued effect function by a specified number of milliseconds.
`.dequeue()`	Executes a function and removes it from the effects queue.
`.queue()`	Displays functions in or adds functions to the effects queue.
`.stop()`	Stops the currently running function in the animation queue.

increased with the .animate() method, the text fades out and then fades back in with the .fadeOut() and .fadeIn() methods.

```
$("#ad").animate({fontSize: "3em"}, 2000, "linear");
$("#ad").fadeOut(2000);
$("#ad").fadeIn(2000);
```

Note

The fx queue is sufficient for most web pages. For greater control over your animations, you can create your own queue. By default, each of the methods in Table 4.1 operates on the fx queue. However, you can pass to each method a parameter with the name of a custom queue in quotations. For example, to specify a custom queue named customEffects with the .queue() method, you use .queue("customEffects"). Remember that unless you specify a custom queue name, each of the queue methods will operate on the fx queue by default.

If you want to run a custom animation, such as dynamically changing a CSS property, the animation will start before any running built-in effect methods are finished executing. The last statement in following code executes the blinking functionality you saw earlier. However, it will begin executing while the font size of the text is still being increased with the .animate() method.

```
$("#ad").animate({fontSize: "3em"}, 2000, "linear");
$("#ad").fadeOut(2000);
$("#ad").fadeIn(2000);
blinkText = setInterval("$('#ad').toggleClass('blink')", 500);
```

To resolve this issue, you need to manually add a function containing the setInterval() statement to the fx queue with the .queue() method. Then, you need to call the .dequeue() method to execute the function and remove it from the fx queue. The following demonstrates how to use the queue methods with the setInterval() statement:

```
$("#ad").animate({fontSize: "3em"}, 2000, "linear");
$("#ad").fadeOut(2000);
$("#ad").fadeIn(2000);
$("#ad").queue(function() {
   blinkText = setInterval("$('#ad').toggleClass('blink')", 500);
   $(this).dequeue
});
```

The .delay() method is used for delaying the execution of queued effect function. To use the .delay() method, you chain it to a selector, followed by an effect method. You pass to the .delay() method the number of milliseconds you want to delay function execution, or the values fast for 200 milliseconds or slow for 600 milliseconds.

For example, the following statements use the .delay() method to delay execution of the .fadeOut() and .fadeIn() methods on the splash page by 1,000 milliseconds (one second).

```
$("#ad").delay(1000).fadeOut(2000);
$("#ad").delay(1000).fadeIn(2000);
```

The .queue() method gives you more flexibility than using callback functions because it allows you to schedule multiple functions to execute for an element. The following code adds a function that changes the text to "Big Savings!" and restarts the blinking functionality, but with a faster interval. Notice that the new function uses the .delay() method to delay execution for 3,000 milliseconds, which gives the preceding function three seconds to execute. Then the function clears the blinkText interval and reuses the variable to restart the blinking animation with a faster interval of 200.

```
$("#ad").animate({fontSize: "3em"}, 2000, "linear");
$("#ad").delay(1000).fadeOut(2000);
$("#ad").delay(1000).fadeIn(2000);
$("#ad").queue(function() {
   blinkText = setInterval(function(){
      $("#ad").toggleClass("blink");
   }, 500);
   $(this).dequeue();
});
$("#ad").delay(3000).queue(function() {
   clearInterval(blinkText);
   $(this).text("Big Savings!");
   blinkText = setInterval(function(){
      $("#ad").toggleClass("blink");
   }, 200);
   $(this).dequeue();
});
```

The final two jQuery queue methods are .stop() and .clearQueue(). The .stop() method stops the currently running animation in the effects queue, whereas the .clearQueue() method clears the effects queue of any remaining animation functions. On the splash page, you need to include both .stop() and .clearQueue() in the .click() method for the element that displays the text, as follows. This ensures that all animations stop and are cleared from the queue when the user clicks the Skip Advertisement link.

```
$("#a1").click(function(){
   $("#ad").stop();
```

```
$("#ad").clearQueue();
clearInterval(blinkText);
$("#splash").css("visibility", "hidden");
return false;
});
```

Tip

The `.stop()` method includes two additional parameters—`clearQueue` and `jumpToEnd`. The `clearQueue` parameter clears the effects queue, the same as the `.clearQueue()` method, and the `jumpToEnd` parameter jumps to the end of the currently running animation instead of simply stopping it. Both parameters default to `false`. To enable these parameters, pass values of `true` to the `.stop()` method, separated by commas. For example, `.stop(true, true)` enables both parameters. If you are using a custom queue, be sure to pass these parameters after the name of the queue parameter as follows: `.stop("customEffects", true, true)`.

Here is a completed version of the splash page:

```
<head>
<script type="text/javascript" src="jquery-1.7.2.js">
</script>
<style type="text/css">
.blink { visibility: hidden }
</style>
<script type="text/javascript">
/* <![CDATA[ */
var countSeconds;
var blinkText;
$(document).ready(function(){
   var splashElement = $("#splash");
   splashElement.css("position","absolute");
   splashElement.css("top", (($(window).height()
      - splashElement.outerHeight()) / 2)
      + $(window).scrollTop() + "px");
   splashElement.css("left", (($(window).width()
      - splashElement.outerWidth()) / 2)
      + $(window).scrollLeft() + "px");
   var secondsLeft = 15;
   countSeconds = setInterval(function(){
      if (secondsLeft == 1)
         $("#a1").click();
      $("#s1").html(-secondsLeft);
   }, 1000);
   $("#ad").animate({fontSize: "3em"}, 2000, "linear");
   $("#ad").delay(1000).fadeOut(2000);
```

```
    $("#ad").delay(1000).fadeIn(2000);
    $("#ad").queue(function() {
        blinkText = setInterval(function(){
            $("#ad").toggleClass("blink");
        }, 500);
        $(this).dequeue();
    });
    $("#ad").delay(3000).queue(function() {
        clearInterval(blinkText);
        $(this).text("Big Savings!");
        blinkText = setInterval(function(){
            $("#ad").toggleClass("blink");
        }, 200);
        $(this).dequeue();
    });
    $("#a1").click(function(){
        $("#ad").stop();
        $("#ad").clearQueue();
        clearInterval(blinkText);
        $("#splash").css("visibility", "hidden");
        return false;
    });
});
/* ]]> */
</script>
</head>
<body>
<div id="splash" style="background-color: #99CCCC; height:500; width:800">
<p style="text-align: right; padding-right: 20px">
<a id="a1" href="">Skip Advertisement (<span id="s1">15</span>)</a></p>
<p id="ad" style="text-align: center; margin-top: 175px;
font-family: Arial, sans-serif; font-weight: bold; font-size: 1em">
Memorial Day Sale!</p>
</div>
</body>
```

SUMMARY

In this chapter, you learned about the various animation techniques available with jQuery, including how to use timeouts and intervals, create simple animation, and how to use callbacks. You also learned how to create DHTML menus, use sliding and fading techniques, and use queue functions. You will continue to apply these techniques in upcoming chapters.

CHAPTER 5

HANDLING EVENTS

One of the primary ways in which JavaScript is executed on a web page is through events. An *event* is a specific circumstance (such as an action performed by a user, or an action performed by the browser) that is monitored by JavaScript and that your script can respond to in some way. This chapter explains how to handle events with both basic JavaScript and jQuery.

UNDERSTANDING JAVASCRIPT EVENTS

The most common events are actions that users perform. For example, when a user clicks a form button, a `click` event is generated. You can think of an event as a trigger that fires specific JavaScript code in response to a given situation. User-generated events, however, are not the only kinds of events monitored by JavaScript. Events that are not direct results of user actions, such as the `load` event, are also monitored. The `load` event, which is triggered automatically by a web browser, occurs when a document finishes loading in a web browser. Table 5.1 lists some JavaScript events and explains what triggers them.

Writing Event Handler Code

Events are associated with XHTML elements. The events that are available to an element vary. The `click` event, for example, is available for the `<a>` element and form controls created with the `<input>` element. In comparison, the `<body>` element does not have a `click` event, but it does have a `load` event, which occurs when a web page finishes loading, and an `unload` event, which occurs when a web page is unloaded.

Table 5.1   JavaScript Events

Event	Triggered When
abort	The loading of an image is interrupted.
blur	An element, such as a radio button, becomes inactive.
click	The user clicks an element once.
change	The value of an element, such as a text box, changes.
error	An error occurs when a document or image is being loaded.
focus	An element, such as a command button, becomes active.
load	A document or image loads.
mouseout	The mouse moves off an element.
mouseover	The mouse moves over an element.
reset	A form's fields are reset to its default values.
select	A user selects a field in a form.
submit	A user submits a form.
unload	A document unloads.

When an event occurs, your script executes the code that responds to that particular event. Code that executes in response to a specific event is called an *event handler*. You include event handler code as an attribute of the element that initiates the event. For example, you can add to a `<button>` element a `click` attribute that is assigned some sort of JavaScript code, such as code that changes the color of some portion of a web page. The syntax of an event handler within an element is:

```
<element event_handler ="JavaScript code">
```

Event handler names are the same as the name of the event itself, plus a prefix of `on`. For example, the event handler for the `click` event is `onclick`, and the event handler for the `load` event is `onload`. Like all XHTML code, event handler names are case sensitive and must be written using all lowercase letters in order for a document to be well formed. Table 5.2 lists various XHTML elements and their associated event handlers.

The JavaScript code for an event handler is contained within the quotation marks following the name of the JavaScript event handler. The following statement uses the `<input>` element to create a push button. The element also includes an

Table 5.2   XHTML Elements and Their Associated Events

Element	Description	Event
`<a>`	Anchor	onfocus, onblur, onclick, ondblclick, onmousedown, onmouseup, onmouseover, onmousemove, onmouseout, onkeypress, onkeydown, onkeyup
`<img>`	Image	onclick, ondblclick, onmousedown, onmouseup, onmouseover, onmousemove, onmouseout, onkeypress, onkeydown, onkeyup
`<body>`	Document body	onload, onunload, onclick, ondblclick, onmousedown, onmouseup, onmouseover, onmousemove, onmouseout, onkeypress, onkeydown, onkeyup
`<form>`	Form	onsubmit, onreset, onclick, ondblclick, onmousedown, onmouseup, onmouseover, onmousemove, onmouseout, onkeypress, onkeydown, onkeyup
`<input>`	Form control	tabindex, accesskey, onfocus, onblur, onselect, onchange, onclick, ondblclick, onmousedown, onmouseup, onmouseover, onmousemove, onmouseout, onkeypress, onkeydown, onkeyup
`<textarea>`	Text area	onfocus, onblur, onselect, onchange, onclick, ondblclick, onmousedown, onmouseup, onmouseover, onmousemove, onmouseout, onkeypress, onkeydown, onkeyup
`<select>`	Selection	onfocus, onblur, onchange

`onclick` event handler that executes the JavaScript `window.alert()` method, in response to a `click` event (which occurs when the button is clicked). The value of the literal string or variable is then displayed in the alert dialog box.

```
<input type="button" onclick="window.alert('You clicked a button!')">
```

The `window.alert()` method is the only statement being executed in the preceding event handler. You can, however, include multiple JavaScript statements in an event handler, as long as semicolons separate the statements. For example, to include two statements in the event handler example—a statement that creates a variable and another statement that uses the `window.alert()` method to display the variable— you would type the following:

```
<p><input type="button" onclick="var message='You clicked a button';
    window.alert(message)" value="Click Me"></p>
```

Creating Event Handler Functions

If an event handler includes multiple statements, it's usually more efficient to create an event handler function, as shown in the following example:

```
...
<script type="text/javascript">
/* <![CDATA[ */
function messageFunction() {
    var message='You clicked a button';
    window.alert(message);
}
/* ]]> */
</script>
...
<p><input type="button" onclick="messageFunction()" value="Click Me"></p>
```

You should already be more than familiar with how to use the `click` event with form controls, such as radio buttons, to execute JavaScript code. However, keep in mind that the `click` event can be used with other types of elements. The `click` event is often used for the anchor element. In fact, the primary event associated with the anchor element is the `click` event. When a user clicks a link, the web browser handles execution of the `onclick` event handler automatically, so you do not need to add an `onclick` event handler to your anchor elements.

There may be times, however, when you want to override an anchor element's automatic `onclick` event handler with your own code. For instance, you may want to warn the user about the content of a web page that a particular link will open. In order to override the automatic click event with your own code, you add to the <a> element an onclick event handler that executes custom code. When you override an internal event handler with your own code, your code must return a value of true or false, using the return statement. With the <a> element, a value of true indicates that you want the web browser to perform its default event-handling operation of opening the URL referenced in the link. A value of false indicates that you do not want the <a> element to perform its default event-handling operation. For example, the <a> element in the following code includes an onclick event handler. The warnUser() function that is called by the onclick event handler returns a value generated by the window.confirm() method. Recall that when a user clicks the OK button in a confirm dialog box, a value of true is returned. When a user clicks the Cancel button, a value of false is returned. Notice that there are two return statements in the following code. The return statement in the warnUser() function returns a value to the onclick event handler. The return statement in the onclick event handler returns the same value to the web browser.

```
...
<script type="text/javascript">
/* <![CDATA[ */
function warnUser() {
    return window.confirm("This link is only for Red Sox fans. ↵
        Are you sure you want to continue?");
}
/* ]]> */
</script>
</head>
<body>
<p><a href="redsox.html" onclick="return warnUser();">Red Sox Fan Club</a></p>
</body>
</html>
```

UNDERSTANDING THE JAVASCRIPT EVENT MODEL

The W3C defines an *event propagation model* that determines how browsers handle events.

This model provides more advanced capabilities for manipulating events. You use the Event object to access and manipulate the event propagation model. When you call an event handler function, you can pass an argument named event, which is an object that contains information about the event that occurred. For example, the Event object contains a type property that specifies the type of event that occurred. The button in the following code calls a statement named eventFunction() and passes to it the event argument. The function then uses the type property of the Event object to display the type of event that occurred. Clicking the button displays "You generated a click event." in an alert dialog box.

```
<script type="text/javascript">
/* <![CDATA[ */
function eventFunction(event) {
    window.alert ('You generated a ' + event.type + ' event.')
}
/* ]]> */
</script>
...
<p><input type="button" onclick="eventFunction(event)" value="Click Me" /></p>
```

Note

You must refer to the Event object in your JavaScript statements with lowercase letters.

You can use the following properties with the Event object:

altKey	clientY	layerY[*]	prevValue	toElement[†]
attrChange	ctrlKey	metaKey	relatedNode	timeStamp
attrName	currentTarget	newValue	relatedTarget	type
bubbles	detail	offsetX[†]	screenX	view
button	eventPhase	offsetY[†]	screenY	wheelDelta[†]
cancelable	fromElement[†]	originalTarget[*]	shiftKey	which[*]
charCode[*]	keyCode[†]	pageX[*]	srcElement[†]	
clientX	layerX[*]	pageY[*]	target	

[*]Mozilla-based browsers
[†]Internet Explorer

Caution

The properties listed in the preceding table are not available for all event types. If you attempt to access a property that does not exist for a particular event, its value will be undefined.

The majority of the preceding properties are W3C compatible, which makes them available to most current web browsers. However, notice that several of the properties are available only to Mozilla-based browsers or Internet Explorer. If you try to access a property that is not available in the current browser, its value will also be undefined.

Need More on These Object Properties?

For detailed descriptions of the W3C-compatible `Event` object properties, refer to the W3C's Document Object Model (DOM) Level 2 Events Specification at www.w3.org/TR/DOM-Level-2-Events/Overview. html#contents.

For detailed descriptions of the Mozilla-specific `Event` object properties, refer to the Gecko DOM Reference on the Mozilla Developer Network (MDN) at developer.mozilla.org/en/Gecko_DOM_Reference.

For detailed descriptions of the Internet Explorer-specific `Event` object properties, refer to the HTML and DHTML Reference on the Microsoft Developer Network (MSDN) at msdn.microsoft.com/en-us/library/ ms533050(v=VS.85).aspx.

One of the major challenges with JavaScript and the `Event` object is that until Version 9, Internet Explorer implemented a different event model than other browsers that conform to the W3C event model. This meant that if you wanted to use advanced event-handling techniques, you needed to write two sets of code: one for Internet Explorer and another for browsers that support the W3C event model. Although Internet Explorer Version 9 supports the W3C event model, at the time of this writing it is used by less than 5 percent of web users. Therefore, if you want your custom event handler code to function in older versions of Internet Explorer, you must still write two sets of code.

Note

As you learn in the next section, jQuery greatly simplifies event-handling techniques across all current browsers.

Advanced event-handling techniques require the use of the `addEventListener()` method for W3C-compatible browsers and the `attachEvent()` method for Internet Explorer browsers earlier than Version 9. First, you will learn about the `addEventListener()` method.

Capturing Events with W3C-Compliant Browsers

The majority of today's browsers, with the exception of Internet Explorer versions earlier than Version 9, support event capturing with the `addEventListener()` method. The syntax for the `addEventListener()` method is as follows:

```
element.addEventListener ("eventType", function, useCapture)
```

The `element` portion of the syntax identifies the element for which you want to create a listener. In most cases, you should use the `getElementById()` method of the `Document` object to identify the element. The `"eventType"` argument specifies a string containing the event type, such as "click" and the `function` argument can be either the name of a function or an anonymous function that executes the code in response to the event. The `useCapture` is a Boolean argument that determines whether the handler should execute using the capturing (`true`) or bubbling (`false`) event order. Event orders are discussed later in this section. All three arguments of the `addEventListener()` method are required.

Note

The `addEventListener()` method does not return a value.

To capture events with the `addEventListener()` method, you place the method within a script section and create the associated function. Note that when you use the `addEventListener()` method to capture events, you do not need to add an event handler to the associated element. As an example, consider the following code, which creates a mouse trail that follows the cursor as it moves around a web page. The first few statements create global variables that track the mouse trail. The `for` loop contains a single `document.write()` statement that creates the number of `<div>` elements that will make up the mouse trail according to the value assigned to the `trailInterval` variable. Each `<div>` element is assigned a unique ID value of `trail + i` (the `i` represents the current counter). Because the `trailInterval` variable is assigned a value of 12, the `for` loop creates 12 `<div>` elements with ID values of `trail0` through `trail11`. Each `<div>` element's `position` property is assigned a value of `absolute` so that it can be dynamically positioned and the `background-color` property is assigned a value of "blue". The `top` and `left` properties are assigned the values of the `xPosition` and `yPosition` variables, respectively. (The initial value assigned to these variables is −10, a setting that hides the `<div>` elements when the web page first loads.)

Notice the values that are assigned to the `width`, `height`, and `font-size` properties. Each of these properties is assigned a value of `i` (the `for` loop counter variable) divided by 2. This creates 12 `<div>` elements, starting with a very small element consisting of a width, height, and font size of .5 and ending with a final element consisting of a width, height, and font size of 6. The `addEventListener()` method following the `for` statement captures the `mousemove` events for the `trailWin` ID, which is assigned to the `<html>` element. This allows the event listening to capture all mouse movements within the document window. Statements within the anonymous function use the `Event` object `clientX` and `clientY` properties to return the horizontal and vertical coordinates of the cursor when the `mousemove` event occurs, and to call a function named `genTrail()`.

```
<html xmlns="http://www.w3.org/1999/xhtml" id="trailWin">
<head>
...
<script type="text/javascript">
/* <![CDATA[ */
var trailInterval = 20;
var xPosition = -10;
var yPosition = -10;
var animationStarted = false;
for (i = 1; i <= trailInterval; i++) {
    document.write("<div id='trail" + i
        + "' style='position:absolute;background-color:blue;top:"
        + yPosition + "px;left:" + xPosition + "px;width:"
        + i/2 + "px;height:" + i/2
        + "px; font-size:" + i/2 + "px'></div>");
}
document.getElementById("trailWin").addEventListener("mousemove",
    function (event) {
        xPosition = event.clientX + 15;
        yPosition = event.clientY + 20;
        if (!animationStarted) {
            animationStarted = true;
            genTrail();
        }
    },false);
/* ]]> */
</script>
</head>
```

The addEventListener() method in the preceding code calls the following genTrail() function, which creates the mouse trail animation effect. The function declares two local variables, div1 and div2. The for loop iterates through the <div> element and changes its value to the value of the previous <div> element. This causes each <div> element to replace the previous <div>, which creates the mouse trail. The last statement in the function uses the setTimeout() method to execute the function every 40 milliseconds. Figure 5.1 shows the mouse trail on a web page.

```
function genTrail(){
    var div1, div2;
    for (i = 1; i <= trailInterval; i++){
        div1 = document.getElementById("trail"+i);
        if (i < trailInterval){
            div2 = document.getElementById("trail"+(i+1));
            div1.style.top = div2.style.top;
```

```
            div1.style.left = div2.style.left;
        }
        else {
            div1.style.top = yPosition + "px";
            div1.style.left = xPosition + "px";
        }
    }
    setTimeout("genTrail()",40);
}
```

Capturing Events with Internet Explorer Browsers

Although Internet Explorer versions 9 and higher support the addEventListener()
method, you must use the attachEvent() for older versions of the browser. The
syntax for the attachEvent() method is as follows:

variable = *element*.attachEvent ("*eventType*", *function*)

As with the addEventListener() method, the element portion of the
attachEvent() method identifies the element for which you want to create a

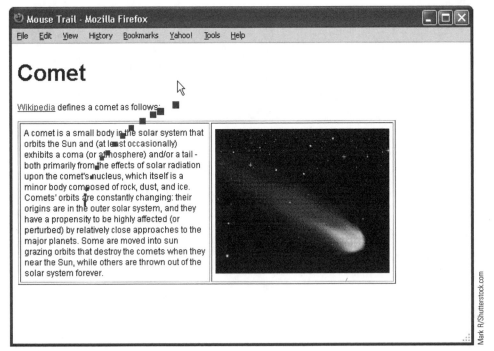

Figure 5.1
Mouse trail web page

listener, the "eventType" argument specifies a string containing the event type, and the function argument can be either the name of a function or an anonymous function that executes the code in response to the event.

Caution

An important difference between the addEventListener() and attachEvent() methods involves the "eventType". With the attachEvent() method, you must precede the event type with on. For example, with the addEventListener() method, you refer to the mouse move event type as mousemove and with the attachEvent() method, you refer to the event as onmousemove.

The following code demonstrates how to use the attachEvent() method to create an event listener for the mouse trail example for use with older versions of Internet Explorer:

```
document.getElementById("trailWin").attachEvent("onmousemove",
    function (event) {
        xPosition = event.clientX + 15;
        yPosition = event.clientY + 20;
         if (!animationStarted) {
             animationStarted = true;
             genTrail();
         }
    },false);
```

To create event listener code that is compatible with W3C browsers and earlier versions of Internet Explorer, you can use an if...else statement to determine whether to execute the addEventListener() or attachEvent() method. To determine which event listener code to use, check whether the browser includes document.addEventListener or document.attachEvent, as follows. W3C-compatible browsers and Internet Explorer 9 execute the addEventListener() code and Internet Explorer versions earlier than 9 execute the attachEvent() code.

```
if (document.addEventListener) {
    document.getElementById("trailWin").addEventListener("mousemove",
        function (event) {
            xPosition = event.clientX + 15;
            yPosition = event.clientY + 20;
            if (!animationStarted) {
                animationStarted = true;
                genTrail();
            }
        },false);
```

```
}
else if (document.attachEvent) {
    document.getElementById("trailWin").attachEvent("onmousemove",
        function (event) {
            xPosition = event.clientX + 15;
            yPosition = event.clientY + 20;
            if (!animationStarted) {
                animationStarted = true;
                genTrail();
            }
        },false);
}
```

Tip

Remember that the if...else statement that determines which event handler method to use—addEventListener() or attachedEvent()—does not need to be placed within a function. Instead, it can be added to any JavaScript section in the document, as long as the associated elements have already been rendered in the browser window.

Understanding the Event Propagation Model

The origins of the event propagation model made an evolutionary split with earlier versions of Netscape and Internet Explorer. Both browsers took a different approach to execute events within nested elements. Consider the following document body. The four elements—<body>, <form>, <p>, and <input>—each contain a click event using the basic JavaScript event model. In its current form, each event executes only when its containing element is clicked.

```
<body onclick="window.alert('body click event')" >
    <form id="f1" onclick="window.alert('form click event')" >
        <p id="p1" onclick="window.alert('para click event')" >
            <input id="b1" type="Button" value="Event Propagation"
                onclick="window.alert('button click event')" /><br />
        </p>
    </form>
</body>
```

If you want to execute the click events for each of the <input> element's ancestor elements when you click the button, you must use the addEventListener() and attachEvent() methods, as follows:

```
if (document.addEventListener) {
        document.getElementById("b1").addEventListener("click", function(){
```

```
            window.alert("button click event");}, true);
        document.getElementById("p1").addEventListener("click", function(){
            window.alert("para click event");}, true);
        document.getElementById("f1").addEventListener("click", function(){
            window.alert("form click event");}, true);
        document.body.addEventListener("click", function(){
            window.alert("body click event");}, true);
}
else if (document.attachEvent) {
        document.getElementById("b1").attachEvent("onclick", function(){
            window.alert("button click event");});
        document.getElementById("p1").attachEvent("onclick", function(){
            window.alert("para click event");});
        document.getElementById("f1").attachEvent("onclick", function(){
            window.alert("form click event");});
        document.attachEvent("onclick", function(){
            window.alert("body click event");});
}
```

When executing the preceding code, the W3C addEventListener() method uses capturing propagation while Internet Explorer uses bubbling propagation.

- *Capturing propagation* begins executing the event at the earliest ancestor that contains the event and works its way down to the source element.

- *Bubbling propagation* begins executing the event at the source element and then "bubbles" up to the earliest ancestor that includes the event. Figure 5.2 conceptually illustrates both propagation models.

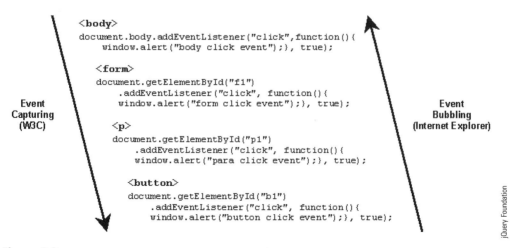

Figure 5.2
Conceptual example of capturing and bubbling event propagation models

The W3C modified Netscape's propagation model so it supports both capturing and bubbling propagation. The following steps represent the three phases of the event propagation model:

1. *Capturing phase*—A DOM ancestor of the event target captured by the event
2. *Target phase*—Event handlers attached to the event target execute
3. *Bubbling phase*—The originating element captures the event

With the `addEventListener()` method, you can specify the event propagation type by assigning to the third argument a value of `true` for capturing propagation and `false` for bubbling propagation.

Tip

Internet Explorer's `attachEvent()` method only supports bubbling propagation.

HANDLING EVENTS WITH JQUERY

jQuery greatly simplifies event handling by implementing various methods that allow you to bind an event to a particular event handler, and that will work across all browsers. The most basic method for binding an event to a particular event handler is the `.bind()` method. The basic syntax for the `.bind()` method is `$("selector").bind("event", [data,] function)`. The following code demonstrates how to create a basic script that uses the `.bind()` method to display an alert dialog box when a button is clicked:

```
...
<script type="text/javascript">
/* <![CDATA[ */
$(document).ready(function(){
    $("#b1").bind("click", function() {
            var message="You clicked a button";
            window.alert(message);
    });
});
/* ]]> */
</script>
...
<p><input type="b1" onclick="messageFunction()" value="Click Me"></p>
```

Although this approach is not commonly used, you can pass data to an event handler function by including it as a second parameter to the `.bind()` method. However, you must define the data from inside a set of curly braces. Within the curly braces, you assign a value to a name with a colon, separating multiple property names with a comma. The data is sent as properties of the event.data object, so you must include the Event as an argument of the called function. The following example demonstrates how to pass a property named message, containing the text "You clicked a button", to the anonymous function called by the .bind() method:

```
$(document).ready(function(){
    $("#b1").bind("click", {message: "You clicked a button"}, function(event) {
        window.alert(event.data.message);
    });
});
```

Although the preceding code assigns a text string to the message property, you can also assign a variable name, as follows:

```
var messageString = "You clicked a button";
$(document).ready(function(){
    $("#b1").bind("click", {message: messageString}, function(event) {
        window.alert(event.data.message);
    });
});
```

It's important to understand that the .bind() method and other jQuery event-handling methods use bubbling propagation, not capturing propagation. In other words, all events start at the source element and work up to the earliest ancestor element that is the target of the event type. As an example, consider the following version of the code you saw in the last section, this time using the jQuery .bind() method. When you click the button, the click event for the button fires first, and then the events for each parent element fire in turn.

```
<head>
<script type="text/javascript">
/* <![CDATA[ */
$(document).ready(function(){
    $("#b1").bind("click", function(){
        window.alert("button click event");
    });
    $("#p1").bind("click", function(){
        window.alert("para click event");
    });
    $("#f1").bind("click", function(){
        window.alert("form click event");
    });
```

```
    $("body").bind("click", function(){
        window.alert("body click event");
    });
});
/* ]]> */
</script>
</head>
<body>
    <form id="f1">
        <p id="p1">
            <input id="b1" type="Button" value="Event Propagation" /><br />
        </p>
    </form>
</body>
```

In addition to the .bind() method, jQuery defines the following simple registration methods for common types of events:

.blur()	.focusout()	.mouseenter()	.resize()
.change()	.hover()	.mouseleave()	.scroll()
.click()	.keydown()	.mousemove()	.select()
.dblclick()	.keypress()	.mouseout()	.submit()
.error()	.keyup()	.mouseover()	.unload()
.focus()	.load()	.mouseup()	
.focusin()	.mousedown()	.ready()	

Each of the preceding methods is essentially a shortcut for the .bind() method. For example, the .click() method is a shortcut for .bind("click"). In previous chapters, you've seen examples of several jQuery event registration methods, including the .ready(), .click(), .mouseover(), and .mouseout() methods.

Tip

You can use the same techniques as the .bind() method for passing event data to each of the preceding methods, except the property list must be passed as the first parameter to each method.

Accessing the jQuery Event Object

Referring to the Event object in jQuery is the same as JavaScript syntax in that you need to pass the event argument to a jQuery function. The following code demonstrates how to capture the .bind() method for a click event and pass the Event object to an anonymous function:

```
<script type="text/javascript">
/* <![CDATA[ */
function messageFunction() {
$(document).ready(function(){
    $("#b1").bind("click", function(event) {
        window.alert('You generated a ' + event.type + ' event.');
    });
});
/* ]]> */
</script>
```

Similarly, the following code demonstrates passing the Event object with the .click() method:

```
<script type="text/javascript">
/* <![CDATA[ */
$(document).ready(function(){
    $("#b1").click(function(event){
        window.alert('You generated a ' + event.type + ' event.');
    });
});
/* ]]> */
</script>
```

Alternately, you can also the jquery.Event() constructor to gain access to an event, as follows:

```
$(document).ready(function(){
    $("#b1").click(function(){
        var e = new jQuery.Event("click");
        window.alert('You generated a ' + e.type + ' event.');
    });
});
```

Note

The new operator is optional with the jquery.Event() constructor, although you should continue to use it as a best practice because other JavaScript constructors require it.

Table 5.3   jQuery Event Properties

Property	Contains
data	The optional data that was passed to an event-handling method.
result	The last value returned by the associated event handler unless the value is undefined.
namespace	The namespace specified when the event was raised.

Using the jQuery Event Properties

In addition to the standard JavaScript properties, the jQuery Event object also includes the three unique properties described in Table 5.3.

WORKING WITH MOUSE EVENTS

This section explains how to work with jQuery mouse event methods. Each of the jQuery mouse event methods is described in Table 5.4.

Table 5.4   jQuery Mouse Event Methods

Method	Fires When
.click()	An element is clicked.
.dblclick()	A element is double clicked.
.hover()	The mouse moves over and off an element.
.mousedown()	The mouse button is pressed.
.mouseenter()	The mouse enters an element.
.mouseleave()	The mouse leaves an element.
.mousemove()	The mouse moves inside an element.
.mouseout()	The mouse moves off of an element.
.mouseover()	The mouse moves over an element.
.mouseup()	The mouse button is released.
.toggle()	A click event executes.

Working with Click Events

The jQuery click event methods include `.click()`, `.dblclick()`, `.mousedown()`, `.mouseup()`, and `.toggle()`. By now, you should be more than familiar with the jQuery `.click()` method. You first saw the `.click()` method in Chapter 2 with the following example, which demonstrates how to use the method with a form's radio and checkbox controls:

```
$(document).ready(function(){
  $("input:radio").click(function(){
    $("input:checkbox").each(function(){
      if ($(this).attr("disabled") == "disabled")
        $(this).attr("disabled", false);
      else
        $(this).attr("disabled", "disabled");
    });
  });
});
```

Using the dblclick Event

The `dblclick` event works the same as the `click` event, except that users need to double click the mouse instead of single clicking it. The `dblclick` event is rarely used. They're not generally used with links, because as you know, links are driven by single mouse clicks, and they are rarely used in other situations because, from the user's point of view, single clicks are much easier than double clicks.

Toggling Click Events

In Chapter 4, you learned how to use the `.toggle()` method . When used without any arguments, the `.toggle()` method simply toggles between displaying and hiding the specified elements. However, you can also use the `.toggle()` method to bind two or more event handler functions to a `click` event. Clicking a selector that is associated with a `.toggle()` method cycles between the defined event handler

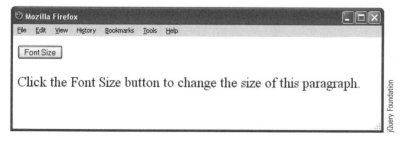

Figure 5.3
Web page with paragraph font size dynamically changed to 18pt

function arguments. You must separate each function name or anonymous function with a comma, as demonstrated in the example, which shows how to cycle a paragraph's font size between 10pt, 14pt, and 18pt. Figure 5.3 shows how the web page appears when the font size is 18 points.

```
<script type="text/javascript">
/* <![CDATA[ */
$(document).ready(function(){
    $("#b1").toggle(
        function () {
            $("#p1").css("fontSize", "14pt");
            },
        function () {
            $("#p1").css("fontSize", "18pt");
            },
        function () {
            $("#p1").css("fontSize", "10pt");
            }
        );
});
/* ]]> */
</script>
</head>
<body>
<form><p><button id="b1">Font Size</button></p></form>
<p id="p1">Click the Font Size button to change the size of this paragraph.</p>
</body>
```

Holding and Releasing the Mouse Button

The mousedown event occurs when you point to an element and hold the mouse button down; the mouseup event occurs when you release the mouse button. In the following example, the paragraph changes when users click and hold their mouse buttons down on the Discount button, and then changes back to the default text when the user releases the button:

```
...
<script type="text/javascript">
/* <![CDATA[ */
$(document).ready(function(){
  $("#b1").mousedown(
    function () {
      $("#p1").html("Congratulations on a 10% discount!");
    }
```

```
    );
  $("#b1").mouseup(
    function () {
      $("#p1").html("Hold your mouse button down on the Discount button.");
    }
  );
});
/* ]]> */
</script>
</head>
<body>
<form><p><button id="b1">Discount</button></p></form>
<p id="p1">Hold your mouse button down on the Discount button.</p>
</body>
```

Capturing Mouse Movement Events

This section describes how to capture mouse movements with jQuery event methods.

Creating Rollovers

You use the mouseover and mouseout events to create rollover effects. A *rollover* is an effect that occurs when your mouse moves over an element. The mouseover event occurs when the mouse passes over an element and the mouseout event occurs when the mouse moves off an element. These events are also commonly used to change an element's style, such as the formatting of a link when the mouse passes over it, as shown in the following code. You can capture the mouseover and mouseout events in jQuery with the .mouseover() and .mouseout() methods. In the following example, the onmouseover event underlines the link when the mouse passes over it, and the onmouseout event removes the link when the mouse passes off of it:

```
...
<style type="text/css">
p { font-family:arial; font-size:14px; color:black; }
a { text-decoration: none }
</style>
<script type="text/javascript">
/* <![CDATA[ */
$(document).ready(function(){
    $("#a1").mouseover(
        function () {
            $(this).css("textDecoration", "underline");
        }
    );
```

```
    $("#a1").mouseout(
        function () {
            $(this).css("textDecoration", "none");
        }
    );
});
/* ]]> */
</script>
</head>
<body>

<p><a id="a1" href="redsox.html">Red Sox Fan Club</a></p>
</body>
```

One of the more common uses of rollovers is to replace (or swap) an image on a web page with another image. Consider the following code. By default, the v500tec.jpg file is displayed. The .mouseover() method changes the image to showroom.jpg, and the .mouseout() method changes the image back to the v500tec.jpg file. Figure 5.4 shows the web page when the mouse is placed on the image. Once the mouse moves off the image, the original image shown in Figure 5.5 is displayed.

Figure 5.4
Web page before the mouse passes over the image

Figure 5.5
Web page with the mouse placed over the image

```
...
<style type="text/css">
p { font-family:arial; font-size:14px; color:black; }
a { text-decoration: none }
</style>
<script type="text/javascript">
/* <![CDATA[ */
$(document).ready(function(){
    $("#banner").mouseover(
        function () {
            $(this).attr("src", "showroom.jpg");
        }
    );
    $("#banner").mouseout(
        function () {
            $(this).attr("src", "v500tec.jpg");
        }
    );
});
/* ]]> */
</script>
</head>
<body>
<p><img id="banner" src="v500tec.jpg" height="90px" width="700px"
alt="Banner images" /></p>
</body>
```

One of the challenges with the mouseover and mouseout events is that they *bubble*. In other words, an element's mouseover and mouseout events will execute whenever the mouse passes over or out of any descendant ancestors that the target element contains. For example, consider the modified version of the web page containing the motorcycle banner image and the output shown in Figure 5.6. The mouseover event should fire only once and increment the counter variable when the mouse enters the box that represents the <div> element. Instead, the event fires whenever users pass their mice over any of the other elements contained within the <div> element.

```
...
<script type="text/javascript">
/* <![CDATA[ */
var counter = 0;
$(document).ready(function(){
    $("#d1").mouseover(
        function () {
            $("#s1").text(counter += 1);
```

```
            }
        );
        $("#banner").mouseover(
            function () {
                $(this).attr("src", "showroom.jpg");
            }
        );
        $("#banner").mouseout(
            function () {
                $(this).attr("src", "v500tec.jpg");
            }
        );
    });
    /* ]]> */
    </script>
    </head>
    <body>
    <div id="d1" style="height: 175px; width: 700px; border:
    5px solid black; padding: 10px">
    <img id="banner" src="v500tec.jpg" height="90px" width="700px"
    alt="Banner images" />
    <p style="font-size:18px; font-weight: bold; ">Welcome to Gosselin Cycles Showroom!</p>
    <p>You have visited this area <span id="s1">0</span> times.</p>
    </div>
    </body>
```

Welcome to Gosselin Cycles Showroom!

You have visited this area 3 times.

Figure 5.6
Web page with counter variable

Internet Explorer implements proprietary `mouseenter` and `mouseleave` events that are virtually identical to the `mouseover` and `mouseout` events except that they do not fire when the mouse passes over any child elements. These events are also available to all jQuery-compatible browsers with the `.mouseenter()` and `.mouseleave()` methods. jQuery also includes a method named `.hover()` that captures both `mouseenter` and `mouseleave` events. You pass to the `.hover()` method two function arguments—the first argument handles `mouseenter` events and the second argument handles `mouseleave` events.

Note

If you pass only one function argument to the `.hover()` method, it will execute for the `mouseenter` and `mouseleave` events.

The following is a modified version of the motorcycle showroom page. In this version, the script captures the `mouseenter` event for the `<div>` element and uses the `.hover()` method to cycle the banner images.

```
...
var i = 0;
$(document).ready(function(){
    $("#d1").mouseenter(
        function () {
            $("#s1").text(i += 1);
        }
    );
    $("#banner").hover(
        function () {
            $(this).attr("src", "showroom.jpg");
        },
        function () {
            $(this).attr("src", "v500tec.jpg");
        }
    );
});
```

Tracking Mouse Movement

Earlier in this chapter you saw a web page that displays a mouse trail whenever the cursor moves across the screen. To capture mouse movement events, the original version of the script used the `addEventListener()` method for W3C-compatible browsers and the `attachEvent()` method for Internet Explorer browsers older than version 9. With jQuery, you can use the `.mousemove()` method to capture mouse movements. You pass to the `.mousemove()` method a function name or anonymous function to handle the mouse movement.

The following code example is a much simpler version that captures the mouse movement event for the mouse trail script. This version includes a single `.mousemove()` method that works with all jQuery compatible browsers.

```
$(document).ready(function(){
    $("html").mousemove(function (event) {
        xPosition = event.clientX + 15;
        yPosition = event.clientY + 20;
        if (!animationStarted) {
            animationStarted = true;
            genTrail();
        }
    });
});
```

MANIPULATING BROWSER AND DOCUMENT EVENTS

This section explains how to work with jQuery browser and document event methods. Each of these methods is described in Table 5.5.

Since Chapter 2, you have seen numerous examples of how to use the `.ready()` method to ensure that the DOM is fully loaded before executing any jQuery statements. As another example of how to use the jQuery browser and document event

Table 5.5 jQuery Browser and Document Event Methods

Method	Fires When
.resize()	The browser window is resized.
.scroll()	A user scrolls to a different location in windows, frames, and elements with the overflow CSS property set to scroll (or auto when the element's explicit height or width is less than the height or width of its contents).
.load()	Loading has finished for any element associated with a URL, including the browser window, images, scripts, frames, and iframes.
.unload()	A user navigates away from the page.
.ready()	The DOM has been fully loaded in a browser.
.error()	An element in not loaded correctly in a browser.

methods, consider the .resize() method, which executes when a user resizes the browser window.

In Chapter 4, you saw a splash animation example that displayed an advertisement for 15 seconds when a user first opened a web page. The following code shows a modified version of the example. In this version, the document.ready() function includes statements that resize the box containing the advertising elements according to the current size of the browser window. The last jQuery function in the script section, window.resize(), reloads the web page if the user resizes the browser window.

```html
<html>
<head>
<script type="text/javascript" src="jquery-1.7.2.js">
</script>
<style type="text/css">
.blink { visibility: hidden }
</style>
<script type="text/javascript">
/* <![CDATA[ */
var countSeconds;
var blinkText;
$(document).ready(function(){
    var splashElement = $("#splash");
    splashElement.css("width", $(window).innerWidth() / 1.5);
    splashElement.css("height", $(window).innerHeight() / 1.5);
    splashElement.css("top", (($(window).innerHeight()
        - splashElement.height()) / 2)
        + $(window).scrollTop());
    splashElement.css("left", (($(window).innerWidth()
        - splashElement.width()) / 2) + $(window).scrollLeft());
    $("#ad").offset({top: (splashElement.offset().top
        + splashElement.height()) / 2});
    var secondsLeft = 15;
    countSeconds = setInterval(function(){
        if (secondsLeft == 1)
            $("#a1").click();
        $("#s1").html(-secondsLeft);
    }, 1000);
    $("#ad").animate({fontSize: "3em"}, 2000, "linear");
    $("#ad").delay(1000).fadeOut(2000);
    $("#ad").delay(1000).fadeIn(2000);
    $("#ad").queue(function() {
        var blinkCount = 0;
```

```
            blinkText = setInterval(function(){
                $("#ad").toggleClass("blink");
                if(blinkCount == 5)
                    clearInterval(blinkText);
                ++blinkCount;
            }, 500);
            $(this).dequeue();
        });
        $("#ad").queue(function() {
            $(this).text("Big Savings!");
            blinkText = setInterval(function(){
                $(this).toggleClass("blink");
            }, 300);
            $(this).dequeue();
        });
        $("#a1").click(function(){
            $("#ad").clearQueue();
            $("#splash").css("visibility", "hidden");
            return false;
        });
        $(window).resize(function() {
            window.location.href=window.location.href;
        });
    });
    /* ]]> */
    </script>
    </head>
    <body>
    <div id="splash" style="background-color: #99CCCC; position: absolute;
    text-align: center">
    <p style="text-align: right; padding-right: 20px"><a id="a1" href="">
    Skip Advertisement (<span id="s1">15</span>)</a></p>
    <span id="ad" style="font-family: Arial, sans-serif;font-weight: bold;
    font-size: 1em; text-align: center; position: relative">Memorial Day Sale!</span>
    </div>
    </body>
    </html>
```

Note

The single statement in the `window.resize()` function in the preceding code uses the standard JavaScript statement `window.location.href=window.location.href` to reload the web page. Technically, you should be able to use the statement `window.location.reload()` to reload the current page. However, at the time of this writing, Firefox and related browsers do not implement this method correctly, although Internet Explorer and other browsers do. Although the `window.location.href=window.location.href` statement is a hack, it works across all browsers, so you should continue to use it if you need to reload a web page with a resize event—at least until Firefox and all other browsers implement the `window.location.reload()` method when used with the `.resize()` method.

CONTROLLING EVENTS

This section covers issues surrounding controlling events—unbinding event handlers and triggering events.

Unbinding Event Handlers

Earlier in this chapter you learned how to use `.bind()` and other jQuery registration methods for handling events. When you use any of the event registration methods to define an event, a handler is attached and never removed until you leave the web page. Handlers that still exist in memory and are no longer used may cause problems with subsequent web page behavior. For example, the resize event handler for the `window` object in the splash animation page you saw in the last section automatically restarts the animation if a user resizes the web page. This behavior occurs as long as the user remains on the page. However, suppose that you only want to ensure that the animation plays out once, or until the user clicks the Skip Advertisement link. To remove an event handler in jQuery, you call the `.unbind()` method. To use the `.unbind()` method, you append it to the selector for which you want to remove a method, and then pass to it a string containing the event name. For instance, to remove the click event handler from an element with an ID of p1, you use the statement `$("#p1").unbind("click");`.

The splash animation ends after 15 seconds or when a user clicks the Skip Advertisement link. The functionality that ends the animation is contained within the following click event handler:

```
$("#a1").click(function(){
    $("#ad").clearQueue();
    $("#splash").css("visibility", "hidden");
    return false;
});
```

The preceding code executes when the user clicks the Skip Advertisement link (which includes an ID of a1) or when the following `setInterval()` code within the `document.ready()` function finishes counting down from 15 to 0. Notice that when the `secondsLeft` variable is equal to 1 the click event handler for the a1 link element is called, ending the animation sequence.

```
var secondsLeft = 15;
countSeconds = setInterval(function(){
    if (secondsLeft == 1)
        $("#a1").click();
    $("#s1").html(-secondsLeft);
}, 1000);
```

The following version of the a1 click event handler demonstrates how to remove the resize event handler for the window object with the .unbind() method.

```
$("#a1").click(function(){
    $(window).unbind("resize");
    $("#ad").clearQueue();
    $("#splash").css("visibility", "hidden");
    return false;
});
```

Triggering Events

As you saw with the splash animation page, you can manually call a jQuery event handler method using a statement similar to $("#a1").click();. jQuery also provides a general method called .trigger() that you can use to manually call a jQuery event handler. The syntax for the .trigger() method is selector.trigger("event"). The following example demonstrates how to use the .trigger() method in the code that cancels the splash animation when the user clicks the Skip Advertisement link:

```
var secondsLeft = 15;
countSeconds = setInterval(function(){
    if (secondsLeft == 1)
        $("#a1").trigger("click");
    $("#s1").html(-secondsLeft);
}, 1000);
```

Note

Manually triggered events perform the same functionality and use the same bubbling propagation as regularly executed events.

Another jQuery method you can use to trigger events is .triggerHandler(). Although the .trigger() method functions the same as if the event were triggered by the user or browser, .triggerHandler() has some important differences. Events triggered with .triggerHandler() do not bubble up through the DOM hierarchy and only operate on the first element in the matching selector. For example, the following .trigger() statement executes the click events for all button elements on a web page while the `.triggerHandler()` only executes the click event for the first button on the page:

```
$("button").trigger("click"); // Triggers all button click events
$("button").triggerHandler("click"); // Triggers the first button click event
```

One of the most important differences between the `.trigger()` and `.triggerHandler()` methods is that the `.triggerHandler()` does not execute the event's default functionality. As an example, consider a form's `submit` event. If you use the `.triggerHandler()` to execute a form's `submit` event, the statements within the `submit` event handler method will execute, but the form itself will not be submitted to the server.

As an example, consider the following code, which renders a web page with a simple form. The form includes Submit and Validate buttons. The Submit button calls the form's `submit` event handler, which ensures the form fields contain values before submitting the form. The Validate button's click event handler uses the `.triggerHandler()` to execute the Submit button's event handler code to ensure that the form contains values. Code within the Validate button's click event handler uses the return value of `true` or `false` to determine whether to write the text `"Valid form"` or `"Invalid form"` to the last text element in the form. However, the `.triggerHandler()` statement does not execute the default functionality of the submit event and submit the form to the server.

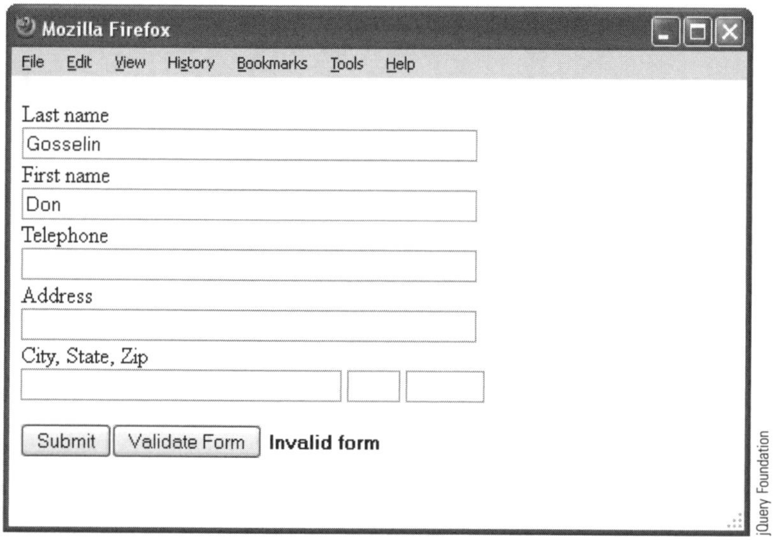

Figure 5.7
A user selected the Validate button without entering values in all of the form fields

The form's submit event handler performs the same tasks, but instead writes the text "Please fill in all fields" if the form is invalid, or submits the form to the server if the form is valid. Figure 5.7 shows how the page appears when a user selects the Validate button without entering values in all of the form fields.

```
<head>
<script type="text/javascript" src="jquery-1.7.2.js">
</script>
<script type="text/javascript">
/* <![CDATA[ */
$(document).ready(function(){
    $("form").submit(function(){
        if ($("#firstName").val() == ""
            || $("#lastName").val() == ""
            || $("#telephone").val() == ""
            || $("#address").val() == ""
            || $("#city").val() == ""
            || $("#state").val() == ""
            || $("#zip").val() == "") {
            $("#message").val("Please fill in all fields.");
            return false;
        }
        else
            return true;
    });
    $("#validate").click(function(){
        var retValue = $("form").triggerHandler("submit");
        if (retValue == true)
            $("#message").val("Valid form");
        else
            $("#message").val("Invalid form");
    });
});
/* ]]> */
</script>
</head>
<body>
<form action="FormProcess.html" method="get"
enctype="application/x-www-form-urlencoded">
<p>Last name<br />
<input type="text" name="lastName" id="lastName" size="50" /><br />
First name<br />
<input type="text" name="firstName" id="firstName" size="50" /><br />
Telephone<br />
```

```
<input type="text" name="telephone" id="telephone" size="50" /><br />
Address<br />
<input type="text" name="address" id="address" size="50" /><br />
City, State, Zip<br />
<input type="text" name="city" id="city" size="34" />
<input type="text" name="state" id="state" size="2" maxlength="2" />
<input type="text" name="zip" id="zip" size="5" maxlength="5" /></p>
<p><input type="submit" value="Submit" /><input type="button"
    id="validate" value="Validate Form" />  
    <input type="text" id="message" style="border: none;
    font-weight: bold" value="test" />
</form>
</body>
```

SUMMARY

This chapter demonstrated both basic and advanced techniques for capturing and handling events in JavaScript. In the next chapter, you will see more event-handling techniques for validating form data.

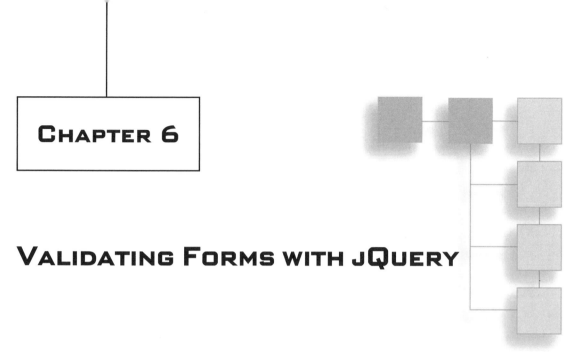

CHAPTER 6

VALIDATING FORMS WITH JQUERY

Forms are one of the most common web page elements used with JavaScript. Typical forms you may encounter on the web include order forms, surveys, and applications. You use JavaScript to make sure that data was entered properly into the form fields and to perform other types of preprocessing before the data is sent to the server. Without JavaScript, the only action that a web page can take on form data is to send it to a server for processing. jQuery helps simplify form validation and manipulation by implementing various methods for use with form elements, including event registration methods and methods for validating and serializing form data. First, you will look at the basic form event registration methods.

WORKING WITH FORM EVENTS

In the past few chapters, you learned about the various types of mouse events that can be used with forms and other types of elements. One of the form examples you saw in Chapter 3 included the following code that uses jQuery `mouseover` and `click` event registration methods to dynamically change the cursor to a help cursor when the mouse pointer passes over form elements and to display context-sensitive help when you click in one of the form fields. Figure 6.1 shows the page after clicking the Password text box.

```
<head>
<script type="text/javascript" src=" jquery-1.7.2.js">
</script>
<script type="text/javascript">
/* <![CDATA[ */
```

```
$(document).ready(function(){
    $("input").mouseover(function() {
        var elementId = $(this).attr('id');
        $("#" + elementId).css("cursor", "help");
    });
    $("input").click(function() {
        var elementId = $(this).attr('id');
        var helpBox = $("#box");
        switch (elementId) {
            case "username":
                helpBox.html("Enter a unique user name that is
                    between 5 and 12 characters.");
                break;
            case "password":
                helpBox.html("Enter a password between 6 and 10
                    characters that contains both upper and lowercase
                    letters and at least one numeric character.");
                break;
            case "password_confirm":
                helpBox.html("Confirm your selected password.");
                break;
            case "challenge":
                helpBox.html("Enter your mother's maiden name.
                    This value will be used to confirm your identity
                    in the event that you forget your password.");
                break;
        }
        helpBox.css("visibility", "visible");
        helpOffset = $("#" + elementId).offset();
        helpBox.css("left", $("#" + elementId).width() + 20);
        helpBox.css("top", helpOffset.top);
    });
});
/* ]]> */
</script>
</head>
<body>
<h1>Form Help</h1>
<div>
<form action="" method="get"
enctype="application/x-www-form-urlencoded">
<p><strong>User name</strong><br />
<input type="text" id="username" name="username" size="50" /></p>
<p><strong>Password</strong><br />
```

```
<input type="password" id="password" name="password" size="50" /></p>
<p><strong>Confirm password</strong><br />
<input type="password" id="password_confirm" size="50" /></p>
<p><strong>What is your mother's maiden name?</strong><br />
<input type="password" id="challenge" name="challenge" size="50" /></p>
</form>
</div>
<div id="box" style="position: absolute; visibility: hidden;
    width: 250px; background-color:#FFFFC0; font-family:Comic Sans MS;
    color: #A00000;border:1px dashed #D00000"></div>
</body>
```

In addition to mouse events, jQuery implements several other event registration methods for specific use with forms, including select, focus, blur, and changes events as well as several keyboard events and the submit event. First, you look at how to handle select events.

Handling Select Events

The select event executes when you select the content of a text box or text area field, or it can be used to select all content contained within a text box or text area field.

Consider the following example. If you type any text in the text box and then select either all or a portion of it using your mouse or keyboard, an alert dialog box will open and display the text you typed, as shown in Figure 6.2.

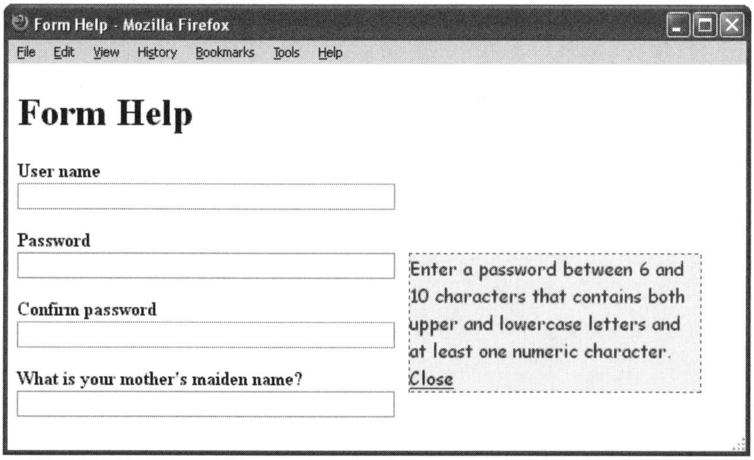

Figure 6.1
Form Help web page

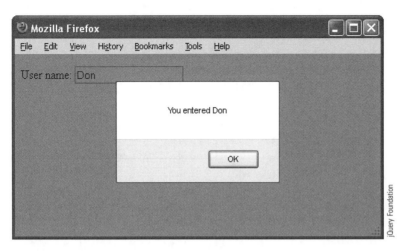

Figure 6.2
Text box with a select event

```
...
<script type="text/javascript" src=" jquery-1.7.2.js">
</script>
<script type="text/javascript">
/* <![CDATA[ */
$(document).ready(function(){
    $("#t1").select(
        function () {
            window.alert("You entered " + $(this).attr("value"));
        }
    );
});

/* ]]> */
</script>
</head>
<body>
<form action="" method="get">
<p>User name: <input type="text" id="t1" name="t1" /></p>
</form>
</body>
```

Note that the preceding code does not select all of the text in the text box; it only triggers the select event in response to some portion of the text being highlighted. To use the select event to highlight all of the text within a text box or text area box, you must call the .select() event registration method without any arguments.

The following modified version of the code includes an <input> button element with a click event handler that executes the .select() event registration method, which highlights all text in the text box before displaying the alert dialog box.

```
<script type="text/javascript">
/* <![CDATA[ */
$(document).ready(function(){
    $("#b1").click(function() {
        $("#t1").select();
    });
        $("#t1").select(function() {
        // Code that validates the entered ID
        window.alert("You entered " + $(this).attr("value"));
        });
});
/* ]]> */
</script>
</head>
<body>
<form action="">
<p>User name: <input type="text" id="t1" name="t1" />
    <input type="button" id="b1" value="Check for duplicate ID" /></p>
</form>
</body>
```

Handling Focus and Blur Events

A focus event triggers when a user selects a form field, either by clicking with the mouse or tabbing to the field, and a blur event triggers when the field loses focus when the user presses the Tab key or clicks on another field. Focus and blur events allow you to capture a user's movement to form fields on a web page, and are often used for performing validation and providing help for specific fields.

JavaScript provides two basic methods—focus() and blur()—for capturing focus and blur events. Similarly, jQuery provides two event registration methods—.focus() and .blur()—for trapping these events. As an example of how to use these methods, consider the following code, which contains two fields: a password field and a password confirmation field. The jQuery section includes a code for a blur event that triggers when the users move their cursors out of the password confirmation field. Statements in the blur event handler compare the values entered into both the password and password confirmation fields. If the values are not the same, the function uses the .focus() method to move the cursor back into the password field, and the `.select()` method to select every-thing in the password text box.

```
<script type="text/javascript" src=" jquery-1.7.2.js">
</script>
<script type="text/javascript">
/* <![CDATA[ */
$(document).ready(function(){
    $("#p2").blur(function() {
        if ($("#p1").attr("value") != $(this).attr("value")) {
            window.alert("You did not enter the same password!");
            $("#p1").focus();
            $("#p1").select();
        }
    });
});
/* ]]> */
</script>
</head>
<body>
<form action="">
<p>Password<br />
<input type="password" id="p1" name="p1" size="50" /></p>
<p>Confirm password<br />
<input type="password" id="p2" size="50" /></p>
<p><input type="submit" /></p>
</form>
</body>
```

For basic types of `focus` and `blur` event handling functionality, the jQuery `.focus()` and `.blur()` event delegation methods are usually sufficient. However, recall from Chapter 5 the discussion on event bubbling. The W3C event propagation model uses capturing propagation, whereas Internet Explorer uses bubbling propagation. Capturing propagation begins by executing the event at the earliest ancestor that contains the event and works its way down to the source element. Bubbling propagation begins executing the event at the source element and then "bubbles" up to the earliest ancestor that includes the event. Neither the `.focus()` or `.blur()` event delegation methods support event bubbling. This means that if you write jQuery code that captures `focus` and `blur` events, and you need those events to bubble in Internet Explorer versions earlier than 9, `.focus()` or `.blur()` event delegation methods will not work. Instead, you must use the jQuery `.focusin()` and `.focusout()` event delegation methods, which are virtually identical to `.focus()` and `.blur()`, except they support event bubbling. Here's a modified version of the password validation code that uses the .focusin() and .focusout() event delegation methods instead of .focus() and .blur():

```
$(document).ready(function(){
    $("#p2").focusout(function() {
        if ($("#p1").attr("value") != $(this).attr("value")) {
            window.alert("You did not enter the same password!");
            $("#p1").focusin();
            $("#p1").select();
        }
    });
});
```

Handling Change Events

A change event occurs when the contents of a form field change. More specifically, a change event is raised when you modify the value of a text box (<input type= "text">) or text area (<textarea>) field, or when you select a different value in a selection list (<select>).

Most form validation with JavaScript takes place when you submit the form. You will learn how to accomplish this kind of validation at the end of this chapter. However, there are some tricks you can use to ensure that users enter the correct information in the first place.

For any fields that require numeric values, for instance, you can use JavaScript's built-in isNaN() function, which determines whether a value is the special value NaN (not a number). The isNaN() function returns a value of true if the value passed to it is not a number and a value of false if the value passed to it is a number. The following function shows a statement that passes the value of a text box named "subtotal" in the first form on a web page to the isNaN() function:

```
isNaN(document.forms[0].subtotal.value);
```

The following script demonstrates how to trap change events for a text box with jQuery. The script calculates miles per gallon. The form contains four text <input> elements: starting mileage, ending mileage, gallons used, and miles per gallon. It also assigned initial starting values of 0 to each of the <input> element's value attribute. The .change() event registration method in the jQuery section declares three variables—startMiles, endMiles, and gallons—and initializes each variable with the value assigned to the starting mileage, ending mileage, and gallons. The if...else statement then uses the isNaN() function within a compound

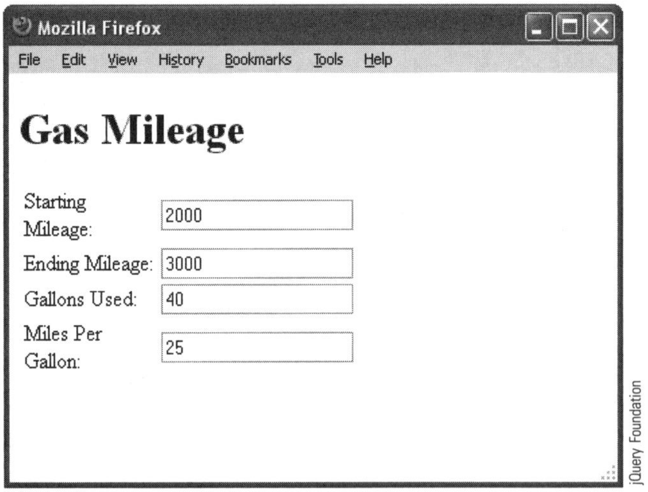

Figure 6.3
Miles-per-gallon calculation page

conditional expression to determine whether the startMiles, endMiles, and gallons variables contain numeric values.

If the variables do not contain numeric variables, an alert dialog box displays informing the users that they must enter numeric values. If the variables do contain numeric values, the else clause performs the miles-per-gallon calculation and assigns the result to the Miles per Gallon text box in the form. The formula for calculating miles per gallon is (endMiles - startMiles) / gallons. The formula includes parentheses to force the order of precedence to calculate the subtraction operation before the division operation. One problem with performing the calculation is that if you attempt to divide by zero, you will receive an error. For this reason, the code includes a nested if statement within the else clause to verify that the gallons variable contains a numeric value greater than zero. If the variable does not contain a value greater than zero, the statements within the if statement will not execute. Figure 6.3 shows the web page in a browser.

```
<script type="text/javascript" src=" jquery-1.7.2.js">
</script>
<script type="text/javascript">
/* <![CDATA[ */
$(document).ready(function(){
    $("input").change(function(){
        var startMiles = parseInt($("#startingMiles").attr("value"));
        var endMiles = parseInt($("#endingMiles").attr("value"));
        var gallons = parseInt($("#gallonsUsed").attr("value"));
        if (isNaN(startMiles) || isNaN(endMiles) || isNaN(gallons))
```

```
                window.alert("You must enter numeric values!");
            else {
                if (gallons > 0) {
                    var mpg = (endMiles - startMiles) / gallons;
                    $("#mpg").attr("value", mpg);
                }
            }
        });
    });
    /* ]]> */
    </script>
    </head>
    <body>
    <h1>Gas Mileage</h1>
    <form action="" name="mileageLog">
    <table border="0px">
    <col span="2" style="width: 100px" />
    <tr><td>Starting Mileage: </td><td><input type="text" id="startingMiles"
        value="0" /></td></tr>
    <tr><td>Ending Mileage: </td><td><input type="text" id="endingMiles"
        value="0" /></td></tr>
    <tr><td>Gallons Used: </td><td><input type="text" id="gallonsUsed"
        value="0" /></td></tr>
    <tr><td>Miles Per Gallon: </td><td><input type="text" id="mpg"
        value="0" /></td></tr>
    </table>
    </form>
    </body>
```

Note

JavaScript does not provide a method for programmatically raising `change` events, although jQuery implements a `.change()` event registration method.

Handling Keyboard Events

jQuery implements the following three keyboard event registration methods:

- `.keydown()`—Executes when a key is pressed
- `.keypress()`—Executes when a key is pressed and released
- `.keyup()`—Executes when a key is released

As an example of how to use the jQuery event registration methods, consider the modified version of the miles-per-gallon page. This version provides more fine-grained control by using the .keypress() method to identify the specific key that the user pressed. The Event object generated by the onkeypress event contains the Unicode character that represents the pressed key in the charCode property. The code returns the Unicode character from the charCode property and then uses the fromCharCode() method of the String class to convert the Unicode character to its equivalent print character. Finally, the code will use a regular expression within the exception-handling structure to determine the type of character the user pressed. If the user did not press a numeric character, the onkeypress event is canceled and a message is displayed to the user.

```
...
<script type="text/javascript" src=" jquery-1.7.2.js">
</script>
<script type="text/javascript">
/* <![CDATA[ */
$(document).ready(function(){
    $("input").keypress(function(event){
        var    enteredKey = event.charCode;
        var    enteredChar = String.fromCharCode(enteredKey);
        if (!/\d/.test(enteredChar) && !/\W/.test(enteredChar)) {
            window.alert("You did not enter a numeric value.");
            this.value="";
        }

    });
});
/* ]]> */
</script>
</head>
<body>
<h1>Gas Mileage</h1>
<form action="" name="mileageLog">
<table border="0px">
<col span="2" style="width: 100px" />
<tr><td>Starting Mileage: </td><td><input type="text" id="startingMiles"
    value="0" /></td></tr>
<tr><td>Ending Mileage: </td><td><input type="text" id="endingMiles"
    value="0" /></td></tr>
<tr><td>Gallons Used: </td><td><input type="text" id="gallonsUsed"
    value="0" /></td></tr>
<tr><td>Miles Per Gallon: </td><td><input type="text" id="mpg"
```

```
        value="0" /></td></tr>
</table>
</form>
</body>
```

Note

The regular expression in the preceding code uses the `\D` class escape character to determine whether an alphabetic key was pressed. It likewise uses the `\W` class escape character to ensure that the pressed key was not an alphanumeric key, such as the Tab key, which the user can press to navigate through the form.

A Note on Unicode

If you are not familiar with the term, *Unicode* is a standardized set of characters from many of the world's languages. A number represents each character in the Unicode character set. For instance, the Unicode numbers for the uppercase letters A, B, and C, are 65, 66, and 67, respectively. In most cases, you can use XHTML numeric character references or character entities to represent Unicode characters in text strings. For example, the copyright symbol (©) can be represented in HTML by the numeric character reference `&#169;` and the character entity is `&copy;`. To assign the text © 1995 – 2006 to a variable named `copyrightInfo` in JavaScript, you can use either of the following statements:

```
copyrightInfo = "<p>&#169; 1995-2006</p>"; // numeric character ref
copyrightInfo = "<p>&copy; 1995-2006</p>"; // character entity
```

Instead of using numeric character references or character entities within text strings, as shown in the preceding example, you can use the `fromCharCode()` method, which constructs a text string from Unicode character codes that are passed as arguments. The `fromCharCode()` method is called a static method because it is not used as a method of any string objects (which can be literal strings or variables) in your scripts. Instead, you must call `fromCharCode()` as a method of the `String` class with the following syntax `String.fromCharCode(char1, char2, …)`. The following statement uses the `fromCharCode()` method to print the word `"JavaScript"` with Unicode characters:

```
document.write("<p>" +
    String.fromCharCode(
    74,97,118,97,83,99,114,105,112,116)
    + "</p>");
```

SUBMITTING FORMS

In Chapter 5, you learned about many of the event handlers that can be used in Java-Script. Two additional event handlers—`onsubmit` and `onreset`—are available for use with the `<form>` element. The `onsubmit` event handler executes when a form is submitted to a server-side script (in other words, when a Submit button is selected on a form). The `onsubmit` event handler is often used to verify or validate a form's data before it is sent to a server. The onreset event handler executes when a Reset button is selected on a form. You use the onreset event handler to confirm that a user really wants to reset the contents of a form. With traditional JavaScript, both the onsubmit and onreset event handlers are placed before the closing bracket of an opening <form> tag. The following code shows how a <form> tag with onsubmit and onreset event handlers is written:

```
<form action="FormProcessor.html" method="post"
    onsubmit="JavaScript statements" onreset="JavaScript statements">
```

The onsubmit and onreset event handlers must return a value of true or false, depending on whether the form should be submitted (true) or reset (false). For example, the onsubmit and onreset event handlers in the following code return values of true or false, depending on whether the user clicks the OK button or the Cancel button in the Confirm dialog box. If the user clicks the OK button, the Confirm dialog box returns a value of true, and the onsubmit or onreset event executes. If the user clicks the Cancel button, the Confirm dialog box returns a value of false, and the onsubmit or onreset event does not execute.

```
<form action="FormProcessor.html" method="get"
    onsubmit="return window.confirm('Are you sure ↵
        you want to submit the form?');"
    onreset="return window.confirm('Are you sure ↵
        you want to reset the form?');">
```

Although the onsubmit event handler is useful for confirming that a user really wants to submit a form, its most important purpose is to validate form data. The validation of form data can mean many things, ranging from simply ensuring that a field is not empty to performing complex validation of credit card numbers. You have already seen several examples of validation at the form level that confirmed that the user entered the same value in the password and password confirmation boxes, along with how to ensure values entered into the miles-per-gallon page were entered as numbers.

Later in this chapter you learn how to perform the final step in the validation of these types of fields: ensuring that they are not empty when the form is submitted.

To submit a form with jQuery, you use the .submit() event registration method. To prevent the form from being submitted, return a value of false, as shown in the following example:

```
<script type="text/javascript" src=" jquery-1.7.2.js">
</script>
<script type="text/javascript">
```

```
/* <![CDATA[ */
$(document).ready(function(){
    $("form").submit(function(event){
      if (window.confirm("Are you sure you want to submit the form?") == false)
      return false;
    });
});
/* ]]> */
</script>
```

Note

---

jQuery does not include an event registration method for the `onreset` event.

VALIDATING TEXT AND PASSWORD BOXES

Chapter 2 discussed the `.val()` accessor method, which gets the attribute value from the first input field in a set of matching elements or sets the attribute value for all matching input fields. The `.val()` method is perhaps the most important jQuery method you will use when working with forms. The following statement demonstrates how to use the `.val()` method to retrieve the value assigned to a text box with an `id` value of `customerEmail`:

```
window.alert("You entered the following e-mail address: "
    + $("#customerEmail").val());
```

To verify that text and password boxes are not empty, you can use the `.val()` method in an `if` statement in the `.submit()` event registration method to check whether the field contains a value. For example, the following code checks whether two text fields (`firstName` and `lastName`) contain text. If they do contain text, a value of `true` is returned and the form is submitted. If they do not contain text, a value of `false` is returned and the form is not submitted. Notice that the conditional expression uses the `||` (Or) operator to confirm that both fields have been filled.

```
<script type="text/javascript" src=" jquery-1.7.2.js">
</script>
<script type="text/javascript">
/* <![CDATA[ */
$(document).ready(function(){
    $("form").submit(function(event){
        if ($("#firstName").val() == "" || $("#lastName").val() == "") {
```

```
                window.alert("You must enter your first and last names!");
                return false;
            }
        else
                return true;
    });
});
/* ]]> */
</script>
</head>
<body>
<form action="FormProcessor.html" method="get">
<p>First <input type="text" id="firstName" name="firstName" /><br />
Last <input type="text" id="lastName" name="lastName" /><br />
<input type="submit" /></p>
</form>
</body>
```

Validating Radio Buttons

When multiple form elements share the same name, JavaScript creates an array out of the elements using the shared name. Radio buttons, for instance, share the same name so that a single name=value pair can be submitted to a server-side script. When you have an array that is created from a group of buttons that share the same name, you can use the checked property to determine which element in a group is selected. The checked property returns a value of true if a check box or radio button is selected, and a value of false if it is not.

In Chapter 2, you saw the following example, which uses an onsubmit event handler similar to the following to determine whether one of the radio buttons in the group is selected:

```
<head>
<script type="text/javascript">
/* <![CDATA[ */
function submitForm() {
    var maritalStatusSelected = false;
    for (var i=0; i<5; ++i) {
        if (document.forms[0].maritalStatus[i].checked == true) {
            maritalStatusSelected = true;
            break;
        }
    }
    if (maritalStatusSelected == false) {
```

```
            window.alert("You must select your marital status.");
            return false;
      }
      else
            return true;
}
/* ]]> */
</script>
</head>
<body>
<form action="FormProcessor.html" method="get"
enctype="application/x-www-form-urlencoded" onsubmit="submitForm()">
<p>What is your current marital status?<br />
<input type="radio" name="maritalStatus"
      value="single" />Single<br />
<input type="radio" name="maritalStatus"
      value="married" />Married<br />
<input type="radio" name="maritalStatus"
      value="divorced" />Divorced<br />
<input type="radio" name="maritalStatus"
      value="separated" />Separated<br />
<input type="radio" name="maritalStatus"
      value="widowed" />Widowed</p>
<p><input type="submit" /></p>
</form>
</body>
```

To create the same programmatic functionality with jQuery, you need to use the input:checked filter, as follows. Notice that the code calls the submit event handler of the Form element and that it uses the standard JavaScript array length property to determine the number of returned elements. If there is at least one returned element, it indicates that one of the radio buttons is selected.

```
$(document).ready(function(){
    $("form").submit(function(){
        if ($("input:checked").length > 0)
                return true;
        else {
                window.alert("You must select your marital status.");
                return false;
        }
    });
});
```

Another method of determining whether a radio button in a group is selected is to use the `.val()` method with the `:input` selector as follows. Notice the syntax that selects all checked radio buttons with a `name` attribute of `maritalStatus`. If the conditional expression in the `if` statement returns a value of `undefined`, no radio button is selected.

```
$(document).ready(function(){
    $("form").submit(function(event){
        if ($("input:radio[name=maritalStatus]:checked").val() != undefined)
                return true;
        else {
                window.alert("You must select your marital status.");
                return false;
        }

    });
});
```

Validating Check Boxes

As with radio buttons, you can group check boxes by giving each check box the same name value, although each check box can have a different value. Unlike when using radio buttons, users can select as many check boxes in a group as they like. When multiple check boxes on a form share the same name, multiple name=value pairs, each using the same name, are submitted to a web server, as with the following example, shown in Figure 6.4. Note that the Fundraising check box is checked when the form first loads because it includes the `checked` attribute.

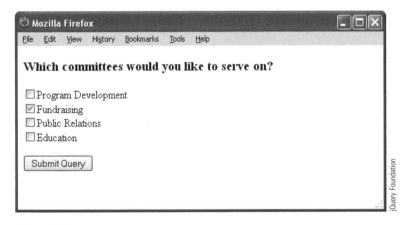

Figure 6.4
Check box form

```
<form action="FormProcessor.html" method="get">
<h3>Which committees would you like to serve on? </h3>
<p><input type="checkbox" name="committees"
     value="program_dev" />Program Development<br />
<input type="checkbox" name="committees"
     value="fundraising" checked="checked" />Fundraising<br />
<input type="checkbox" name="committees"
     value="pub_relations" />Public Relations <br />
<input type="checkbox" name="committees"
     value="education" />Education</p>
<p><input type="submit" /></p>
</form>
```

In the preceding example, if the Fundraising and Public Relations check boxes are selected, two name=value pairs—committees=fundraising and committees=pub_relations—are submitted. Note that you are not required to group check boxes with the same name attribute. Although a common group name helps you to identify and manage groups of check boxes, it is often easier to keep track of individual values when each check box has a unique name attribute.

You can use the checked property to determine whether an individual check box has been selected. If check boxes are part of a group, you can validate them using the same functionality as the validation code for radio buttons, because JavaScript creates an array out of elements with the same name. The following standard JavaScript onsubmit event handler determines whether at least one check box in a group of check boxes named "committees" is selected:

```
function submitForm() {
    var committeesSelected = false;
    for (var i=0; i<4; ++i) {
        if (document.forms[0].committees[i].checked == true) {
            committeesSelected = true;
            break;
        }
    }
    if (committeesSelected == false) {
        window.alert("You must select at least one committee.");
        return committeesSelected;
    }
    else
        return committeesSelected;
}
```

Here's a jQuery version of the preceding code that uses the `input:checkbox:checked` selector to determine whether at least one check box with a `name` attribute of `committees` is selected:

```
$(document).ready(function(){
    $("form").submit(function(event){
        if ($("input:checkbox[name=committees]:checked").val() != undefined)
            return true;
        else {
            window.alert("You must select at least one committee.");
            return false;
        }

    });
});
```

Summary

In this chapter, you saw how to use form events to manipulate user input and validate submitted field data. In the next chapter, you learn how to work with AJAX to manipulate web page content dynamically, without having to reload a web page from the server.

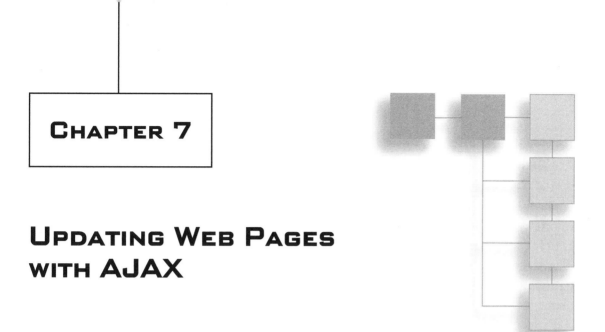

CHAPTER 7

UPDATING WEB PAGES
WITH AJAX

The most recent version of the JavaScript language is ECMAScript Edition 3, which was first released in December of 1999. The next major edition of the JavaScript language will be ECMAScript Edition 4, although at the time of this writing, the developers of the language have not made a great deal of progress on the new version, and it is not known when it will be complete. Although there have been numerous browser enhancements since Edition 3 was released in 1999, the core JavaScript language has remained essentially unchanged for almost a decade. This is unusual with software development technologies, because the web developers who use these technologies are constantly looking for new and better tools for writing their programs. Unwilling to simply await the arrival of Edition 4, JavaScript programmers have managed to accommodate their own demand for increased JavaScript functionality by combining JavaScript with other technologies.

One such technology is DHTML, which makes web pages dynamic by combining JavaScript, XHTML, CSS, and the Document Object Model. DHTML does a great job of making web pages more dynamic and will continue to be a vital web page development technique. The fact that DHTML runs entirely within a user's web browser used to be considered an advantage, because it made external resources, such as server data, unnecessary. However, as the Internet matured and broadband access became commonplace, web developers began demanding a way to make their web pages interact more dynamically with a web server. For example, consider a web browser's request for a web page. In response, the web server returns the requested page. If the user wants to refresh the web page, the web server returns the entire page again—not just the changed portions of the page. For web page data that must always be up to date, such as stock prices, continuously reloading the entire page is too slow, even at broadband speeds. As you will learn in this chapter, the solution is to use AJAX.

INTRODUCTION TO AJAX

Asynchronous JavaScript and XML (AJAX) refers to a combination of technologies that allow web pages displayed on a client computer to quickly interact and exchange data with a web server without reloading the entire web page. Although its name implies a combination of JavaScript and XML, AJAX primarily relies on JavaScript and HTTP requests to exchange data between a client computer and a web server. AJAX gets its name from the fact that XML is often the format used for exchanging data between a client computer and a web server (although it can also exchange data using standard text strings). The other technologies that compose AJAX include XHTML, CSS, and the Document Object Model (DOM). However, these technologies primarily handle the display and presentation of data within the web browser (the same as with DHTML), whereas HTTP and XML are responsible for data exchange. JavaScript ties everything together.

Note

The term AJAX was first used in an article written in 2005 by Jesse James Garrett entitled *Ajax: A New Approach to Web Applications* (http://adaptivepath.com/publications/essays/archives/000385.php). The article discussed how Garrett's company, Adaptive Path, was using a combination of technologies, which they referred to collectively as AJAX, to add richness and responsiveness to web pages. Since then, AJAX has become hugely popular among JavaScript developers.

It's important to note that Garrett and Adaptive Path did not invent anything new. Rather, they improved web page interactivity by combining JavaScript, XML, XHTML, CSS, and the DOM with the key component of AJAX, the XMLHttpRequest object, which is available in modern web browsers. The XMLHttpRequest object uses HTTP to exchange data between a client computer and a web server. Unlike standard HTTP requests, which usually replace the entire page in a web browser, the XMLHttpRequest object can be used to request and receive data without reloading a web page. By combining the XMLHttpRequest object with DHTML techniques, you can update and modify individual portions of your web page with data received from a web server. The XMLHttpRequest object has been available in most modern web browsers since around 2001. However, Garrett's article was the first to clearly document the techniques for combining the XMLHttpRequest object with other techniques in order to exchange data between a client computer and a web server.

Figure 7.1
Google Suggest list box

Another factor contributing to AJAX's popularity was the release in 2005 of Google Suggest search functionality, making Google one of the first commercial websites to implement an AJAX application. As you type a search item in the Google website, Google Suggest lists additional search suggestions based on the text you type. For example, if you type "JavaScript," the search suggestions shown in Figure 7.1 appear. The important thing to understand about Google Suggest is that as you type each letter, JavaScript code uses the XMLHttpRequest object to send the string in the text box to the Google server, which attempts to match the typed characters with matching suggestions. The Google server then returns the suggestions to the client computer (without reloading the web page), and JavaScript code populates the suggestion list with the response text.

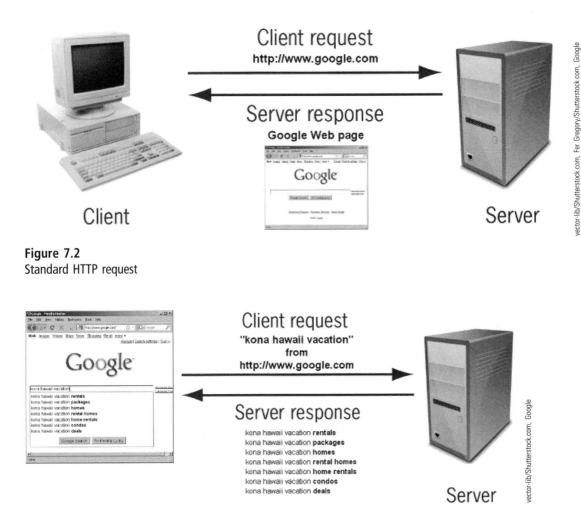

Figure 7.2
Standard HTTP request

Figure 7.3
HTTP request with the XMLHttpRequest object

Figures 7.2 and 7.3 conceptually illustrate the difference between a standard HTTP request and an HTTP request with the XMLHttpRequest object. In Figure 7.2, the client makes a standard HTTP request for the http://www.google.com web page, which is returned from the server and displayed in the client's web browser. Figure 7.3 illustrates the request process with Google when a user types the text "kona Hawaii vacation" into the text box. Instead of requesting an entire web page, the XMLHttpRequest object only requests recommended search terms for the 'kona Hawaii vacation' string. The server returns the recommended search terms to the client, which in turn uses JavaScript to display the terms in the suggestion list.

Running AJAX from a Web Server

Throughout this book, you have opened web pages directly from your local computer or network with your web browser. However, in this chapter, you will open files from a web server. Opening a local file in a web browser requires the use of the file:/// protocol. Because AJAX relies on the `XMLHttpRequest` object to retrieve data, you must open your AJAX files from a web server with the HTTP (http://) or HTTPS (https://) protocols instead. You can turn a computer into a web server by installing web server software on it. The most popular web server software used on the Internet is Apache HTTP Server (typically referred to as Apache), which is used by more than half of today's websites. The second most popular web server is Microsoft Internet Information Services (IIS) for Windows operating systems, which is used on about one third of today's websites.

Understanding AJAX's Limitations

The same origin policy restricts how JavaScript code in one window or frame accesses a web page in another window or frame on a client computer. For windows and frames to view and modify the elements and properties of documents displayed in other windows and frames, they must have the same protocol (such as HTTP) and exist on the same web server. Because JavaScript is the basis of AJAX programming, you cannot use the `XMLHttpRequest` object to directly access content on another domain's server; the data you request with the `XMLHttpRequest` object must be located on the web server where your JavaScript program is running. In other words, you cannot directly bypass your own web server and grab data from someone else's web server. However, the same origin policy only applies to JavaScript and not to any other programs running on your web server. This means that you can use a server-side script as a proxy to access data from another domain. The term *proxy* refers to someone or something that acts or performs a request for another thing or person. The server-side proxy script can then return the data to the client computer as it is requested with the `XMLHttpRequest` object.

Accessing Content on a Separate Domain

The purpose of the same origin policy is to prevent malicious scripts from modifying the content of other windows and frames and to prevent the theft of private browser information and information displayed on secure web pages. However, the ability for one web server to access web pages and data on another web server is the foundation of the World Wide Web. Although you should never attempt to pass off the content from another website as your own, there are legitimate reasons why you would use a server-side script to access data from another domain, particularly when it comes to accessing web services and RSS feeds. A *web service,* or *XML web service,* is a software component that resides on a web server. Web services do not contain any sort of graphical user interface or even a command-line interface. Instead, they simply provide services and data in the form of methods and properties; it is up to the client accessing a web service to provide an implementation for a program that calls a web service.

As an example of a web service, consider a web page that displays the prices of commodities that you want to track, such as crude oil, natural gas, gold, or silver. The web page may periodically call methods of a web service that return the most recent trading price for each type of commodity. The developer of a server-side script only needs to know which method of the web service to call for each type of commodity (such as a `getSilverPrice()` method that returns the current price of silver). The web service itself does not care what you do with the data once you receive it; it is up to you to display it on a web page, store it in a database, or use it in some other way in your application. In the case of AJAX, you might pass the data to a JavaScript program running on a client.

Tip

To find the methods and properties that are available for a particular web service, visit the website of the web service provider.

This chapter includes an AJAX example that displays streaming stock quote information from Yahoo! Finance. When you enter a stock quote into Yahoo! Finance, the returned results include a link that allows you to download a CSV (comma-separated values) file containing the basic stock quote information such as opening price and average volume. The default URL format for a CSV file downloaded from Yahoo! Finance is as follows:

```
http://finance.yahoo.com/d/quotes.csv?s={ticker symbols separated by+}
    &f={data format tags}&e=.csv
```

By default, the CSV file is named quotes.csv, and it is assigned three name=value pairs:

- *s* for ticker symbols
- *f* for data formats
- *e* for file extension (`.csv`)

You separate the ticker symbols assigned to the name=value pair for the ticker symbols with plus signs (+). The data that is downloaded from Yahoo! Finance to a CSV file is determined by the special tags that are assigned to the data format's name=value pair. By default, the values s1l1d1t1c1ohgv are assigned to the data format's name=value pair and represent the ticker symbol (s), last price (l1), date (d1), time (t1), change (c1), open price (o), daily high (h), daily low (g), and volume (v). Notice that the data format symbols are not separated by spaces or any other symbols. For example, the URL for a CSV file downloaded from Yahoo! Finance for Oracle Corp. (ORCL) is as follows:

```
http://download.finance.yahoo.com/d/quotes.csv?
    s=ORCL&f=s1l1d1t1c1ohgv&e=.csv
```

Tip

Although the download data link from Yahoo! Finance returns the ticker symbol, last price, date, time, change, open price, daily high, daily low, and volume by default, you can compose your own URL that downloads additional data for the specific ticker symbols. See http://www.dividendgrowth.org/ FundamentalAnalysis/YahooData.htm for a complete list of data format symbols that you can use when downloading a CSV file from Yahoo! Finance.

Because the returned CSV file from Yahoo! Finance is a simple text file, with each entry separated by commas, you can use a script to parse the file and use the values in your web pages. You will study the stock quote web page throughout this chapter. For now, you need to understand that the web page relies on a server-side PHP script to retrieve and parse stock information from Yahoo! Finance. The PHP script executes when it is passed a stock ticker with the XMLHttpRequest object. After the PHP script retrieves the information for the specified stock, it returns the data to the JavaScript code that called it. When you first open the stock quote web page, it defaults to the quote data for the NASDAQ Composite Index (^IXIC), as shown in Figure 7.4.

Entering a new ticker symbol and clicking the Get Quote button automatically retrieves the quote data for the specified stock from the Yahoo! Finance page. Figure 7.5 displays the updated stock quotes page after entering the ticker symbol for Oracle Corporation, ORCL.

The design of the stock quote page is quite involved and uses multiple tables to manage the layout of the navigation links and other elements on the page.

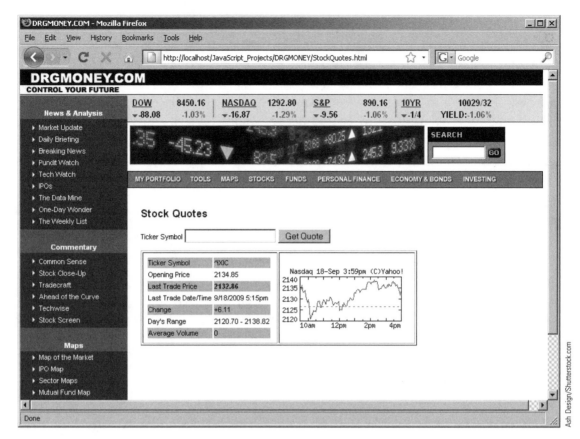

Figure 7.4
Stock quote page displaying the default NASDAQ Composite Index quote data

For the purposes of this chapter, the AJAX functionality only applies to the following text and elements that appear in the main body of the page:

```
<h2>Stock Quotes</h2>
<form action="" method="get" enctype="application/x-www-form-urlencoded">
<p>
    Ticker Symbol
    <input type="text" name="symbol" value="^IXIC" />
    <input type="button"
           onclick="getStockQuote(document.forms[0].symbol.value)"
        value="Get Quote" /></p>
<table cellpadding="5">
    <colgroup width="215px" />
    <tr>
        <td style="outline-style: ridge">
            <table id="tickerTable" border="0">
```

```
            <tr style="background-color: cyan">
                <td>Ticker Symbol</td>
                <td id="ticker"> </td>
            </tr>
            <tr>
                <td>Opening Price</td>
                <td id="openingPrice"> </td>
            </tr>
            <tr style="background-color: cyan">
                <td>Last Trade Price</td>
                <td id="lastTrade"></td>
            </tr>
            <tr>
                <td>Last Trade Date/Time</td>
                <td id="lastTradeDT"> </td>
            </tr>
            <tr style="background-color: cyan">
                <td>Change</td>
                <td id="change"> </td>
            </tr>
            <tr>
                <td>Day's Range</td>
                <td id="range"> </td>
            </tr>
            <tr style="background-color: cyan">
                <td>Average Volume</td>
                <td id="volume"> </td>
            </tr>
        </table>
    </td>
    <td id="chart" style="outline-style: ridge">
        <img src="http://ichart.finance.yahoo.com/t?s=%5EIXIC"
            alt="Stock line chart from Yahoo.com." />
    </td>
    <td>
    <p><img id="loader" src="preloader.gif" alt="Visual formatting image"
        style="display: none; cellpadding:0" /></p>
    </td>
</tr>
</table>
</form>
```

The stock quote page relies on the following PHP script to retrieve data from the Yahoo! Finance page. The script downloads a CSV (comma-separated values) file

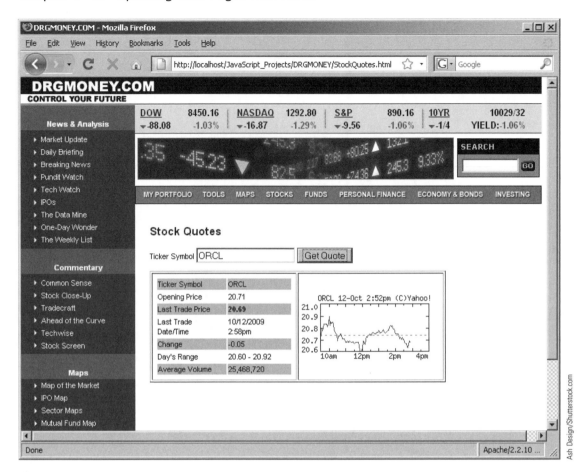

Figure 7.5
Stock quote page displaying quote data for the Oracle Corporation

from the Yahoo! Finance page that displays the quote data. Then, the script builds an XML tree from the CSV file and returns the result to the client with an `echo` statement, which is similar to JavaScript's `document.write()` statement. The focus of this book is jQuery programming, not PHP programming, so you will not analyze the following code any further. However, PHP shares a lot of similarities with JavaScript, so you can probably figure out most of the statements in the following code on your own.

```php
<?php
header("Content-Type: text/xml");
$QuoteXML = "<?xml version='1.0' ⏎
    encoding='iso-8859-1' standalone='yes' ?>\n";
$TickerSymbol = $_GET["checkQuote"];
```

```php
$Quote = fopen("http://finance.yahoo.com/d/quotes.csv?s ↵
    =$TickerSymbol&f=sl1d1t1c1p2ohgv&e=.csv", "r");
$QuoteString = fread($Quote, 2000);
fclose($Quote);
$QuoteString = str_replace("\"", "", $QuoteString);
$QuoteArray = explode(",", $QuoteString);
$QuoteXML .= "<quote>\n";
$QuoteXML .= "<ticker>{$QuoteArray[0]}</ticker>\n";
$QuoteXML .= "<lastTrade>{$QuoteArray[1]}</lastTrade>\n";
$QuoteXML .= "<lastTradeDate>{$QuoteArray[2]}</lastTradeDate>\n";
$QuoteXML .= "<lastTradeTime>{$QuoteArray[3]}</lastTradeTime>\n";
$QuoteXML .= "<change>{$QuoteArray[4]}</change>\n";
$QuoteXML .= "<changePercent>{$QuoteArray[5]}</changePercent>\n";
$QuoteXML .= "<open>{$QuoteArray[6]}</open>\n";
$QuoteXML .= "<rangeHigh>{$QuoteArray[7]}</rangeHigh>\n";
$QuoteXML .= "<rangeLow>{$QuoteArray[8]}</rangeLow>\n";
$QuoteXML .= "<volume>{$QuoteArray[9]}</volume>\n";
$QuoteXML .= "<chart>http://ichart.yahoo.com/t?s ↵
    =$TickerSymbol</chart>\n";
$QuoteXML .= "</quote>";
header("Content-Length: " . strlen($QuoteXML));
header("Cache-Control: no-cache");
echo $QuoteXML;
?>
```

When you run the preceding PHP script, it builds an XML tree containing the data for the stock ticker symbol that is passed to it. Then, the AJAX code in your Java-Script program uses node-manipulation techniques to parse the data. Following is an example of the XML tree that the PHP script generates when you pass the ticker symbol ORCL (for Oracle Corporation) to it:

```xml
<quote>
    <ticker>ORCL</ticker>
    <lastTrade>21.81</lastTrade>
    <lastTradeDate>10/16/2009</lastTradeDate>
    <lastTradeTime>4:00pm</lastTradeTime>
    <change>+0.49</change>
    <changePercent>+2.30%</changePercent>
    <open>21.23</open>
    <rangeHigh>22.03</rangeHigh>
    <rangeLow>21.18</rangeLow>
    <volume>65051668</volume>
    <chart>http://ichart.yahoo.com/t?s=</chart>
</quote>
```

UNDERSTANDING AJAX AND JAVASCRIPT

In order to be successful manipulating AJAX with jQuery, it helps to understand how to manipulate AJAX with JavaScript. First, you need to understand how to request server data.

Requesting Server Data with JavaScript

The `XMLHttpRequest` object is the key to turning your JavaScript script into an AJAX program because it allows you to use JavaScript and HTTP to exchange data between a web browser and a web server. More specifically, you use the methods and properties of an instantiated `XMLHttpRequest` object with JavaScript to build and send request messages and to receive and process response messages. The first step to using AJAX to exchange data between an HTTP client and a web server is to instantiate an `XMLHttpRequest` object.

Instantiating an XMLHttpRequest Object

For Mozilla-based browsers, such as Firefox, and for Internet Explorer 7, you instantiate an `XMLHttpRequest` object with the `XMLHttpRequest` constructor, as follows:

```
var httpRequest = new XMLHttpRequest();
```

Unfortunately, although the `XMLHttpRequest` object is available in most modern web browsers, it is not standardized by the W3C or any other standards organization. Thankfully, Internet Explorer 7 now uses the same syntax for instantiating an `XMLHttpRequest` object that Mozilla-based browsers use. However, for older versions of Internet Explorer, to instantiate an `XMLHttpRequest` object in Internet Explorer, you must instantiate the `XMLHttpRequest` object as an ActiveX object. *ActiveX* is a technology that allows programming objects to be easily reused with any programming language that supports Microsoft's Component Object Model. (The `Component Object Model` (`COM`) is an architecture for cross-platform development of client/server applications.) For Internet Explorer 6, you use the following syntax to instantiate an `XMLHttpRequest` object by passing a value of `"Msxml2.XMLHTTP"` to the ActiveX object constructor:

```
var httpRequest = new ActiveXObject("Msxml2.XMLHTTP");
```

Because Internet Explorer 6 is still used by a small percentage of the browser market, your code should test for and instantiate an `XMLHttpRequest` object according to the following rules:

1. For Mozilla-based browsers or Internet Explorer 7, use the `XMLHttpRequest` constructor.

2. For Internet Explorer 6, pass a value of `"Msxml2.XMLHTTP"` to the ActiveX object constructor.

3. For all other browsers, inform the users that their browsers do not support AJAX.

Most JavaScript programmers use a series of nested `try…catch` statements to instantiate an `XMLHttpRequest` object according to the web browser that is running the script. For example, the following code declares a variable named `httpRequest` and then attempts to use the `XMLHttpRequest` constructor in the `try` statement to declare an `XMLHttpRequest` object. If the web browser running the code does not contain an `XMLHttpRequest` constructor, it is neither a Mozilla-based browser nor Internet Explorer 7. If this is the case, the `try` statement throws an exception to the `catch` statement. Notice that the `catch` statement contains a nested `try…catch` statement. The nested `try` statement attempts to declare an `XMLHttpRequest` object by passing a value of `"Msxml2.XMLHTTP"` to the ActiveX object constructor.

If the web browser running the code does not support a value of `"Msxml2.XMLHTTP"` with the ActiveX object constructor, it is not Internet Explorer. If this is the case, the `try` statement throws an exception to the nested `catch` statement. Finally, if the nested `try` statement cannot instantiate an `XMLHttpRequest` object with the ActiveX object constructor, the nested `catch` statement prints `"Your browser does not support AJAX!"`

```
var httpRequest;
// instantiate an object for Mozilla-based browsers
// and Internet Explorer 7
try {
     httpRequest = new XMLHttpRequest();
}
// instantiate an ActiveX object for Internet Explorer 6
catch (requestError) {
     try {
             httpRequest = new ActiveXObject("Msxml2.XMLHTTP");
     }
     catch (requestError) {
             document.write("<p>Your browser does ↵
               not support AJAX!</p>");
             return false;
     }
}
```

Opening and closing HTTP connections takes up a lot of computer memory and processing time. To improve performance between client requests and server responses, HTTP/1.1 automatically keeps the client-server connection open until it is specifically closed by the client or server. It does this by assigning a value of `close` to the

Connection header. This means that you can make your AJAX programs faster by reusing an instantiated XMLHttpRequest object instead of recreating it each time you send a server request.

The following code demonstrates how to create a global variable named curRequest, which is assigned an instantiated XMLHttpRequest object in a function named getRequestObject(). The getRequestObject() function is only called once, when the web page first loads. After the getRequestObject() function creates the appropriate XMLHttpRequest object, the last statement in the function returns the curRequest variable to a calling statement. Notice the if statement that follows the getRequestObject()function. If the curRequest variable is equal to false, it has not been instantiated with the XMLHttpRequest object and the getRequestObject() function is called. However, if the curRequest variable is *not* equal to false (meaning that the web page has already been loaded), the getRequestObject() function is bypassed because the XMLHttpRequest object already exists.

```
var curRequest = false;
function getRequestObject() {
    try {
        httpRequest = new XMLHttpRequest();
    }
    catch (requestError) {
        try {
            httpRequest = new ActiveXObject(
                    "Msxml2.XMLHTTP");
        }
        catch (requestError) {
            try {
                httpRequest = new
                        ActiveXObject(
                        "Microsoft.XMLHTTP");
            }
            catch (requestError) {
                window.alert("Your browser ⏎
                        does not support AJAX!");
                return false;
            }
        }
    }
    return httpRequest;
}
if (!curRequest)
    curRequest = getRequestObject();
```

Opening and Sending a Request

After you instantiate an XMLHttpRequest object, you use the open() method with the instantiated XMLHttpRequest object to specify the request method (such as "get" or "post") and URL. The following statement is the open() method used by the stock quotes web page. The statement specifies the "get" method and a URL named StockCheck.php, which is the PHP script that retrieves the stock information from Yahoo! Finance. The requested stock is appended to the URL as a query string in the format checkQuote=tickerSymbol. The value assigned to the tickerSymbol variable is passed with the Get Quote button's onclick event to a function containing the XMLHttpRequest code.

```
stockRequest.open("get","StockCheck.php?" + "checkQuote=" + tickerSymbol);
```

The open() method also accepts three optional arguments. The first two optional arguments— a username and password—are necessary only if the web server requires authentication. The third optional argument, the async argument, can be assigned a value of true or false to determine whether the request will be handled synchronously or asynchronously. A *synchronous request* stops the processing of the JavaScript code until a response is returned from the server. Compared to a synchronous request, an *asynchronous request* allows JavaScript to continue processing while it waits for a server response. Assigning a value of true to the async argument performs the request asynchronously, whereas a value of false performs the request synchronously. If you omit the async argument, it defaults to a value of true, which performs the request asynchronously. The following statement demonstrates how to specify that the request will be handled synchronously and how to pass a username ("dongosselin") and password ("rosebud") to the open() method:

```
stockRequest.open("get","StockCheck.php?" + "checkQuote="
        + tickerSymbol, false, "dongosselin", "rosebud");
```

Caution

Although synchronous responses are easier to handle, they have a major drawback in that a script will not continue processing until the response is received. This means that if the server doesn't respond for some reason (perhaps because it is running slowly due to high traffic or maintenance requirements), your web page will appear to be dead in the water. Users can stop the script by clicking the browser's Stop button. However, a synchronous request does not contain any sort of mechanism for specifying the length of time that is allowed for receiving a response. To ensure that your script continues running in the event of a server problem, you should use asynchronous requests.

When you reuse an existing XMLHttpRequest object, it is possible that the object may already have been in the process of sending a request to the server. To improve performance, you should call the abort() method of the XMLHttpRequest object to cancel any existing HTTP requests before beginning a new one. Append the abort() method to an instantiated XMLHttpRequest object and call the method before calling the open() method, as follows:

```
stockRequest.abort();
stockRequest.open("get","StockCheck.php?"
    + "checkQuote=" + tickerSymbol, false, "dongosselin", "rosebud");
```

After you have defined the basic request criteria with the open() method, you use the send() method with the instantiated XMLHttpRequest object to submit the request to the server. The send() method accepts a single argument containing the message body. If "get" is specified with the open() method, you must pass a value of null to the send() method, as follows:

```
stockRequest.send(null);
```

When a web browser submits an HTTP request, it usually includes various response and message body headers. When running basic "get" requests with the XMLHttpRequest object, you do not usually need to specify any additional HTTP headers. For example, the following statements are all you need to open and send a request with the stock quotes web page:

```
stockRequest.abort();
stockRequest.open("get","StockCheck.php?"
    + "checkQuote=" + tickerSymbol);
stockRequest.send(null);
```

"Post" requests are a little more involved. With form data, a web browser automatically handles the task of creating name=value pairs from form element name attributes and field values. When submitting form data as the message body with the XMLHttpRequest object, you must manually build the name=value pairs that will be submitted to the server. The first statement in the following code creates a variable named requestBody that is assigned the value "checkQuote=" and the URI-encoded value assigned to the tickerSymbol variable. The last statement then passes the requestBody variable as an argument to the send() method.

```
var requestBody = "checkQuote=" + encodeURIComponent(tickerSymbol);
    stockRequest.send(requestBody);
```

With "post" requests, you must at least submit the Content-Type header before executing the send() method to identify the MIME type of the message body. You should also submit the Content-Length header to specify the size of the message body and the Connection header to specify that the connection with the server be closed after the response is received. You use the `setRequestHeader()` method to specify HTTP headers and values to submit with the HTTP request. You pass two arguments to the `setRequestHeader()` method: the name of the header and its value. For example, the following code uses the `setRequestHeader()` method to define the `Content-Type`, `Content-Length`, and `Connection` headers before submitting the request for the stock quotes web page:

```
stockRequest.abort();
stockRequest.open("post","StockCheck.php");
var requestBody = "checkQuote=" + encodeURIComponent(tickerSymbol);
stockRequest.setRequestHeader("Content-Type",
    "application/x-www-form-urlencoded");
stockRequest.setRequestHeader("Content-Length", requestBody.length);
stockRequest.setRequestHeader("Connection", "close");
stockRequest.send(requestBody);
```

Receiving Server Data

After you submit a request with the `XMLHttpRequest` object, the message body in the server response is assigned to the `XMLHttpRequest` object's `responseXML` or `responseText` properties. The `responseXML` property contains the HTTP response as an XML document, whereas the `responseText` property contains the HTTP response as a text string. Note that the message body is assigned to the `responseXML` property only if the server response includes the `Content-Type` header, assigned a MIME type value of `"text/xml"`. You can process the contents of the `responseXML` property by using node-manipulating techniques. For example, the following statements demonstrate how to manipulate the value assigned to the `responseXML` property for the stock quotes web page. The first statement assigns the value of the returned `responseXML` property to a variable named `stockValues`. The remaining statements then use the `innerHTML()` method and node properties to assign the values of the XML document stored in the `stockValues` variable to the appropriate element.

```
var stockValues = stockRequest.responseXML;
document.getElementById("ticker").innerHTML
    = stockValues.getElementsByTagName("ticker")[0]
    .childNodes[0].nodeValue;
document.getElementById("openingPrice")
    .innerHTML = stockValues.getElementsByTagName(
    "open")[0].childNodes[0].nodeValue;
document.getElementById("lastTrade").innerHTML
    = "<strong>" + stockValues.getElementsByTagName(
```

```
    "lastTrade")[0].childNodes[0].nodeValue
    + "</strong>";
document.getElementById("lastTradeDT").innerHTML
    = stockValues.getElementsByTagName(
    "lastTradeDate")[0].childNodes[0].nodeValue
    + " " + stockValues.getElementsByTagName(
    "lastTradeTime")[0].childNodes[0].nodeValue;
document.getElementById("change").innerHTML
    = stockValues.getElementsByTagName(
    "change")[0].childNodes[0].nodeValue;
document.getElementById("range").innerHTML
    = stockValues.getElementsByTagName(
    "rangeLow")[0].childNodes[0]
    .nodeValue + " - "
    + stockValues.getElementsByTagName(
    "rangeHigh")[0].childNodes[0].nodeValue;
var volume = parseInt(stockValues
    .getElementsByTagName(
    "volume")[0].childNodes[0].nodeValue);
document.getElementById("volume").innerHTML
    = volume.toLocaleString();
document.getElementById("chart").innerHTML
    = "<img src=" + stockValues
    .getElementsByTagName("chart")[0]
    .childNodes[0].nodeValue
    + " alt='Stock line chart from Yahoo.com.' />";
```

To receive a response for an asynchronous request, you must use the XMLHttpRequest object's readyState property and onreadystatechange event. The readyState property contains one of the following values, which represent the state of the HTTP request: 0 (uninitialized), 1 (open), 2 (sent), 3 (receiving), or 4 (loaded). The onreadystatechange event is triggered whenever the value assigned to the readyState property changes. You assign to the onreadystatechange event the name of a function that will execute whenever the readyState property changes. For example, the open() method in the following code defines an asynchronous request because it includes a value of true as the method's third argument. The third statement assigns a function named fillStockInfo() as the event handler function for the onreadystatechange event.

```
stockRequest.abort();
stockRequest.open("get","StockCheck.php?" + "checkQuote=" + tickerSymbol);
stockRequest.send(null);
stockRequest.onreadystatechange=fillStockInfo;
```

The value assigned to the readyState property is updated automatically according to the current statement of the HTTP request. However, you cannot process the response until the readyState property is assigned a value of 4, meaning that the response is finished loading. For this reason, you include an if statement in the fillStockInfo() function that checks the value assigned to the readyState property. As shown in the following example, once the readyState property is assigned a value of 4 and the status property is assigned a value of 200, the statements in the body of the if statement process the response:

```
function fillStockInfo() {
    if (stockRequest.readyState==4
        && stockRequest.status == 200) {
        var stockValues = stockRequest.responseXML;
        document.getElementById("ticker").innerHTML
            = stockValues.getElementsByTagName(
            "ticker")[0].childNodes[0].nodeValue;
    ...
    }
}
```

Refreshing Server Data Automatically

To automatically refresh data that is obtained from an HTTP server, you use Java-Script's setTimeout() or setInterval() methods to send a request to the server, and read and process the data returned from the server. As an example, the following code contains a completed version of the JavaScript section that gives the stock quotes web page its functionality. A global variable named tickerSymbol is declared at the beginning of the script section and retrieves the default value assigned to the text field with an ID of symbol. (The default value of ^IXIC is the ticker symbol for the NASDAQ Composite Index.) The getStockQuote() function, which calls the getRequestObject() function and also opens and submits the HTTP request, is initially called from an onload event in the <body> tag and is subsequently called each time a user clicks the Get Quote button. The last statement in the getStockQuote() function uses a setTimeout() method to call the getStockQuote() function every 10,000 milliseconds (or every 10 seconds). The setTimeout() method reinitializes each time the getStockQuote() function executes.

```
<script type="text/javascript">
/* <![CDATA[ */
var stockRequest = false;
var tickerSymbol = document.getElementById("symbol").value;
```

```
function getRequestObject() {
    try {
        httpRequest = new XMLHttpRequest();
    }
    catch (requestError) {
        try {
            httpRequest = new ActiveXObject(
            "Msxml2.XMLHTTP");
        }
        catch (requestError) {
            window.alert("Your browser does not support AJAX!");
            return false;
        }
    }
    return httpRequest;
}
function getStockQuote(newTicker) {
    if (!stockRequest)
        stockRequest = getRequestObject();
    if (newTicker)
        tickerSymbol = newTicker;
    stockRequest.abort();
    stockRequest.open("get","StockCheck.php?"
        + "checkQuote=" + tickerSymbol, true);
    stockRequest.send(null);
    stockRequest.onreadystatechange=fillStockInfo;
    clearTimeout(updateQuote);
    var updateQuote = setTimeout(
        "getStockQuote", 10000);
}
function fillStockInfo() {
    if (stockRequest.readyState==4
        && stockRequest.status == 200) {
        var stockValues = stockRequest.responseXML;
    document.getElementById("ticker").innerHTML
        = stockValues.getElementsByTagName(
        "ticker")[0].childNodes[0].nodeValue;
    document.getElementById("openingPrice")
        .innerHTML = stockValues
        .getElementsByTagName("open")[0]
        .childNodes[0].nodeValue;
    document.getElementById("lastTrade").innerHTML
        = "<strong>" + stockValues
        .getElementsByTagName(
```

```
        "lastTrade")[0].childNodes[0].nodeValue
        + "</strong>";
    document.getElementById("lastTradeDT")
        .innerHTML = stockValues
        .getElementsByTagName("lastTradeDate")[0]
        .childNodes[0].nodeValue + " "
        + stockValues.getElementsByTagName(
        "lastTradeTime")[0].childNodes[0]
        .nodeValue;
    document.getElementById("change").innerHTML
        = stockValues.getElementsByTagName(
        "change")[0].childNodes[0].nodeValue;
    document.getElementById("range").innerHTML
        = stockValues.getElementsByTagName(
        "rangeLow")[0].childNodes[0].nodeValue
        + " - " + stockValues
        .getElementsByTagName("rangeHigh")[0]
        .childNodes[0].nodeValue;
    var volume = parseInt(stockValues
        .getElementsByTagName(
        "volume")[0].childNodes[0].nodeValue);
    document.getElementById("volume").innerHTML
        = volume.toLocaleString();
    document.getElementById("chart").innerHTML
        = "<img src=" + stockValues
        .getElementsByTagName("chart")[0]
        .childNodes[0].nodeValue
        + " alt='Stock line chart from Yahoo.com.' />";
    }
}
/* ]]> */
</script>
```

IMPLEMENTING AJAX FUNCTIONALITY WITH JQUERY

Thankfully, jQuery makes it much easier to implement AJAX functionality with jQuery, which handles all of the instantiation requirements for the XMLHttpRequest object. The most basic jQuery AJAX utility is the .load() method, which is discussed first.

Using the .load() Method

The .load() inserts the returned content from an AJAX call into a specified selector. The syntax for the .load() method is as follows:

```
$(selector).load(url[, data][, function(response, status, xhr)])
```

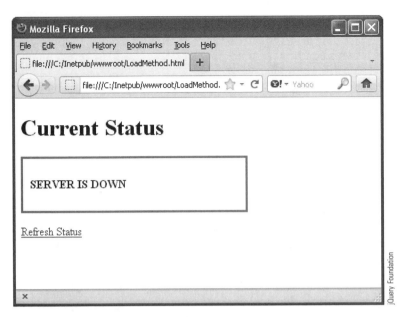

Figure 7.6
Status web page after clicking the Refresh Status button

The only required argument for the .load() method is the URL that contains the data you want to load into the specified selector. The data parameter contains data that is sent to the selector along with the request. The function parameter is a callback function that executes after the returned content is inserted into the specified selector. The following simple example demonstrates how to use the .load() method to load the contents of a document named CurrentStatus.html into a <div> element with an ID of statusBox. By default, the <div> element contains <p>No current status updates</p>. Assuming that the CurrentStatus.html file contains a single paragraph element, <p>SERVER IS DOWN</p>, clicking the Refresh Status link updates the web page as shown in Figure 7.6.

```
<script src="jquery-1.6.1.js"></script>
<script type="text/javascript">
/* <![CDATA[ */
$(document).ready(function(){
    $("#check").click(function() {
        $("#statusBox").load("CurrentStatus.html");
    return false;
    });
});
/* ]]> */
```

```
</script>
</head>
<body>
<h1>Current Status</h1>
<div id="statusBox" style="border:3px solid red; width:300px; padding:10px">
<p>No current status updates</p></div>
<p><a href="" id="check">Refresh Status</a></p>
</body>
```

By default, the .load() method inserts the entire contents of a specified web page into a matching selector. However, you can specify that jQuery only insert a specific element and its contents by appending the element's ID to the URL, separated by a space. For example, assume that the CurrentStatus.html page contains the following elements, and that each paragraph element contains the status of a specific server identified by its ID attribute:

```
<p id="s001"><strong>SERVER IS DOWN</strong></p>
<p id="s002"><strong>SERVER UNDER HEAVY LOAD</strong></p>
<p id="s003"><strong>SERVER AVAILABLE</strong></p>
```

If you modify the .load() method as follows, only the second paragraph element and its contents are inserted into the <div> element:

```
$("#statusBox").load("CurrentStatus.html #s002");
```

You can pass the server ID to the .load() method and a PHP page, as follows. The PHP page could then use the server ID to retrieve current status information.

```
$("#statusBox").load("CurrentStatus.php", "s002");
```

The .load() method and the utility functions that are covered in the next section all accept a *function* argument that can be either the name of a function or an anonymous function that executes the code in response to the event. The function or anonymous function can return three optional arguments: returned data, status text, and an object representing the XMLHttpRequest. The status text can be one of the following values:

- success—Request was successful.
- notmodified—Request was successful but the server returned an HTTP "Not Modified" response.
- error—Request was unsuccessful.
- timeout—Request was not completed within the timeout interval.
- parsererror—Request was successful but parsing failed.

The following code demonstrates how to use all three arguments with the `.load()` method's callback function for the status web page. Notice that the code uses the `.html()` method to assign the response text to the `<div>` element and that the `else...if` clause uses properties of the `XMLHttpRequest` object to return the status code and status text in the event that the jQuery status response returns an error.

```
$(document).ready(function(){
    $("#check").click(function() {
        $("#statusBox").load("CurrentStatus.html #s003",
                function(response, status, xhr) {
            if (status == "success")
                $("#statusBox").html(response);
            else if (status == "error")
                $("#statusBox").html("<p><strong>Error "
                                + xhr.status + "; " + xhr.statusText);
        });
    return false;
    });
});
```

Working with the jQuery AJAX Utility Functions

jQuery includes two utility functions—`.get()` and `.post()`—which are very similar to the `.load()` method. As their names imply, the `.get()` function performs a GET request while the `.post()` function performs a POST request. Both methods accept the same parameters as the `.load()` method, except that they can also accept a fourth parameter that identifies the type of returned data: xml, html, text, script, json, or jsonp. In most cases, the data type parameter is not necessary because jQuery can usually identify the type of returned data.

Note

Keep in mind that a *method* is associated with an object, whereas a *function* is usually standalone, depending on the programming language. For example, the AJAX `.load()` method is available only to elements that match a specified selector. In comparison, functions such as `.get()` and `.post()` can be executed independently of any specific object.

The following code demonstrates how to use the `.post()` function with the stock quotes web page you saw earlier. In this version, the `.ready()` function initially calls the `getStockQuote()` function to retrieve the data for the ^IXIC ticker symbol, and also contains a `.click()` event that triggers when users click the Get Quote button. The `.post()` function in the `getStockQuote()` function handles the

AJAX functionality. Notice that the statements in the previous `fillStockInfo()` function are now incorporated into the `getStockQuote()` function and that they now use jQuery syntax to assign values to the HTML elements that display the stock info.

```
$(document).ready(function(){
    getStockQuote();
    $("#getButton").click(getStockQuote);
    function getStockQuote() {
        tickerSymbol = $("#symbol").attr("value");
        $.get("StockCheck.php", {checkQuote:tickerSymbol},
            function(stockValues, status) {
                if (status == "success") {
                    $("#ticker").html(stockValues.getElementsByTagName(
                        "ticker")[0].childNodes[0].nodeValue);
                    $("#openingPrice").html(stockValues.getElementsByTagName(
                        "open")[0].childNodes[0].nodeValue);
                $("#lastTrade").html("<strong>"
                    + stockValues.getElementsByTagName(
                        "lastTrade")[0].childNodes[0].nodeValue + "</strong>");
                $("#lastTradeDT").html(stockValues.getElementsByTagName(
                    "lastTradeDate")[0].childNodes[0].nodeValue + " "
                        + stockValues.getElementsByTagName(
                        "lastTradeTime")[0].childNodes[0].nodeValue);
                $("#change").html(stockValues.getElementsByTagName(
                    "change")[0].childNodes[0].nodeValue);
                $("#range").html(stockValues.getElementsByTagName(
                    "rangeLow")[0].childNodes[0].nodeValue + " - "
                    + stockValues.getElementsByTagName(
                    "rangeHigh")[0].childNodes[0].nodeValue);
                var volume = parseInt(stockValues.getElementsByTagName(
                    "volume")[0].childNodes[0].nodeValue);
                $("#volume").html(volume.toLocaleString());
                $("#chart").html("<img src="
                    + stockValues.getElementsByTagName(
                    "chart")[0].childNodes[0].nodeValue + "
                    alt='Stock line chart from Yahoo.com.' />");
            }
        });
        clearTimeout(updateQuote);
        var updateQuote = setTimeout("getStockQuote", 10000);
    }
});
```

Capturing Events with the jQuery AJAX Event Registration Methods

jQuery includes the event handling methods listed in Table 7.1 that allow you to capture events initiated by AJAX.

Essentially, you can use the JavaScript AJAX event registration methods to capture and handle events that occur when executing an AJAX call.

Unlike the `.get()` and `.post()` methods, which can be called independently of a selector, you must append the JavaScript AJAX event registration methods to a selector. However, it makes no difference which selector you append it to, as long as the selector exists in the current document. Unfortunately, the jQuery organization offers no explanation for this behavior, so your best bet is to append the JavaScript AJAX event registration methods to the element that initiated the AJAX event.

The table that displays the stock information on the stock quote page includes the following `<td>` element, which displays an animated GIF image with the text `"Loading"` that is intended to run while AJAX is retrieving stock information. The stock quote page examples you have seen so far have not used this image because the CSS `display` style is assigned a value of `none` by default.

```
<td><p><img id="loader" src="preloader.gif"
alt="Visual formatting image" style="display: none; cellpadding: 0" />
</p></td>
```

With the AJAX event registration methods, you can use the `.ajaxStart()` method to display the animated GIF image while AJAX is retrieving stock information and then use the `.ajaxComplete()` method to hide the image when the AJAX call is

Table 7.1 JavaScript AJAX Event Registration Methods

Event	Triggered When
`.ajaxComplete()`	An AJAX call completes.
`.ajaxError()`	An error is returned from an AJAX call.
`.ajaxSend()`	An AJAX call is sent.
`.ajaxStart()`	An AJAX call starts.
`.ajaxStop()`	An AJAX call stops.
`.ajaxSuccess()`	An AJAX call completes successfully.

complete. The following statements demonstrate how to use these methods with the animated GIF image.

```
$("body").ajaxStart(function(){
    $("#loader").css("display","block");
});
$("body").ajaxComplete(function(){
    $("#loader").css("display","none");
});
```

Using the .ajax() Method

jQuery includes several other AJAX methods that require a more advanced knowledge of AJAX. However, one method you should be familiar with is the .ajax() method, which is the ancestor method that all other AJAX methods—including .load(), .get(), and .post()—utilize to perform their functionality. You will rarely need to use the .ajax() method, but you should be aware of it in case you need to implement some AJAX functionality that is beyond the capabilities of the .load(), .get(), and .post() methods.

The basic syntax for the .ajax() method is as follows:

```
$.ajax(url: url [, {name:value, name:value, ... }])
```

The .ajax() method accepts a number of parameters that are thoroughly described on the page: http://api.jquery.com/jQuery.ajax/. Three of the most commonly used parameters are url, data, and success. The url parameter identifies the URL to which the AJAX request is sent, the data parameter identifies a set of data to be sent to the server along with the AJAX request, and the success parameter identifies a function to be called if the request succeeds.

As a basic example of how to use the .ajax() method, the following example shows the getStockQuote() method on the stock quote page using the .ajax() method. Notice that all parameters passed to the .ajax() method use the *name:value* syntax, and that the values are either enclosed within quotations or contained within a set of curly braces.

```
function getStockQuote() {
    tickerSymbol = $("#symbol").attr("value");
    $.ajax({
        url: "StockCheck.php",
        data: {checkQuote: tickerSymbol},
        success: function(stockValues) {
            $("#ticker").html(stockValues.getElementsByTagName(
```

```
            "ticker")[0].childNodes[0].nodeValue);
        $("#openingPrice").html(stockValues.getElementsByTagName(
            "open")[0].childNodes[0].nodeValue);
        $("#lastTrade").html("<strong>"
            + stockValues.getElementsByTagName(
                "lastTrade")[0].childNodes[0].nodeValue + "</strong>");
        $("#lastTradeDT").html(stockValues.getElementsByTagName(
            "lastTradeDate")[0].childNodes[0].nodeValue + " "
                + stockValues.getElementsByTagName(
                "lastTradeTime")[0].childNodes[0].nodeValue);
        $("#change").html(stockValues.getElementsByTagName(
            "change")[0].childNodes[0].nodeValue);
        $("#range").html(stockValues.getElementsByTagName(
            "rangeLow")[0].childNodes[0].nodeValue + " - "
            + stockValues.getElementsByTagName(
            "rangeHigh")[0].childNodes[0].nodeValue);
        var volume = parseInt(stockValues.getElementsByTagName(
            "volume")[0].childNodes[0].nodeValue);
        $("#volume").html(volume.toLocaleString());
        $("#chart").html("<img src=" + stockValues.getElementsByTagName(
            "chart")[0].childNodes[0].nodeValue
            + " alt='Stock line chart from Yahoo.com.' />");
        }
    });
    clearTimeout(updateQuote);
    var updateQuote = setTimeout('getStockQuote()', 10000);
}
```

Summary

This chapter covered a great deal of territory when it comes to working with AJAX. Keep in mind that AJAX is a complex subject, and this chapter only scratched the surface of its capabilities. However, you should have gained enough knowledge to begin creating your own AJAX web pages.

CHAPTER 8

MANIPULATING WEB PAGE CONTENT

As you learned earlier in this book, almost every jQuery script begins by selecting one or more nodes from the DOM. After you select some nodes, you can then perform some sort of action using JavaScript or jQuery techniques. The DOM represents the HTML or XML of a web page that is displayed in a browser. The Document Object Model that represents HTML content is referred to as the HTML DOM, and the Document Object Model that represents XML content is referred to as the XML DOM. The W3C formally recommends using the XML DOM instead of the HTML DOM. Nonetheless, it's easier to use the HTML DOM with basic types of DHTML techniques. In fact, throughout this book you have seen various examples of how to use the HTML DOM to select and filter elements, manipulate CSS, create visual effects, and perform other functions by accessing nodes through the HTML DOM. However, for more sophisticated node manipulation, you must use the XML DOM.

WORKING WITH THE XML DOM

HTML was originally based on an older language called *Standard Generalized Markup Language,* or *SGML,* which defines the data in a document independent of how the data will be displayed. In other words, SGML separates the data in a document from the way that data is formatted. Each element in an SGML document is marked according to its type, such as paragraphs, headings, and so on. Like SGML, HTML was originally designed as a way of defining the elements in a document independent of how they would appear. HTML was not intended to be used for designing the actual appearance of the pages in a web browser, but the language gradually evolved to have this capability.

HTML first became an Internet standard in 1993 with the release of version 1.0. The next version, HTML 2.0, was released in 1994 and included many core HTML features, such as forms and the ability to bold and italicize text. Yet, many of the standard features that are widely used today, such as using tables to organize text and graphics on a page, were not available until the release of HTML 3.2 in 1996. Version 4.01 was released in 1999.

An application that can retrieve and process web pages is called a *user agent*. A user agent can be a traditional web browser, a mobile phone, a tablet computer, or even an application such as a crawler for a search engine that simply collects and processes data instead of displaying it. Although user agents other than browsers can process HTML, they are not ideally suited to the task, primarily because HTML is more concerned with how data appears than with the data itself.

As web browsers have evolved over the years, they have added *extensions* (elements and attributes) to HTML to provide functionality for displaying and formatting web pages. For instance, one extension to the original HTML language is the <font> element, which allows you to specify the font for data in an HTML document. The <font> element has nothing to do with the type of data in an HTML document. Instead, its sole purpose is to display data in a specific typeface within a web browser.

For two primary reasons, HTML is not suitable for user agents other than web browsers:

- First, HTML originally evolved into a markup language that focused more on the appearance of data than with the data itself because HTML is based on SGML, which defines the data in a document independently of how it will be displayed. Tags like the <font> tag violate this rule.

- Second, most web browsers allow you to write sloppy HTML code. For instance, all HTML documents should begin with <html> and end with </html>, and should include <head>... </head> and <body>... </body> tag pairs. In practice, however, you can omit any of these tags from an HTML document and a web browser will still render the page correctly. In fact, although many tags require a closing tag, you can often omit it and the web page will usually render properly.

HTML was the first language used for creating traditional web pages that are displayed in web browsers on desktop computers and workstations. However, a few years ago the W3C's stated goal was that HTML 4.01 would be the last version and would be replaced with *Extensible Hypertext Markup Language*, or *XHTML*, which was supposed to be the next-generation markup language for creating web pages. XHTML version 1.0 was introduced in 2000, and is a stricter form of HTML that requires web page syntax to adhere to a specific set of rules and XML standards, making it compatible with all user agents that support it. Ideally, you would always use XHTML because its stricter rules will make your web pages compatible with user agents other than traditional web browsers. XHTML also makes your web pages compatible with the Americans with Disabilities Act (ADA), allowing handicapped people to read them. For this reason, many corporate websites began publishing their web pages using XHTML.

Although the noble goal of XHTML was to make the web accessible to all via any sort of user agent, vendors were reluctant to implement the new XHTML features. One of the main reasons for this reluctance was because many of the countless websites out there were not yet willing to spend the time or resources to convert to XML standards.

Although every HTML page can be reproduced with XHTML if you know the rules, for smaller websites, it is often faster and easier to use basic HTML. Another major reason that XHTML wasn't widely adopted was because Microsoft did not add true XHTML support to Internet Explorer until Version 9. Although Firefox is now the dominant web browser, in the early years of XHTML, Internet Explorer was still the main player in the game, and web developers had no choice but to create web pages that were compatible with it.

Because of the reluctance of the web community to adopt XHTML, in 2004 the Web Hypertext Application Technology Working Group (WHATWG) was formed independently of the W3C to promote the development of HTML separately from XHTML. The standard that WHATWG developed eventually became known as HTML5 includes an XHTML implementation, and is endorsed by the web's original architect, Tim Berners-Lee. In 2007, the W3C voted to recognize WHATWG's HTML5 specification as the standard for the next generation of HTML. Then, in 2009, the W3C stopped work on XHTML 2.0 and officially recognized that HTML5 would be the next-generation standard for both HTML and XHTML.

Like XHTML, HTML5 documents can also conform to XML requirements. This ensures that all user agents can read your web pages, and that you can use XML node manipulation techniques with JavaScript and jQuery.

Note

HTML5 is the first version of the language that is not based on SGML.

Understanding XML

Languages based on SGML use a Document Type Definition, or DTD, to define the tags and attributes that you can use in a document and the rules the document must follow when it includes them. When a document conforms to an associated DTD, it is said to be valid. When a document does not conform to an associated DTD, it is invalid. For example, you may have a DTD that defines tags and elements in a document that will be used by a Human Resources department. The DTD may include tags such as <employee_name>, <position>, and <salary>. The DTD may also define attributes such as employeeID that can be used in the <employee_name> tag. Additionally, the Human Resources DTD may define rules about how the tags and attributes can be used in a document. For instance, it may require that the <employee_name>, <position>, and <salary> tags be contained within a <department> tag.

All XML elements must conform to the following rules in order to be valid:

- All XML documents must have a root element.
- XML is case sensitive.
- All XML elements must have a closing tag.
- XML elements must be properly nested.
- Attribute values must appear within quotation marks.
- Empty elements must be closed.

When you open an HTML or XHTML document in a web browser, the browser does not parse the code as it would an XML document. Instead, if the XHTML document is not well formed, the browser simply ignores the errors and renders the web page. To ensure that a web page is well formed and that its elements are valid, you need to use a *validating parser*. *Validation* checks that your document is well formed, and that the elements in your document are written correctly according to the element definitions in an associated Document Type Definition, or DTD, which defines the tags and attributes that you can use in a document and the rules the document must follow when it includes them. Because earlier versions of HTML were based on SGML, it requires a DTD, and the HTML5 DTD is built directly into web browsers. The HTML DTD defines tags such as <html>, <head>, and <body> and defines rules that you must follow when authoring your documents. For instance, one rule in the HTML DTD states that you must include a <title> tag with a <head> tag. However, because most web browsers allow you to write sloppy code, this rule—and almost every other rule defined in the HTML DTD—is usually ignored. Note that you cannot edit the HTML DTD or create your own version, although other SGML-based languages do allow you to create your own DTDs.

Note

Some languages that are based on SGML are not required to use DTDs. XML documents, for instance, can be created with or without a DTD.

You are not required to validate web page documents. If you do not validate a web page and it contains errors, most web browsers will probably treat it as an HTML document, ignore the errors, and render the page anyway. However, validation can help you spot errors in your code. Even the most experienced web authors frequently introduce typos or some other error into XHTML documents that prevent the document from being well formed and valid. Remember that if your document is not well formed, user agents such as mobile phones may have trouble rendering it.

Tip

Many validating parsers exist. One of the best available is the W3C Markup Validation Service, a free service that validates both HTML and XHTML. The W3C Markup Validation Service is located at http://validator.w3.org. The main web page for the service allows you to validate a web page by entering its URI in the Address box and selecting various options. Once you validate a document, the W3C Markup Validation Service displays a results page that lists warnings or errors found in the document. The W3C Markup Validation Service also includes a separate page that you can use to validate XHTML files by uploading them from your computer. You can open the File Upload page of the W3C Markup Validation Service by clicking the Validate by File Upload tab at the top of the main page or by entering the following URL in your browser's Address box: http://validator.w3.org/#validate_by_upload.

The structure of an XML document is arranged in a hierarchical tree, and each element and attribute in an XML document tree is referred to as a *node*. The document's root element is referred to as the *root node*. Individual nodes in an XML document tree can contain other nodes; similar to the way a folder on a hard drive can contain subfolders. An XML document tree is really just another way of looking at nested elements. However, the tree structure is important to understand because it is critical to how you can use JavaScript and jQuery to access and manipulate web pages. As an example, consider the following XML document that organizes Winter Olympic medal counts by country:

```
<olympics>
    <event>Winter Olympics</event>
    <medals>Olympic Medal Counts</medals>
    <countries>
        <country name="Germany">
```

```
            <gold>12</gold>
            <silver>16</silver>
            <bronze>7</bronze>
        </country>
        <country name="USA">
            <gold>10</gold>
            <silver>13</silver>
            <bronze>11</bronze>
        </country>
        <country name="Norway">
            <gold>11</gold>
            <silver>7</silver>
            <bronze>6</bronze>
        </country>
    </countries>
</olympics>
```

In the preceding example, the root node is the <olympics> element. Figure 8.1 presents a conceptual illustration of how the preceding XML document appears in the concept of a tree structure.

The structure of an HTML document is also arranged in a hierarchical tree. Each element and attribute in an HTML document tree is referred to as a node. The <!DOCTYPE> declaration for HTML5 is simply <!DOCTYPE HTML> and is referred to as the root node. The tree structure is important to understand because it is critical to how you can use JavaScript and jQuery to manipulate individual nodes. First, consider the following HTML version of the Winter Olympics web page:

```
<!DOCTYPE HTML>
<html>
    <head>
        <title>Winter Olympics</title>
        <style type="text/css">
            td {text-align:center}
        </style>
    </head>
    <body>
        <h1>Winter Olympics</h1>
        <h2>Olympic Medal Counts</h2>
        <table width="50%" border="1">
            <tr>
                <th>Country</th>
                <th>Gold</th>
                <th>Silver</th>
                <th>Bronze</th>
```

```
        </tr>
        <tr>
            <td>Germany</td>
            <td>12</td>
            <td>16</td>
            <td>7</td>
        </tr>
        <tr>
            <td>USA</td>
            <td>10</td>
            <td>13</td>
            <td>11</td>
        </tr>
        <tr>
            <td>Norway</td>
            <td>11</td>
            <td>7</td>
            <td>6</td>
        </tr>
    </table>
  </body>
</html>
```

The root node for the preceding document is `<html>` and it can be represented visually in a tree, as shown in Figure 8.2.

Tip

> Remember to use a validating parser, such as the W3C Markup Validation Service at http://validator.w3.org, to validate your documents.

Now that you better understand how HTML and XML are represented by a tree structure, you can examine some of the techniques for working with nodes.

Traversing the XML DOM

The jQuery selectors and filters are usually robust enough to handle any element and attribute selection tasks. However, there will be times when you need more fine-grained control when selecting elements, particularly when it comes to manipulating web page items by document hierarchy. jQuery includes a *traversing API* that contains methods for manipulating element sets that were returned with a selector.

The term "traversing" refers to the ability to access and control the individual elements on a web page. To access a specific element according to its position in

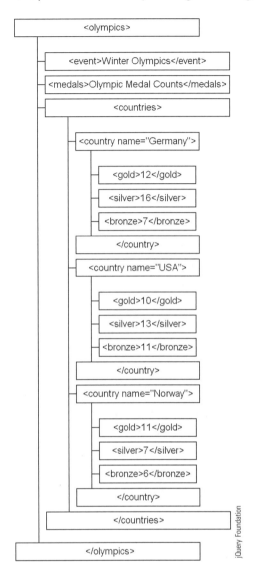

Figure 8.1
Winter Olympics XML document in a tree structure

the XML DOM, you must use the traversing API. For example, if you want to retrieve the last name of someone who subscribed to your website, you must use a traversing API method to access his or her name, according to the element that contains it. When you call a traversing method, a jQuery object representing the elements is returned. You can then use other traversing methods to expand or reduce the elements within the jQuery object, according to specified criteria.

It is important to understand that, like the basic jQuery selectors and filters, the traversing methods do not actually modify the elements; their primary purpose is to

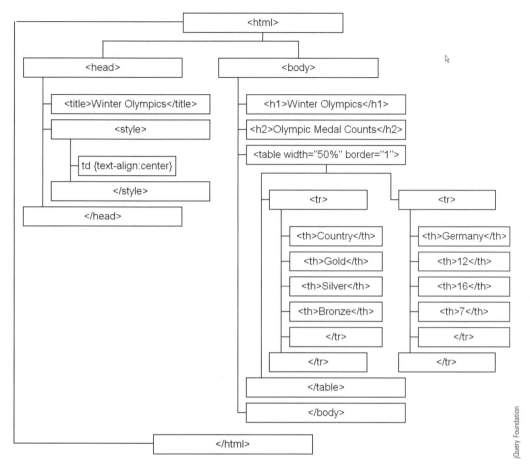

Figure 8.2
Winter Olympics HTML document in a tree structure

control which elements are accessible through the jQuery object. To modify the elements represented in the jQuery object, you must use other methods such as the .html() and .css() methods—or the XML DOM manipulation methods discussed in the next section—to manipulate the element and attribute contents. Table 8.1 lists the jQuery traversing API accessor methods.

Note

The .is() method is the only traversing method that does not return a jQuery object.

To better understand the jQuery traversing API methods, consider the getElementById() method that you have seen several times in earlier chapters. This method is JavaScript's method for accessing nodes by ID in the HTML DOM. To access an element with an ID of lastName in the HTML DOM, you use a

Table 8.1 jQuery Traversing API Accessor Methods

Method	Description
.add()	Adds elements that match a specified selector to the set of matched elements.
.andSelf()	Adds the previous set of elements to the current set of elements.
.children()	Reduces the set of matched elements to the children of each element, optionally filtered by a selector parameter.
.closest()	Reduces the set of matched elements to the first element that matches a specified selector, starting at the current element and progressing up through the DOM.
.contents()	Reduces the set of matched elements to the children of each element, including text nodes.
.end()	Ends the most recent filtering operation in the current chain and returns the set of matched elements to its previous state.
.eq()	Reduces the set of matched elements to the element that matches a specified index.
.filter()	Reduces the set of matched elements to the descendants of each element that match a specified selector or passes a function's test.
.find()	Reduces the set of matched elements to the descendants of each element that match a specified selector.
.first()	Reduces the set of matched elements to the first element.
.has()	Reduces the set of matched elements to the descendants of each element that match a specified selector or DOM element.
.is()	Determines whether at least one element in the set of matched elements matches a specified selector, jQuery object, or element; returns true or false.
.last()	Reduces the set of matched elements to the last element.
.map()	Creates a new jQuery object by filtering the set of matched elements with a specified function.
.next()	Reduces the set of matched elements to the following immediate sibling, optionally filtered by a selector parameter.
.nextAll()	Reduces the set of matched elements to all following siblings, optionally filtered by a selector parameter.
.nextUntil()	Reduces the set of matched elements to all following siblings, up to but not including a specified selector, jQuery object, or element.
.not()	Reduces the set of matched elements to all elements that do not match a specified selector, jQuery object, or element.

Table 8.1   jQuery Traversing API Accessor Methods (*Continued*)

Method	Description
.offsetParent()	Reduces the set of matched elements to the closest ancestor element with a CSS position attribute that is assigned a value of relative, absolute, or fixed.
.parent()	Reduces the set of matched elements to the parent elements, optionally filtered by a selector parameter.
.parents()	Reduces the set of matched elements to all ancestor elements, optionally filtered by a selector parameter.
.parentsUntil()	Reduces the set of matched elements to all ancestor elements, up to but not including a specified selector, jQuery object, or element.
.prev()	Reduces the set of matched elements to the previous immediate siblings, optionally filtered by a selector parameter.
.prevAll()	Reduces the set of matched elements to all previous siblings, optionally filtered by a selector parameter.
.prevUntil()	Reduces the set of matched elements to all previous siblings, up to but not including a specified selector, jQuery object, or element.
.siblings()	Reduces the set of matched elements to all siblings, optionally filtered by a selector parameter.
.slice()	Reduces the set of matched elements to those that match a range of specified indices.

statement similar to document.getElementById("lastName"). To access an element with the same ID with a jQuery traversing API method, you can use the .find() method using a statement such as $("body").find("#lastName").

As another example of how to use the traversing methods, consider the following version of the Winter Olympics web page. This version highlights each table row when the mouse passes over it and then removes the highlighting when the mouse passes off of it.

The jQuery section includes mouseover and mouseout event handlers for the table row and uses standard selectors to select the <tr> elements. Then, the .children() traversing method is applied to the returned selectors, which narrows the set of matched elements to the child elements in the <tr> elements. The mouseover event handler further restricts the returned result set to <td> elements so that the table header row is not highlighted when the mouse passes over it. Figure 8.3 shows how the page appears when the USA row is highlighted.

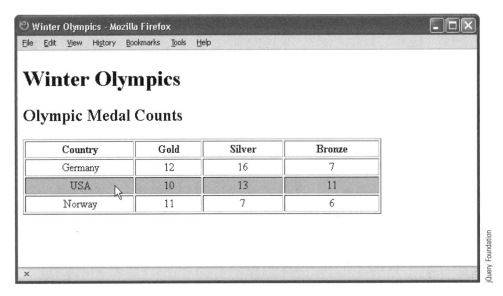

Figure 8.3
Winter Olympics HTML document with row highlighted using traversing methods

```
<!DOCTYPE html PUBLIC "-//W3C//DTD HTML 4.01//EN">
<html>
    <head>
        <title>Winter Olympics</title>
        <style type="text/css">
            td {text-align:center}
        </style>
        <script src="http://code.jquery.com/jquery-latest.js"></script>
        <script type="text/javascript">
        /* <![CDATA[ */
            $(document).ready(function(){
                $("tr").mouseover(function (event) {
                    $(this).children("td").css({ backgroundColor:'cyan' });
                });
                $("tr").mouseout(function (event) {
                    $(this).children().css({ backgroundColor:'white' });
                });
            });
        /* ]]> */
        </script>
    </head>
    <body>
        <h1>Winter Olympics</h1>
```

```
        <h2>Olympic Medal Counts</h2>
        <table width="50%" border="1">
            <tr>
                <th>Country</th>
                <th>Gold</th>
                <th>Silver</th>
                <th>Bronze</th>
            </tr>
            <tr>
                <td>Germany</td>
                <td>12</td>
                <td>16</td>
                <td>7</td>
            </tr>
            ....
        </table>
    </body>
</html>
```

The traversing methods give you a great deal of flexibility when it comes to selecting elements, and several of the methods can perform the same function. For example, the following code demonstrates how to create the row highlighting functionality using the .has() method instead of the .child() method:

```
<script type="text/javascript">
/* <![CDATA[ */
    $(document).ready(function(){
        $("tr").mouseover(function (event) {
            $(this).has("td").css({ backgroundColor:'cyan' });

        });
        $("tr").mouseout(function (event) {
            $(this).has("td").css({ backgroundColor:'white' });

        });
    });
/* ]]> */
</script>
```

MANIPULATING THE XML DOM

Whereas the preceding section explained the techniques for accessing DOM elements, this section describes how to add, delete, and modify elements with the manipulation API.

Adding and Removing Elements

Table 8.2 lists the jQuery-manipulation API methods that you can use to add and remove elements from a document. So why would you need to add or remove elements from a web page? Suppose you are a teacher and you are developing a web page that lists the top five students in your class, according to the grade of your most recent assignment. You would write a jQuery script that automatically lists the top five students according to grades you input.

The following example demonstrates how to use both the `.append()` and `.remove()` methods with the Winter Olympics page. This version includes a link

Table 8.2 jQuery-Manipulation API Methods for Adding and Removing Elements

Method	Description
`.after()`	Inserts elements after each element that matches a specified selector.
`.append()`	Inserts elements at the end of each element that matches a specified selector.
`.appendTo()`	Inserts each element that matches a specified selector at the end of a specified target.
`.before()`	Inserts elements before each element that matches a specified selector.
`.clone()`	Creates a copy of all elements and their descendants that match a specified selector.
`.detach()`	Removes all DOM elements that match a specified selector, but stores them for later reuse.
`.empty()`	Removes all child nodes of any elements that match a specified selector.
`.insertAfter()`	Inserts each element that matches a specified selector after a specified target.
`.insertBefore()`	Inserts each element that matches a specified selector before a specified target.
`.prepend()`	Inserts elements at the beginning of each element that matches a specified selector.
`.prependTo()`	Inserts each element that matches a specified selector at the beginning of a specified target.
`.remove()`	Removes all DOM elements that match a specified selector.

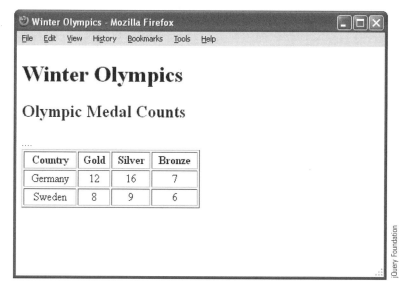

Figure 8.4
Winter Olympics page after adding Sweden

with the text Add Sweden (see Figure 8.4). Clicking the link invokes a click event that uses the `.append()` method to add the text and elements for Sweden to the end of the table. The `.remove()` method then removes the paragraph containing the link from the DOM tree.

```
<!DOCTYPE html PUBLIC "-//W3C//DTD HTML 4.01//EN">
<html>
    <head>
        <title>Winter Olympics</title>
        <style type="text/css">
            td {text-align:center}
        </style>
        <script src="http://code.jquery.com/jquery-1.7.2.js"></script>
        <script type="text/javascript">
        /* <![CDATA[ */
            $(document).ready(function(){
                $("#as").click(function (event) {
                    $("table").append(
                        "<tr><td>Sweden</td><td>8</td><td>9</td><td>6</td></tr>");
                    $("#ps").remove();
                    return false;
                });
            });
```

```
            /* ]]> */
            </script>
        </head>
        <body>
            <h1>Winter Olympics</h1>
            <h2>Olympic Medal Counts</h2>
            <table width="50%" border="1">
                <tr>
                    <th>Country</th>
                    <th>Gold</th>
                    <th>Silver</th>
                    <th>Bronze</th>
                </tr>
                <tr>
                    <td>Germany</td>
                    <td>12</td>
                    <td>16</td>
                    <td>7</td>
                </tr>
                ....
            </table>
            <p id="ps"><a href="" id="as">Add Sweden</a></p>
        </body>
    </html>
```

The following jQuery script shows another version of the code that adds the Swedish data to the table. This version inserts the data to the beginning of the table by using the .first() traversing method with a selector that selects the first <tr> element, which represents the table's header row. Then, the .after() method inserts the Swedish data after the header row.

```
/* <![CDATA[ */
    $(document).ready(function(){
        $("#as").click(function (event) {
            $("tr").first().after(
                "<tr><td>Sweden</td><td>8</td><td>9</td><td>6</td></tr>");
            $("#ps").remove();
            return false;
        });
    });
/* ]]> */
</script>
```

Figure 8.5
Web page before clicking the Cookie Check link

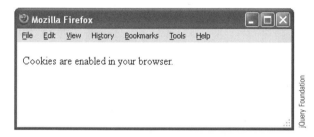

Figure 8.6
Web page after clicking the Cookie Check link

Replacing Elements

Although you can normally use the `.html()` method or one of the traversing API methods to dynamically change elements on a web page, there will be times when you simply want to replace one or more elements instead of using one of these methods to modify them. For example, consider the following web page. The `<div>` element contains a `<span>` element with a link that users can click to determine whether their browsers are enabled for cookies. The click event handler in the jQuery section uses the `cookieEnabled` property of the `Navigator` object, along with the `.html()` method, to change the anchor element to a paragraph element with either `"Cookies are enabled in your browser"` or `"Cookies are not enabled in your browser"`, depending on the value returned by the `cookieEnabled` property. Figure 8.5 shows the page before clicking the link and Figure 8.6 shows the page after clicking the link in a browser where cookies are enabled.

```
<!DOCTYPE html>
<html xmlns="http://www.w3.org/1999/xhtml">
<head>
<script type="text/javascript" src="jquery-1.7.2.js"></script>
<script type="text/javascript">
/* <![CDATA[ */
$(document).ready(function(){
```

```
    $("a").click(function(){
        if (navigator.cookieEnabled)
            $("#cookieCheck").html("<p>Cookies are enabled in your
                browser.</p>");
        else
            $("#cookieCheck").html("<p>Cookies are not enabled in
                your browser.</p>");
        return false
    });
});
/* ]]> */
</script>
</head>
<body>
<div><span id="cookieCheck"><a id="test" href="">
        Are cookies enabled in my browser?</a></span></div>
</body>
</html>
```

Instead of using the .html() method to change the elements, you can use one of the two manipulation API methods described in Table 8.3 to replace the elements.

The following code demonstrates how to use the .replaceWith() method with the code that determines whether cookies are enabled:

```
$(document).ready(function(){
    $("a").click(function(){
        if (navigator.cookieEnabled)
            $("#cookieCheck").replaceWith("<p>Cookies are enabled in your
                browser.</p>");
        else
            $("#cookieCheck").replaceWith("<p>Cookies are not enabled in
                your browser.</p>");
        return false
    });
});
```

Table 8.3 jQuery Manipulation API Methods for Replacing Elements

Method	Description
content.replaceAll(*target*)	Replace each target element with the set of matched elements.
target.replaceWith(*content*)	Replace each element in the set of matched elements with the provided new content.

When called with an HTML string parameter, the `.html()` method only returns the HTML of the first element in the set of matched elements. However, when you do pass an HTML string to the `.html()` element, it replaces the HTML of all matched elements, the same as the `.replaceWith()` method. Although you can use either method to replace elements, a best practice is to use the `.html()` method to retrieve element content, but use the `.replaceWith()` method to replace element content.

The `.replaceAll()` method performs the same functionality as the `.replaceWith()` method except that the source and target are reversed. In other words, you append the `.replaceAll()` method to the replacement content, but pass to the `.replaceAll()` method the selector whose content you want to replace. The following function shows how to use the `.replaceAll()` method instead of the `.replaceWith()` method with the code that determines whether cookies are enabled:

```
$(document).ready(function(){
    $("a").click(function(){
        if (navigator.cookieEnabled)
            $("<p>Cookies are enabled in your browser.</p>")
                .replaceAll("#cookieCheck");
        else
            $("<p>Cookies are not enabled in your browser.</p>")
                .replaceAll("#cookieCheck");
        return false
    });
});
```

Wrapping Elements

If you have not spent much time with XML or well-formed web pages, the concept of *element wrapping* can be a little hard to get used to. Essentially, the concept refers to elements that contain other elements. A common use of wrapping is to change the appearance of text, such as bolding or unbolding it, which requires wrapping the content within a `<strong>` element. Or you may need to dynamically position some content, such as text and images, after a page renders, in which case you need to wrap it in a `<div>` element and use dynamic CSS positioning.

Remember that all XML elements must be properly nested, and this specifically refers to element wrapping. For example, in the following code, the `<em>` element is nested within the `<strong>` element, whereas the `<strong>` element is nested within the `<p>` element.

```
<p><strong><em>This paragraph is bold and italicized.</em></strong></p>
```

Table 8.4 jQuery-Manipulation API Methods for Wrapping Elements

Method	Description
.unwrap()	Removes the DOM parent elements from the elements that match a specified selector.
.wrap()	Wraps selected elements with a specified element.
.wrapAll()	Wraps all selected elements as a group with a specified element.
.wrapInner()	Wraps the contents of selected elements with a specified element.

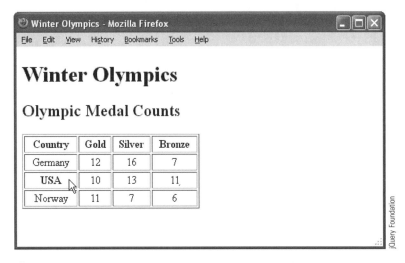

Figure 8.7
Winter Olympics page with .wrapInner() and .unwrap() methods

Table 8.4 lists the manipulation API methods that are used for wrapping DOM elements.

The following example demonstrates how to use the .wrapInner() and .unwrap() methods to wrap and unwrap the contents of any <td> elements with a <strong> element. If you add this code to the Winter Olympics web page, the contents of each cell will be bolded and unbolded as you move your mouse over and off the cell. Figure 8.7 shows the page with the mouse held over the USA cell.

```
$(document).ready(function(){
    $("td").mouseover(function (event) {
        $(this).wrapInner("<strong />");
    });
```

```
    $("td").mouseout(function (event) {
        $(this).children().contents().unwrap();
    });
});
```

Notice the preceding `mouseout` event handler function uses the `.children()` and `.contents()` traversing methods to select the contents of each `<td>` element.

Tip

The preceding example simply serves to show how to use the jQuery manipulation API methods to wrap elements. You can accomplish the preceding functionality more easily by manipulating styles with the `.css()` method. For example, the following code uses the `.css()` method to bold and unbold each cell using the CSS `fontWeight` property.

```
$(document).ready(function(){
        $("td").mouseover(function (event) {
            $(this).css("fontWeight", "bold");
        });
        $("td").mouseout(function (event) {
            $(this).css("fontWeight", "normal");
        });
});
```

Note

There is an important difference between the `.wrap()` and `.wrapAll()` methods that requires further explanation. Assume that you have a document with three `<p>` elements and you select all of them and then use the `.wrap()` method to apply a `<div>` element. The `.wrap()` method wraps each `<p>` element within a `<div>` element, such as `<div><p></p></div>` `<div><p></p></div>` `<div><p></p></div>`. In comparison, if you call the `.wrapAll()` method, all three `<p>` elements are wrapped within a *single* `<div>` element as follows: `<div><p></p><p></p><p></p></div>`.

Using Data with XML DOM Elements

One of the more powerful aspects of jQuery when used with the DOM is its ability to store arbitrary data in selected DOM elements. If you have ever needed to store data for later reuse or that the user does not need to see, you have probably used hidden form fields, global JavaScript variables, or some other hack. Some of the types of data you may need to store temporarily include user names, addresses, color preferences, and so on, although you should never use these or any other methods to store sensitive data such as credit cards or social security numbers, which should be sent to the server immediately. However, the ability to store arbitrary data with the specific

Table 8.5   jQuery Data Methods

Selector	Description
`.data()`	Stores and retrieves data in DOM elements.
`.hasData()`	Determines whether an element contains stored jQuery data.
`.removeData()`	Removes jQuery data from DOM elements.

element to which it applies makes your code neater and more manageable, and can help improve the functionality of your code.

Table 8.5 lists the jQuery methods that are used for managing data with DOM elements.

You store data with the `.data()` method by assigning it to a selected element and passing a key and a value that you want to store. For example, the following statement stores a person's gender in a key named `gender` with a `<form>` element:

```
$("form").data("gender", "male");
```

To retrieve an element's data, you append the `.data()` method to an element and just pass the key name, as follows:

```
window.alert($("form").data("gender"));
```

To store multiple data values with an element, enclose the values within a pair of curly braces following the key name. Then, assign name=value pairs with a colon, separating by a comma. For example, the following demonstrates how to store two keys, gender and age, in a key named `formData`:

```
$("form").data("formData" { "gender": "male", "age": 21 );
```

To retrieve a value from an element in which you have stored multiple values, append its name to the `.data()` method as property, like this:

```
window.alert("You are a " + $("form").data("formData").gender + " year old "
  + $("form").data("formData").gender);
```

Note

The data you store with a DOM element is not actually saved as a property of the element, but rather is stored in an empty object called `$.cache`. Each DOM element in which you store data is assigned a unique ID that is saved in the `$.cache` object.

SUMMARY

This chapter explained how to gain detailed control of your web pages by manipulating the XML DOM, including how to use basic traversing methods to work with the XML DOM. You also learned some valuable techniques for adding, removing, replacing, and wrapping elements, and learned how to store arbitrary data with associated elements. The next chapter discusses more advanced web page manipulation techniques through the use of jQuery utilities.

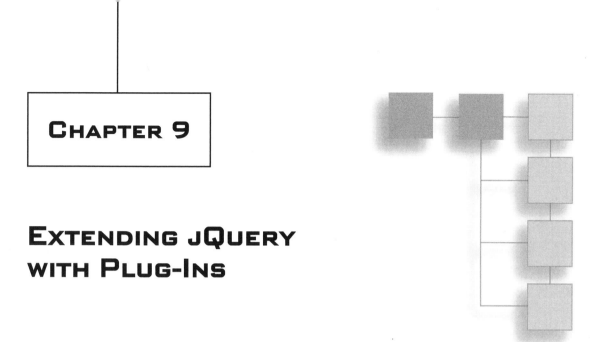

CHAPTER 9

EXTENDING JQUERY WITH PLUG-INS

Up to this point in the book you have seen many of the ways in which the jQuery library can be used to simplify and accomplish various JavaScript tasks. In addition to the base functionality defined with the jQuery library, you can also extend jQuery by using and developing plug-ins.

As mentioned in Chapter 1, developing plug-ins with basic JavaScript is a major endeavor because you need to write the add-on according to a particular framework, such as the Netscape Plug-in Application Programming Interface (NPAPI), which is supported by today's most popular browsers, with the exception of Internet Explorer. Although Internet Explorer supports plug-ins, it primarily uses ActiveX controls to execute embedded objects. The challenge with developing plug-ins using NPAPI, ActiveX, or any other framework is that you need to understand the underlying programming technology to be successful. jQuery mitigates this problem by providing a framework that uses standard JavaScript programming techniques for developing and deploying plug-ins.

OBTAINING AND USING PLUG-INS

The jQuery development community has created and posted thousands of plug-ins on the web, both public and commercial, that add a wide range of functionality to jQuery and JavaScript. You can find existing plug-ins for almost any conceivable task, including simple utilities that help style documents, and more complex plug-ins for use with multimedia, Ajax, and many other tasks. The first place to look for jQuery plug-ins is on the plug-ins page at the main jQuery at http://plugins.jquery.com. This page includes features such as user ratings, versioning, and bug reporting.

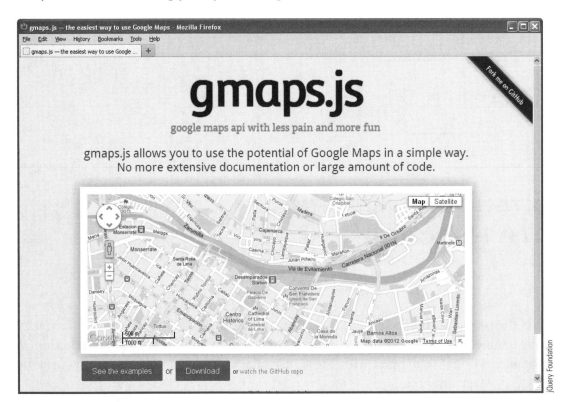

Figure 9.1
gmaps.js web page

Many of the listed plug-ins include links to demos, example code, and tutorials to help you get started. You can also find more plug-ins by searching the web for "jQuery plug-ins".

Although it is impossible to select any bestselling or most popular jQuery plug-ins, there are several standouts. One popular jQuery plug-in is gmaps.js, which allows you to incorporate Google mapping technology into your web page. Figure 9.1 shows the homepage for gmaps.js, http://hpneo.github.com/gmaps/, along with an example of the Google mapping technology that you can incorporate into your web pages.

Plug-ins are created using JavaScript source files, usually in the format jquery.*plugin_ name*.js. You first need to download the plug-in .js file and then add another `<script>` element to the jQuery page from which you want to access the plug-in. You can then access the plug-in's methods with the same syntax you use to access other jQuery methods.

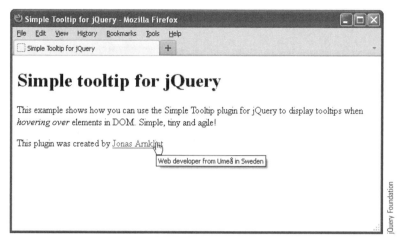

Figure 9.2
Page that uses the simple tooltip plug-in

As a simple example of how to use a jQuery plug-in, consider the simple tooltip plug-in, jquery.simple-tooltip.js, that you can download from the jQuery plug-ins page. This plug-in was written by Jonas Arnklint, and at the time of this writing is listed as one of the most popular plug-ins on the jQuery plug-ins page. The simple tooltip plug-in contains a single method, simpleTooltip(), which creates a tooltip for the selected element.

The following code shows a sample of an HTML page that uses the plug-in. In this case, the value assigned to the title attribute of the <a> element is passed as the text to display in the tooltip, but you can pass any other string value. The stylesheet determines the actual appearance of the tooltip. Figure 9.2 shows the page in a browser with the mouse over the link.

```
<!DOCTYPE html PUBLIC "-//W3C//DTD HTML 4.01//EN">
<html>
<head>
<title>Simple Tooltip for jQuery</title>
<meta http-equiv="Content-Type" content="text/html; charset=utf-8">
<script type="text/javascript" src="jquery-1.6.1.js" />
<script type="text/javascript" src="jquery.simple-tooltip.js">
<script type="text/javascript">
      jQuery(document).ready(function() {
        $("#my-link, p span").simpleTooltip($(this).attr("title"));
      });
</script>
<style type="text/css">
```

```
#v-tooltip {
    position:absolute;
    background:#000;
    padding:3px 5px;
    color:#fff;
    font-size: 11px;
    font-family: Arial, Verdana, sans-serif;
    display:none;
    -moz-border-radius: 3px;
    -webkit-border-radius: 3px;
    }
    p span {
        font-style: italic;
    }
</style>
</head>
<body>
<h1>Simple tooltip for jQuery</h1>
<p>This example shows how you can use the Simple Tooltip
    plugin for jQuery to display tooltips when
    <span>hovering over</span> elements in DOM. Simple,
    tiny and agile!</p>
<p>This plugin was created by <a href="http://arnklint.com"
    id="my-link" title="Web developer from Ume&#229; in Sweden"
    name="my-link">Jonas Arnklint</a></p>
</body>
</html>
```

Tip

Most plug-ins come with detailed documentation that specifies the parameters you can pass to the plug-in methods in order to customize functionality.

There are two basic types of API elements you can create with jQuery plug-in functionality: global functions and object methods. Next, you will learn how to create global functions.

CREATING GLOBAL JQUERY FUNCTIONS

Throughout this book you have seen examples of both global functions and object methods. The primary difference between them is that *global functions* apply to the jQuery object, whereas *object methods* apply to selected DOM elements. In other words, global functions can be called without being appended to a selected element.

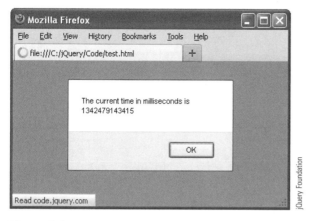

Figure 9.3
Dialog box displaying results from the .now() utility

A typical example of a global function is the .now() utility method, which returns the current time in milliseconds. To call the .now() utility, you simply append it to the $ alias as follows:

```
window.alert("The current time in milliseconds is " + $.now());
```

The preceding example generates an alert dialog box similar to Figure 9.3.

Note

> Global functions are essentially the same as utility methods because both types of constructs apply to the jQuery object itself and not to the selected DOM elements. This book uses the term "global functions" to clearly distinguish plug-ins from the built-in jQuery utility methods.

To understand how to create a global jQuery function, consider the following code, which defines a global jQuery function named tickTock() that adds a digital clock to a web page. This function is defined in a JavaScript source file named jQuery.DigitalClock.js. The first two statements in the function determine whether a form with an ID of clockForm exists within the document body. If not, it is added. The remaining statements use the JavaScript Date object to instantiate a date object and extract the second, minute, and hour values. The final statement adds the time string to an input field named readout in the form named clockForm.

```
jQuery.tickTock = function() {
    if ($("body").has("#clockForm").length == 0)
        $("body").prepend("<form action='' id='clockForm'><p><input
            type='text' size='30' id='readout' /></p></form>");
    var dateObject = new Date();
```

```
        var curTime = "";
        var secondsValue = dateObject.getSeconds();
        var minuteValue = dateObject.getMinutes();
        var hourValue = dateObject.getHours();
        if (secondsValue < 10)
            secondsValue = "0" + secondsValue;
        if (minuteValue < 10)
            minuteValue = "0" + minuteValue;
        if (hourValue < 12)
            curTime = hourValue + ":" + minuteValue + ":" + secondsValue + " AM";
        else if (hourValue == 12)
            curTime = hourValue + ":" + minuteValue + ":" + secondsValue + " PM";
        else if (hourValue < 17)
            curTime = (hourValue-12) + ":" + minuteValue + ":" + secondsValue
                + " PM"
        else
            curTime = (hourValue-12) + ":" + minuteValue + ":" + secondsValue
                + " PM"
        $("#readout").val(curTime);
}
```

The following code demonstrates how to call the DigitalClock plug-in from a web page. A setInterval() method repeatedly calls the DigitalClock function through the tickTock() method to update the digital clock every second.

Notice that the plug-in is not called until after the load event executes for the Window object. Figure 9.4 shows how the clock appears in a web browser.

```
...
<script src="jquery-1.7.2.js"></script>
<script src="jQuery.DigitalClock.js" type="text/javascript"></script>
<script type="text/javascript">
/* <![CDATA[ */
$(document).ready(function() {
  $(window).load(function() {
    var tick = setInterval("$.tickTock()", 1000);
  });
});
/* ]]> */
</script>
...
```

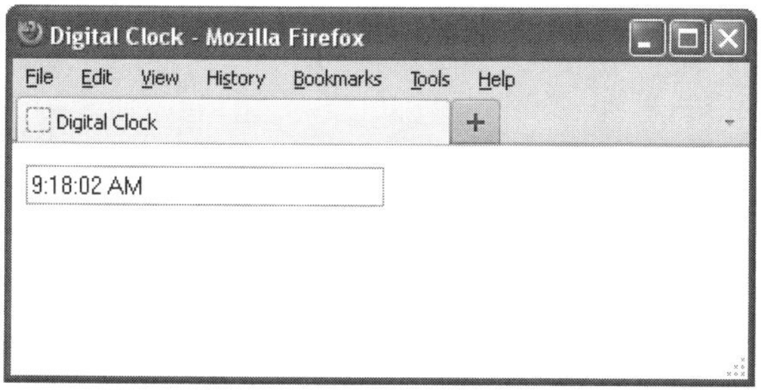

Figure 9.4
Digital clock plug-in

Using the $ Alias

An important item that is missing from the DigitalClock plug-in is the use of the $ alias. Instead of the `tickTock()` function beginning with the $ symbol, it begins with `jQuery.tickTock()`. As you might recall, the $ symbol is simply a reference for the jQuery object. With most jQuery code, you can use either the $ symbol or `jQuery` to identify jQuery code. By default, jQuery does not support the $ alias, mainly because the `$.noConflict()` method can be used to globally relinquish jQuery's control over the $ symbol. In other words, if another script or plug-in that your web page references uses the `$.noConflict()` method to cancel jQuery's use of the $ alias, your plug-in methods will not work.

However, most jQuery developers are used to the $ alias, not only in terms of using the alias by default within their code, but also because it makes code easier to read. For this reason, you can locally define and invoke a function, known as an *Immediately Invoked Function Expression (IIFE),* that allows you to use the $ alias.

To accomplish this, you need to wrap your function definitions within an IIFE that defines the $ alias as a function, as follows:

```
(function($) {
  // code
})(jQuery);
```

For example, to use the $ alias with the DigitalClock plug-in, you wrap the `tickTock()` function within an IIFE, as follows:

```
(function($) {
    $.tickTock = function() {
        if ($("body").has("#clockForm").length == 0)
            $("body").prepend("<form action='' id='clockForm'>
                <p><input type='text' size='30' id='readout' /></p></form>");
        var dateObject = new Date();
```

```
            var curTime = "";
            var secondsValue = dateObject.getSeconds();
            var minuteValue = dateObject.getMinutes();
            var hourValue = dateObject.getHours();
            if (secondsValue < 10)
                secondsValue = "0" + secondsValue;
            if (minuteValue < 10)
                minuteValue = "0" + minuteValue;
            if (hourValue < 12)
                curTime = hourValue + ":" + minuteValue + ":" + secondsValue
                    + " AM";
            else if (hourValue == 12)
                curTime = hourValue + ":" + minuteValue + ":" + secondsValue
                    + " PM";
            else if (hourValue < 17)
                curTime = (hourValue-12) + ":" + minuteValue + ":" + secondsValue
                    + " PM";
            else
                curTime = (hourValue-12) + ":" + minuteValue + ":" + secondsValue
                    + " PM"
            $("#readout").val(curTime);
    }
})(jQuery);
```

Defining Multiple Global jQuery Functions

When it comes to XML documents, a *namespace* is used to organize the elements and attributes into separate groups.

Because you define your own elements, if an XML document combines multiple XML documents, conflicts among elements can occur. For instance, two separate XML documents may both define an element named <company>. If you combine both XML documents into a single document, how does a web browser know which version of the <company> element to use? To address this problem, you identify each <company> element by the namespace to which it belongs. Programming languages must also use namespaces to manage identifiers, which refer to the names of programmatic constructs such as methods and properties. Different programs may use the same identifiers for methods, properties, and other items. With a large and complex program, then, it is only a matter of time before your program encounters two elements with identical names. This challenge also applies to jQuery plug-in development. For example, if your web page uses two plug-ins, both of which have a global function named calcShipping(), how does JavaScript know which function to execute?

To define additional global jQuery functions, you can simply add them to the jQuery object. For example, the following code defines two global functions for the DigitalClock plug-in—one that displays 12-hour time and another that displays 24-hour time:

```
(function($) {
    $.tickTock12 = function() {
        if ($("body").has("#clockForm").length == 0)
            $("body").prepend("<form action='' id='clockForm'>
                <p><input type='text' size='30' id='readout' /></p></form>");
        var dateObject = new Date();
        var curTime = "";
        var secondsValue = dateObject.getSeconds();
        var minuteValue = dateObject.getMinutes();
        var hourValue = dateObject.getHours();
        if (secondsValue < 10)
            secondsValue = "0" + secondsValue;
        if (minuteValue < 10)
            minuteValue = "0" + minuteValue;
        if (hourValue < 12)
            curTime = hourValue + ":" + minuteValue + ":"
                + secondsValue + " AM";
        else if (hourValue == 12)
            curTime = hourValue + ":" + minuteValue + ":"
                + secondsValue + " PM";
        else if (hourValue < 17)
            curTime = (hourValue-12) + ":" + minuteValue + ":"
                + secondsValue + " PM"
        else
            curTime = (hourValue) + ":" + minuteValue + ":"
                + secondsValue + " PM"
        $("#readout").val(curTime);
    }
    $.tickTock24 = function() {
        if ($("body").has("#clockForm").length == 0)
            $("body").prepend("<form action='' id='clockForm'>
                <p><input type='text' size='30' id='readout' /></p></form>");
        var dateObject = new Date();
        var curTime = "";
        var secondsValue = dateObject.getSeconds();
        var minuteValue = dateObject.getMinutes();
        var hourValue = dateObject.getHours();
        if (secondsValue < 10)
            secondsValue = "0" + secondsValue;
        if (minuteValue < 10)
```

```
        minuteValue = "0" + minuteValue;
    curTime = hourValue + ":" + minuteValue + ":" + secondsValue
    $("#readout").val(curTime);
    }
})(jQuery);
```

To call either of the preceding functions, you can just change the name of the function that the main HTML document calls, as follows:

```
$(document).ready(function() {
  $(window).load(function() {
    var tick = setInterval("$.tickTock24()", 1000);
  });
});
```

Although the DigitalClock plug-in will execute, the function names run the risk of conflicting with functions of the same name that may exist in other plug-ins referenced by the page.

There is only a slight chance that your JavaScript code will call two plug-ins that include identical function names, such as tickTock24(). Nevertheless, the creators of jQuery strongly discourage plug-ins from defining more than one namespace. Instead, a best practice is to define all the functions for a single plug-in within an object literal, and then call each function by passing the name of each function as a string.

To define an object literal for a plug-in, you use the following syntax:

```
$.pluginName = {functionName1: function() {code},
    {functionName1: function() {code}, additional functions
};
```

The preceding syntax creates a namespace object named *pluginName*, which becomes a property of the global jQuery object. Although defined functions are really methods of the defined by *pluginName*, they are still normally referred to as global jQuery functions.

The DigitalClock plug-in essentially claims two namespaces—one for the 12-hour clock and another for the 24-hour clock. The following code demonstrates how to define the functions within a namespace object called digitalClock.

```
(function($) {
    $.digitalClock = {
        tickTock12: function() {
            if ($("body").has("#clockForm").length == 0)
                $("body").prepend("<form action='' id='clockForm'><p>
                    <input type='text' size='30' id='readout' /></p></form>");
```

```
            var dateObject = new Date();
            var curTime = "";
            var secondsValue = dateObject.getSeconds();
            var minuteValue = dateObject.getMinutes();
            var hourValue = dateObject.getHours();
            if (secondsValue < 10)
                secondsValue = "0" + secondsValue;
            if (minuteValue < 10)
                minuteValue = "0" + minuteValue;
            if (hourValue < 12)
                curTime = hourValue + ":" + minuteValue + ":"
                    + secondsValue + " AM";
            else if (hourValue == 12)
                curTime = hourValue + ":" + minuteValue + ":"
                    + secondsValue + " PM";
            else if (hourValue < 17)
                curTime = (hourValue-12) + ":" + minuteValue + ":"
                    + secondsValue + " PM"
            else
                curTime = (hourValue) + ":" + minuteValue + ":"
                    + secondsValue + " PM"
            $("#readout").val(curTime);
        },
        tickTock24: function() {
            if ($("body").has("#clockForm").length == 0)
                $("body").prepend("<form action='' id='clockForm'><p>
                    <input type='text' size='30' id='readout' /></p></form>");
            var dateObject = new Date();
            var curTime = "";
            var secondsValue = dateObject.getSeconds();
            var minuteValue = dateObject.getMinutes();
            var hourValue = dateObject.getHours();
            if (secondsValue < 10)
                secondsValue = "0" + secondsValue;
            if (minuteValue < 10)
                minuteValue = "0" + minuteValue;
            curTime = hourValue + ":" + minuteValue + ":" + secondsValue
            $("#readout").val(curTime);
        }
    };
})(jQuery);
```

To call a global function defined within an object namespace, you need to append the function name to the object, as follows:

```
$(document).ready(function() {
  $(window).load(function() {
    var tick = setInterval("$.digitalClock.tickTock24()", 1000);
  });
});
```

ADDING JQUERY OBJECT METHODS

The procedures for defining jQuery object methods in your plug-ins are very similar to the procedures for defining global functions. The one primary difference is that instead of defining the function as part of the global jQuery object, you define it as part of the jQuery.fn object, which is the prototype object for all jQuery objects. Any functions that you add to the jQuery.fn object become jQuery methods. Keep in mind that object methods primarily differ from global functions because they operate on selected elements, whereas global functions are not associated with selected elements and only apply to the jQuery object.

Tip

All of the syntax and best practice recommendations that you have seen so far for global functions, including the use of the $ alias and namespace recommendations, are also applicable to object methods.

In Chapter 5, you saw an example of a program that creates a mouse trail, which follows the cursor as it moves around a web page. The code to create the mouse trail is fairly involved and would be much more useful if it could be easily invoked with a plug-in.

As an example of the plug-in version of the program, consider the following code:

```
var trailInterval = 20;
var xPosition = -10;
var yPosition = -10;
var animationStarted = false;
(function($) {
    $.fn.mouseTrail = function(event) {
        if (!animationStarted) {
            for (i = 1; i <= trailInterval; i++) {
                $("body").append("<div id='trail" + i
                    + "' style='position:absolute;background-color:blue;top:"
```

```
                    + yPosition + "px;left:" + xPosition + "px;width:"
                    + i/2 + "px;height:" + i/2
                    + "px; font-size:" + i/2 + "px'></div>");
            }
            animationStarted = true;
        }
        xPosition = event.clientX + 15;
        yPosition = event.clientY + 20;
        genTrail();
    };
})(jQuery);
function genTrail() {
    var div1, div2;
    for (i = 1; i <= trailInterval; i++){
        if (i < trailInterval){
            $("#trail"+i).css("top", $("#trail"+(i+1)).css("top"));
            $("#trail"+i).css("left", $("#trail"+(i+1)).css("left"));

        }
        else {
            $("#trail"+i).css("top", yPosition + "px");
            $("#trail"+i).css("left", xPosition + "px");
        }
    }
    setTimeout("genTrail()",40);
}
```

Figure 9.5 shows the result in a browser.

As with the original, the first few statements create global variables that track the mouse trail. Within the function definition of $.fn.mouseTrail(), the if statement determines whether the animation has started. The for loop uses the .prepend() method to add to the beginning of the <body> element the number of <div> elements that will make up the mouse trail according to the value assigned to the trailInterval variable.

Each <div> element is assigned a unique ID value of trail + *i* (the *i* represents the current counter). Because the trailInterval variable is assigned a value of 12, the for loop creates 12 <div> elements with ID values of trail0 through trail11. Each <div> element's position property is assigned a value of absolute so that it can be dynamically positioned and the background-color property is assigned a value of blue. The code then retrieves the mouse coordinates from the Event object and calls the genTrail() function, which uses a setTimeout() method to update

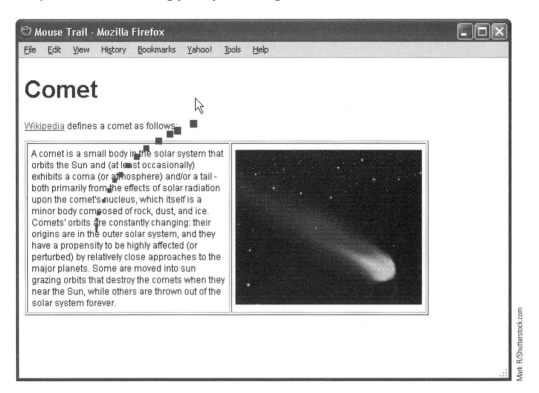

Figure 9.5
Mouse trail web page

the `top` and `left` properties of each `<div>` element in order to simulate the animation.

To execute the `mouseTrail()` method, you call it using the `this` reference, which refers to the `<html>` doc as it is raised with the `mouseMove` event, as follows:

```
$(document).ready(function() {
    $("html").mousemove(function(event) {
        $(this).mouseTrail(event);
    });
});
```

Note

An important point to mention when it comes to jQuery object methods is that the `this` reference implicitly refers to the selected element that called the plug-in. In other words, you do not need to explictly define the `this` reference using `$(this)` in order to reference the element that called the plug-in method.

DEFINING METHOD PARAMETERS

Like other types of functions and methods, jQuery global functions and object methods can accept multiple arguments. One of the challenges with providing an argument list for a function or method—especially to consumers of a plug-in—is understanding the order in which to pass the arguments. A better solution is to create a *parameter map,* which requires plug-in users to provide specific names for each passed argument. With this approach, the order in which you pass an argument list makes no difference to the consuming function or method.

To pass a parameter map to a method, you enclose the method in brackets and include name:value pairs, with each parameter separated by a comma. For example, consider a more complex version of the mouse trail script that uses Scalable Vector Graphics. *Scalable Vector Graphics (SVG)* is an XML specification for defining static and dynamic two-dimensional vector graphics, which are made up of simple objects. These objects include shapes such as polygons and circles, and objects such as lines, points, and curves. In comparison, raster graphics, such as photographs, are made up of arrays of pixels. Even though they are made up of simple objects, vector graphics can be extremely complex. Figure 9.6 displays an image of the Olympic Rings created with vector graphics, and Figure 9.7 displays a typical raster image of a photograph in JPEG format.

Figure 9.6
Vector image

Figure 9.7
Raster image

Whereas raster graphics typically represent a static image, vector graphics can be edited with programs such as Adobe Illustrator. SVG allows you to define a vector image using XML; you do not need to include an accompanying image file to display an SVG image. Inline SVG refers to the ability to render SVG XML elements from inside a web page. Note that because inline SVG is an XML application, web pages that include inline SVG must use a file extension of .xhtml or .xml in order for web browsers to recognize the page as XML.

Inline SVG is available in all major browsers except for Internet Explorer. Support for Inline SVG is expected to be added in Internet Explorer 9. You define an SVG image with the `<svg>` element, and you must include the `xmlns="http://www.w3.org/2000/svg"` namespace within the opening `<svg>` tag. You can also use the attributes listed in Table 9.1.

Note

SVG is defined by the SVG 1.1 specification, which is published by the W3C at www.w3.org/TR/SVG11/.

Table 9.1 Attributes of the <svg> Element

Attribute	Description
height	Defines the height of the object using pixels or a percentage of the screen height.
width	Defines the width of the object using pixels or a percentage of the screen width.
version	Identifies the SVG language version.
baseProfile	Identifies the minimum SVG language profile.
x	Specifies the horizontal location of the upper-left corner of the object box.
y	Specifies the vertical location of the upper-left corner of the object box.

The following code demonstrates how to pass a parameter consisting of two parameters, shape and color, to the .mouseTrail() method.

```
$(document).ready(function() {
    $("html").mousemove(function() {
      $(this).mouseTrail({
        color: "blue",
        shape: "rect"
      });
  });
});
```

To access the parameter map from the called method, you need to pass an arbitrary parameter name representing the map to the method. For example, the following code uses a parameter named option to access the contents of the parameter map. Notice that a nested if statement uses the <svg> element's options parameter with the shape parameter to determine the shape (rectangle or circle) of the mouse trail object. Another nested if statement uses the color parameter to determine the color of the mouse trail.

```
(function($) {
  $.fn.mouseTrail = function(options) {
    return this.each(function() {
      if ($("#trail1").length == 0) {
        for (var i=1; i <= trailInterval; i++) {
```

```
        if (options.shape == "rect") {
          $("body").append("<svg xmlns='http://www.w3.org/2000/svg'
              height='100px' width='100px'"
                + " style='position:absolute; top:-20px; left: -20px'
                id='trail" + i + "'>" + "<rect style='fill:"
                  + options.color + "' width='" + i/2
                  + "px' height='" + i/2 + "px' /></svg>");
        }
        else if (options.shape == "circle") {
          $("body").append("<svg xmlns='http://www.w3.org/2000/svg'
              height='100px' width='100px'" + " style='position:absolute;
              top:-20px; left: -20px' id='trail" + i + "'>"
              + "<circle fill='" + options.color
              + "' cx='10px' cy='10px' r='" + i/2 + "px' /></svg>");
        }
      }
    }
    $(this).mousemove(function(event) {
      xPosition = event.clientX + 15;
      yPosition = event.clientY + 20;
    });
    genTrail();
    });
  };
})(jQuery);
```

Notice that the preceding code uses a different syntax to instantiate an Event object. Instead of passing an Event object as an argument to the .mouseTrail() method, a new anonymous function wraps the two statements that define the xPosition and yPosition variables, as follows:

```
$(this).mousemove(function(event) {
  xPosition = event.clientX + 15;
  yPosition = event.clientY + 20;
});
```

Figure 9.8 shows how the mouse trail plug-in appears as a red circle.

When you do use a parameter map with a plug-in, it is always good practice to provide default settings. This allows users to exclude any or all parameters when calling the plug-in. To define parameter defaults, you use the .extend() method, which merges the contents of two or more objects into a single object.

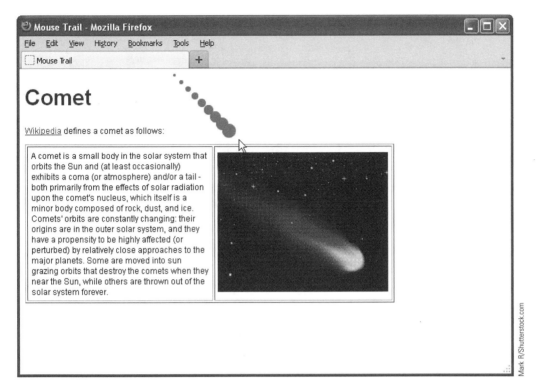

Figure 9.8
Mouse trail plug-in with a red circle

For example, consider the following code that defines within the .mouseTrail() method a variable named defaults that contains default values for the shape and color parameters:

```
(function($) {
    $.fn.mouseTrail = function(params) {
        var defaults = {
            "shape" : "rect",
            "color" : "blue"
        };
        var options = $.extend(defaults, params);
        return this.each(function() {
...
```

Notice the statement that calls the .extend() method in the preceding example. The statement defines an options variable and passes to the .extend() method first the defaults variable and then the params argument (which represents the values passed by the users to the .mouseTrail() method). This allows any parameters that exist in the params variable to override the default values in the `defaults` variable. The remaining code uses the `options` variable to set the `shape` and `color` values.

SUMMARY

In this chapter, you learned how to extend jQuery by using and creating plug-ins, which make your jQuery programs much easier to use by other programmers. All good programmers build a library of their own code that they can use when needed, and plug-ins are an essential tool for you to use in building your own code library. In the next chapter, you go a step further and learn how to use the jQuery UI.

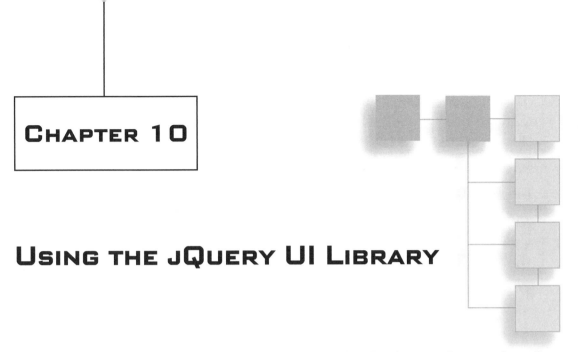

Chapter 10

Using the jQuery UI Library

In Chapter 9, you learned how to extend jQuery by developing plug-ins that allow other JavaScript programmers to easily incorporate new utilities and functionality into their scripts. This chapter takes things a step further by explaining how to use and develop jQuery UI (user interface) plug-ins, which provide advanced animation, effects, and multimedia that JavaScript programmers can use to create web pages with dynamic and interactive functionality. To understand the difference between standard plug-ins and jQuery UI plug-ins, you can think of standard plug-ins as essentially consisting of various types of utilities (which might not include user interface functionality) that you can add to your web pages. In comparison, jQuery UI plug-ins are more advanced user interface elements that provide advanced animation and user interactivity functionality. There is definitely some overlap between standard and jQuery UI plug-ins, so your rule-of-thumb should be to use plug-ins for complex utilities or basic types of animation and effects. For advanced user interface functionality, you should create a jQuery UI plug-in.

Introduction to the jQuery UI Library

Before you can develop your own jQuery UI plug-ins, you need to understand how to use the *jQuery UI library,* which consists of a set of features that is released as part of an official project of the jQuery team. The goal of the project is to create features to solve basic needs. You can find the officially sanctioned plug-ins on the jQuery UI library web page at http://jqueryui.com. This page contains the latest UI code and supporting documentation, along with links to the main jQuery documentation page. To save on file size and download speed, you can download just the code for just the features you need. In addition to the available web development tools, the jQuery UI also supports CSS *themes*, which allow you to create a standard look and feel across all of jQuery UI elements. You can even create your own custom CSS themes to match the fonts, colors, and other design elements on your website. The jQuery UI plug-ins are organized into the following categories:

- **Effects**—Provide animated transitions and easing for rich user interaction.
- **Interactions**—Define complex behaviors such as dragging and dropping, resizing, selecting, and sorting.
- **Utilities**—Provide low-level utilities for building widgets, interactions, and effects.
- **Widgets**—Offer complete UI controls that include multiple options and theming support.

Note

At the time of this writing, the most recent, stable version of the jQuery UI is version 1.8.22.

The basic procedures for incorporating a jQuery UI feature into your web page are as follows:

1. Design the theme you want to use.
2. Select and download the version and modules you need.
3. Incorporate and customize the code for your web page.

The next section takes a look at theme rolling.

Selecting a Theme

One of the coolest aspects of the jQuery UI library is the online ThemeRoller page, which allows you to select preexisting design themes or design ("roll") your own. You can access the ThemeRoller page at http://jqueryui.com/themeroller/. Figure 10.1 shows how the page appears when it first opens.

The ThemeRoller page contains examples of the following types of web page elements, which are called out in Figure 10.2.

- Accordion
- Tabs
- Dialog

Figure 10.1
Default ThemeRoller page

- Overlay and Shadow classes
- Framework icons (content color preview)
- Button
- Autocomplete
- Slider
- Datepicker
- Progressbar
- Highlight/error

By default, each of the proceeding elements is formatted using a basic grayscale color theme. The box on the left side of the ThemeRoller page allows you to design your own theme with the Roll Your Own link or select an existing theme using the Gallery link. The Roll Your Own link is selected by default, and you can see in Figure 10.2

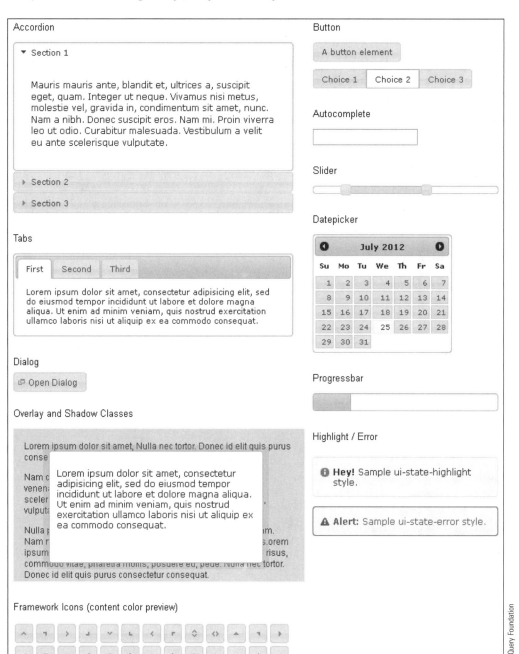

Figure 10.2
ThemeRoller web page elements

Figure 10.3
ThemeRoller page after selecting Dark Hive from the theme gallery

the various design elements, such as fonts and highlighting, that you can customize. Figure 10.3 shows the available predesigned themes after clicking the Gallery link. The figure also shows how the web page elements appear after selecting the Dark Hive theme.

After selecting or customizing your theme, click the Download button to open the Build Your Download page, which is described in the next section.

Building Your Download

The Build Your Download page is where you select the jQuery UI components that you want to use on your website. Unless you have slow Internet connectivity or restricted file space, it's usually safe just to download all the jQuery UI components. However, if you maintain multiple websites with different themes, and each site only uses one or two jQuery UI components, you specify just the individual components you need.

Caution

Each jQuery UI component requires different core modules. For example, the Accordion widget requires the Core and Widget modules. To ensure that you have selected the required modules, first click the Deselect All Components link. Then click the link for the component you need and the page will automatically select any modules required by the selected component.

Figure 10.4 displays the default Build Your Download page. In addition to the component check boxes, the page includes a Theme section where you can select a default theme and define the theme's CSS scope and folder name, along with a Version section where you can select which jQuery UI release you want to download. In most cases, you should always download the most current, stable version (1.8.22 at the time of this writing).

Tip

The CSS scope field on the Build Your Download page allows you to restrict the scope of a theme to a particular portion of the page, although in most cases you would not use multiple themes on the same page. You enter into the CSS scope field an ID, CSS class, or HTML element.

Figure 10.4
The Build Your Download page

Your jQuery UI package downloads as a compressed file, such as jquery-ui-1.8.22. custom-4.zip on PC operating systems. After you download the file, you need to extract it to a location that is accessible to any web page that needs to use the selected theme and components. If you only need to use the package with a single website, you can safely extract it to the site's root folder.

Extracting the jQuery UI package creates the following files and directory structure:

- **css folder**—Contains the CSS definitions for the selected or customized theme.

- **development-bundle folder**—Includes all jQuery UI source code, including demos and documentation. If you do not plan on customizing any of the jQuery UI components, you can safely delete this folder.

- **js folder**—Contains the downloaded jQuery UI component definition code, along with a minimized version of the jQuery library (necessary to run the index.html file, described next).

- **index.html file**—Displays a web page that demonstrates the theme you selected for your jQuery UI components you selected.

Note

Of the preceding items, only the `css` and `js` folders are required for your websites.

An important issue to understand is that, although you may have downloaded your selected theme and UI code, you still need to incorporate these items into your web pages, as described next.

Adding jQuery UI Code to Your Web Pages

So you've selected your theme and downloaded the necessary jQuery UI code. Now how do you incorporate these elements into your plug-in pages? The first thing you need to understand is that your selected jQuery UI themes and components will not automatically incorporate themselves in your plug-in pages. Instead, you must link to the CSS and jQuery UI packages that you downloaded, and then add the appropriate links to your plug-in page file. In addition to including a `<script>` element that calls the jQuery source file, any plug-in pages that use jQuery UI components must also include a `<link>` element to reference the CSS file containing the theme information and another `<script>` element that calls the source file containing the selected jQuery UI component code. The `\css` folder you extracted from the download package contains the CSS file, while the `\js` folder contains both a minimized jQuery library and a minimized version of the selected jQuery UI component definition code. The <link> and <script> sections in your plug-in page that processes the jQuery UI code should appear similar to the following:

```
<link type="text/css" href="css/dark-hive/jquery-ui-1.8.22.custom.css"
    rel="stylesheet" />
<script type="text/javascript" src="js/jquery-1.7.2.min.js"></script>
<script type="text/javascript"
    src="js/jquery-ui-1.8.22.custom.min.js"></script>
```

Tip

As mentioned earlier in this book, although you can reference hosted online jQuery versions, most plug-in developers prefer to have more control of the code that controls their plug-in pages. The same holds true for hosted instances of the jQuery UI. Although you can reference hosted jQuery UI instances, your best bet is to reference local instances so you can maintain tighter control over your plug-in sites.

Although the online ThemeRoller page is really cool, what's even cooler is the Demos & Documentation page at http://jqueryui.com/demos/. This page contains very clear and well written information on how to customize the jQuery UI components using the options, events, methods, arguments, and themes that are available to an individual component. Figure 10.5 displays the page for the Accordion widget.

Figure 10.5
The Accordion Demos & Documentation page

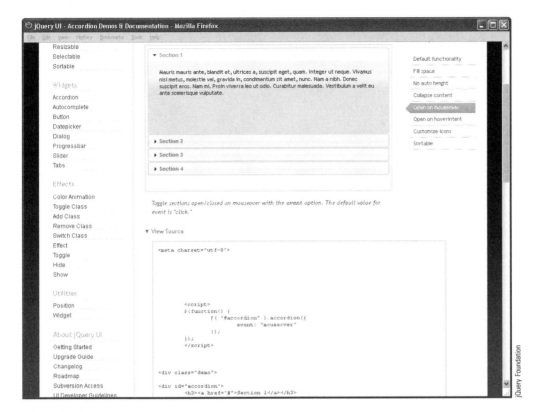

Figure 10.6
The Accordion Demos & Documentation page display example code

At the top of the Demos & Documentation page for a widget is a working example. You can select any of the examples to the right of the displayed component and then click the View Source link to display the required script and HTML elements. Figure 10.6 displays the page after clicking the Open on Mouseover example and then clicking the View Source link just below the Accordion widget example.

If you copy the script and HTML elements from the Demos & Documentation page into a plug-in page, as follows, the page renders as shown in Figure 10.7. As you can see in the following code, the .accordion() function handles literally all functionality.

```
<!DOCTYPE HTML>
<html>
<head>
    <meta http-equiv="content-type" content="text/html; charset=utf-8" />
    <title>Accordion Example</title>
    <link type="text/css"
        href="css/dark-hive/jquery-ui-1.8.22.custom.css" rel="stylesheet" />
```

```
    <script type="text/javascript" src="js/jquery-1.7.2.min.js"></script>
    <script type="text/javascript"
        src="js/jquery-ui-1.8.22.custom.min.js"></script>
    <script type="text/javascript">
    $(function() {
        $( "#accordion" ).accordion({
            event: "mouseover",
            animated: 'bounceslide'
        });
    });
    </script>
</head>
<body>
<div class="demo">
<div id="accordion">
    <h3><a href="#">Section 1</a></h3>
    <div>
        <p>Mauris mauris ante...</p>
    </div>
    <h3><a href="#">Section 2</a></h3>
    <div>
        <p>Sed non urna ...</p>
    </div>
    <h3><a href="#">Section 3</a></h3>
    <div>
        <p>Nam enim risus ...</p>
        <ul>
            <li>List item one</li>
            <li>List item two</li>
            <li>List item three</li>
        </ul>
    </div>
    <h3><a href="#">Section 4</a></h3>
    <div>
        <p>Cras dictum ...</p>
    </div>
</div>
</div><!-- End demo -->
<div class="demo-description">
<p>Toggle sections open/closed on mouseover with the
        <code>event</code> option. The default value for event is "click."</p>
</div><!-- End demo-description -->
</body>
</html>
```

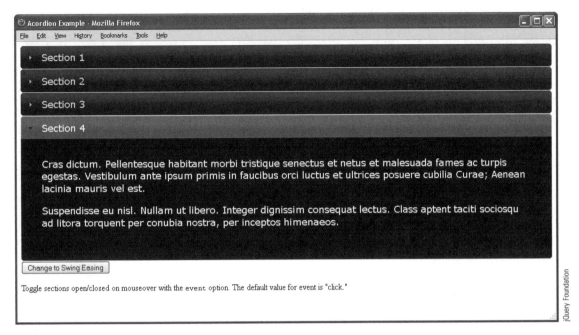

Figure 10.7
Web page rendering according code

Notice that a parameter map consisting of a single event parameter is passed to the `.accordion()` function. Passing parameters using a map is how many of the jQuery UI components can be customized. For example, the following jQuery code contains two additional parameters: `animated` and `autoHeight`. The `animated` parameter is assigned a value of `bounceslide`, which creates a bouncing animation effect instead of the default `slide` effect. The `autoHeight` parameter sets the height of each section to the height of the highest content section.

```
$(function() {
    $("#accordion").accordion({
        event: "mouseover",
        animated: "bounceslide:,
        autoHeight: true
    });
});
```

Note

The `animated` parameter calls the `.animate()` function. As you might recall from Chapter 4, you can assign two built-in easing values to the `.animate()` function—`linear` and `swing`—although many more types of easing functions are available as jQuery plug-ins. For example, the `bounceslide` easing function is part of the UI Effects Core, which is available through the jQuery UI source file you downloaded when you were selecting your jQuery UI components.

Understanding the Common Plug-in Methods

Many of the jQuery UI plug-ins include methods that you can use to control the plug-in's functionality. Table 10.1 lists the methods that are common to all plug-ins.

The important point to understand about the common plug-in methods is that they can be initialized only *after* the plug-in is initialized. For example, consider the `option()` method. The following statements demonstrate how to disable and enable the accordion widget after it has been initialized:

```
$("#accordion").accordion("disable");
$("#accordion").accordion("option", "enable", true);
```

Notice how the preceding statements call the plug-in methods. Instead of using the standard method syntax such as `.enable()`, the name of the method is passed as a string to the plug-in.

You already know that you must use a parameter map to customize a plug-in when it is first initialized. If you want to change a plug-in option after initialization, you must pass the option name and value as additional parameters to the plug-in name. The following statement changes the animation's easing value to `linear`.

```
$("#accordion" ).accordion("option", "animated", "linear");
```

Referencing the Framework Icons

When you refer to an image from an HTML page, you almost always use an `<img>` with an `src` attribute that identifies an image file, such as `<img src="myimage.jpg" />`. However, when referencing a framework icon, you must refer to one of the classes listed in the jquery-ui.version.custom.css file, which in turn pulls the icon from the .png image in the `css/theme/images` directory where

Table 10.1 Common Plug-in Methods

Method	Description
option()	Changes the default plug-in methods after initialization.
enable()	Enables the plug-in.
disable()	Disables the plug-in.
destroy()	Removes the plug-in functionality completely.

Figure 10.8
Button element with an icon

you downloaded your jQuery UI build. For example, the following code for the Button widget, which you study in the next section, uses the icon identified by the `ui-icon-refresh` class to display the image shown in Figure 10.8.

```
$("#b1").button({
    label: "Refresh Stock Quotes" },
    {icons: {primary: "ui-icon-refresh"}});
});
```

USING JQUERY UI WIDGETS

A jQuery UI widget is a self-contained user interface component that you can add to your plug-in pages. The jQuery UI edits are very well developed and robust and they will save you mountains of time since you do not need to create the components yourself. This section describes and demonstrates the available widgets.

Note

The jQuery UI widgets include various options, events, methods, and theming choices. This chapter only includes the most commonly used choices in order to get you started. For more information on what you can do with the jQuery UI widgets, refer to the Demos & Documentation page at http://jqueryui.com/demos/.

The Accordion Widget

You've already seen an example of the accordion widget, which displays content panels one at a time. Accordion widgets present content as a series of stacked, horizontal sections, the same as the expandable menus you saw in Chapter 4. The following code demonstrates the Hall of Fame Players page you saw in Chapter 4 using an accordion widget and Figure 10.9 shows the output in a browser.

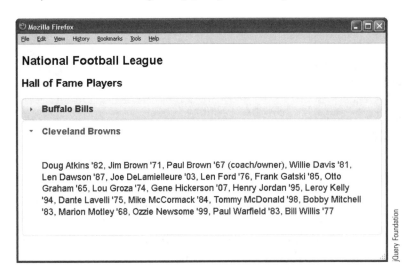

Figure 10.9
Hall of Fame Players page using an accordion widget

The parameter map for the accordion widget initializes the collapsible and autoHeight options. The collapsible option determines whether all of the sections can be closed at once, whereas the autoHeight option determines whether the highest content part is used as height reference for all other parts. In this instance, the collapsible option is assigned a value of true to allow all sections to be closed at once, and the autoHeight option is assigned a value of false, to allow the sections to adjust to the height of their contents.

```
<head>
<meta http-equiv="Content-Type" content="text/html; charset=iso-8859-1" />
<link href="css/blitzer/jquery-ui-1.8.22.custom.css" rel="stylesheet"
    type="text/css" />
<style type="text/css">
h1 { font-family: Arial, sans-serif; font-size: 1.5em }
h2 { font-family: Arial, sans-serif; font-size: 1.3em }
</style>
<script src="js/jquery-1.7.2.min.js" type="text/javascript"></script>
<script src="js/jquery-ui-1.8.22.custom.min.js"
            type="text/javascript"></script>
<script type="text/javascript">
/* <![CDATA[ */
$(document).ready(function(){
```

```
    $( "#accordion" ).accordion({
        collapsible: true,
        autoHeight: false,
        event: "click"
    });
});
/* ]]> */
</script>
</head>
<body>
<h1>National Football League</h1>
<h2>Hall of Fame Players</h2>
<div id="accordion">
<h3><a href="#">Buffalo Bills</a></h3>
<p>Joe DeLamielleure '03, Jim Kelly '02, Marv Levy '01 (coach),
James Lofton '03, Billy Shaw '99, Thurman Thomas '07</p>
<h3><a href="#">Cleveland Browns</a></h3>
<p>Doug Atkins '82, Jim Brown '71, Paul Brown '67 (coach/owner),
Willie Davis '81, Len Dawson '87, Joe DeLamielleure '03, Len Ford '76,
Frank Gatski '85, Otto Graham '65, Lou Groza '74, Gene Hickerson '07,
Henry Jordan '95, Leroy Kelly '94, Dante Lavelli '75,
Mike McCormack '84, Tommy McDonald '98, Bobby Mitchell '83,
Marion Motley '68, Ozzie Newsome '99, Paul Warfield '83,
Bill Willis '77</p>
</div>
</body>
```

Notice in Figure 10.9 that by default, closed sections in the accordion widget include an icon of an arrow pointing right and open sections include an icon of an arrow point down. You can change these default images with the header and headerSelected values of the icons option in the parameter map.

The following code renders the icons shown in Figure 10.10:

```
$(document).ready(function(){
    $( "#accordion" ).accordion({
        collapsible: true,
        autoHeight: false,
        event: "click",
        icons: {header: "ui-icon-circle-arrow-e",headerSelected:
            "ui-icon-circle-arrow-s"}
    });
});
```

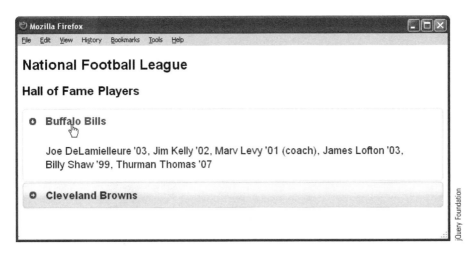

Figure 10.10
Accordion widget on Hall of Fame Players page with custom icons

The Autocomplete Widget

Auto complete is a feature that is often used with AJAX or other server-side scripting technology to retrieve values based on what a user types into a text box. One of the most widely used auto complete features is available on Google's search page, which uses AJAX to send the string in the text box to the Google server. The server then attempts to match the typed characters with matching suggestions. The Google server then returns the suggestions to the client computer (without reloading the plug-in page), and JavaScript code populates the suggestion list with the response text. The jQuery UI Autocomplete widget helps to greatly simplify the task of creating an auto complete field.

The jQuery Autocomplete widget works with the <input> text element to retrieve and display a menu of possible choices, based on what a user enters into the field. How a match is determined depends on the options that are selected when creating the widget.

As a simple example, consider the following code, which is based on a script that the Demos & Documentation Page generates. The code uses a static list created with a JavaScript array that is assigned to a variable named availableTags. If you type **co** into the text box, the widget restricts the displayed items to COBOL and ColdFusion, as shown in Figure 10.11.

```
<link type="text/css"
    href="css/blitzer/jquery-ui-1.8.22.custom.css" rel="stylesheet" />
<script type="text/javascript" src="js/jquery-1.7.2.min.js"></script>
<script type="text/javascript" src="js/jquery-ui-
            1.8.22.custom.min.js"></script>
```

```
<script type="text/javascript">
/* <![CDATA[ */
$(document).ready(function(){
    var availableTags = ["ActionScript","AppleScript","Asp","BASIC","C",
        "C++","Clojure","COBOL","ColdFusion","Erlang","Fortran","Groovy",
        "Haskell","Java","JavaScript","Lisp","Perl","PHP","Python",
        "Ruby","Scala","Scheme"];
    $( "#tags" ).autocomplete({
        source: availableTags
    });
});
/* ]]> */
</script>
</head>
<body>
<div class="ui-widget">
    <label for="tags">Tags: </label>
    <input id="tags">
</div>
</body>
```

Following is a more complex version that uses AJAX with JSON to look up city names from geonames.org. Figure 10.12 shows the page after typing **san**.

```
<script type="text/javascript">
/* <![CDATA[ */
$(document).ready(function(){
  function log( message ) {
      $( "<div/>" ).text( message ).prependTo( "#log" );
      $( "#log" ).scrollTop( 0 );
    }
  $( "#city" ).autocomplete({
    source: function( request, response ) {
      $.ajax({
        url: "http://ws.geonames.org/searchJSON",
        dataType: "jsonp",
        data: {
          featureClass: "P",
          style: "full",
          maxRows: 12,
          name_startsWith: request.term
        },
        success: function( data ) {
          response( $.map( data.geonames, function( item ) {
            return {
```

```
                        label: item.name + (item.adminName1 ? ", "
                                         + item.adminName1 : "")
                                         + ", " + item.countryName,
                  value: item.name
                }
            }));
          }
        });
      },
      minLength: 2,
      select: function( event, ui ) {
        log( ui.item ?
          "Selected: " + ui.item.label :
          "Nothing selected, input was " + this.value);
      },
      open: function() {
        $( this ).removeClass( "ui-corner-all" ).addClass( "ui-corner-top" );
      },
      close: function() {
        $( this ).removeClass( "ui-corner-top" ).addClass( "ui-corner-all" );
      }
    });});
/* ]]> */
</script>
</head>
<body>
<div class="ui-widget">
    <label for="city">Your city: </label>
    <input id="city" />
    Powered by <a href="http://geonames.org">geonames.org</a>
</div></body>
```

Figure 10.11
An Autocomplete widget created with a static list

Figure 10.12
An Autocomplete widget using AJAX

The Button Widget

The primary purpose of the Button widget is to enhance the appearance and functionality of buttons created with the <input>, <button>, <submit>, <reset>, and <a> elements. You can use one of two methods with the Button widget: .button() or .buttonset().

You use the .button() method with individual buttons that are not part of a group, including the <input type="button">, <button>, <submit>, and <reset> elements. The Button widget includes four options: disabled, text, icons, and label. The disabled option accepts a Boolean value to determine whether the button is enabled. The text option also accepts a Boolean value to determine whether to display any text on the button face. Both the disabled and text options are set to false by default. The icons option identifies the icons to display with the button, and label defines the text to display on the button face. The following example demonstrates how to use the Button widget's label option with the <input type="button">, <button>, and <a> elements. Figure 10.13 shows the output.

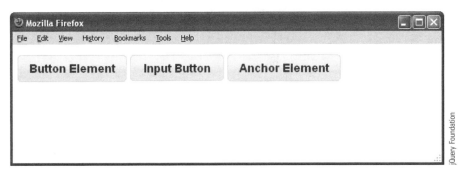

Figure 10.13
Web page with three Button widgets

```
<head>
<meta http-equiv="Content-Type" content="text/html; charset=iso-8859-1" />
<link href="css/blitzer/jquery-ui-1.8.22.custom.css"
      rel="stylesheet" type="text/css" />
<script src="js/jquery-1.7.2.min.js" type="text/javascript"></script>
<script src="js/jquery-ui-1.8.22.custom.min.js"
      type="text/javascript"></script>
<script type="text/javascript">
/* <![CDATA[ */
$(document).ready(function(){
    $("#b1").button({label: "Button Element"});
    $("#i1").button({label: "Input Button" });
    $("#a1").button({label: "Anchor Element"});
});
/* ]]> */
</script>
</head>
<body>
<p><button id="b1"></button>
<input type="button" id="i1" />
<a href="#" id="a1" style="text-decoration: none"></a></p>
</body>
```

You can use two values with the icons option: primary and secondary. The primary value identifies the icon to appear to the left of the label text and the secondary value identifies the icon to appear to the right of the label text. To display a single icon on a button, you use the following syntax, which assigns a label value of Empty Shopping Cart and a primary icon represented by the ui-icon-cart class:

```
<script type="text/javascript">
/* <![CDATA[ */
```

```
$(document).ready(function(){
    $("#b1").button({
        label: "Empty Shopping Cart" },
        {icons: {primary: "ui-icon-cart"}});
    });
/* ]]> */
</script>
</head>
<body>
<button id="b1"></button>
</body>
```

To use both icons with a button, separate them with a comma in the parameter map for the `icons` option, as follows. Figure 10.14 shows how both icons appear on the button.

```
<script type="text/javascript">
/* <![CDATA[ */
$(document).ready(function(){
    $("#b1").button({
        label: "Empty Shopping Cart" },
        {icons: {primary: "ui-icon-cart",secondary: "ui-icon-trash"}
    });
});
/* ]]> */
</script>
</head>
<body>
<button id="b1"></button>
</body>
```

As you learned in Chapter 6, when multiple form elements share the same name, JavaScript creates an array out of the elements using the shared name. Radio buttons, for instance, share the same name so that a single name=value pair can be submitted

Figure 10.14
Button element with primary and secondary icons

to a server-side script. In order for the Button widget to recognize a group of related buttons, you use the `.buttonset()` method. However, an important difference that you need to understand is that the `.buttonset()` method works by selecting the ID of a container element, such as a `<div>` element, that contains the buttons—not by accessing their shared name. The following script uses the `.buttonset()` method to group the radio buttons within a `<div>` element with an ID of `maritalStatus`:

```
<head>
<link type="text/css"
    href="css/blitzer/jquery-ui-1.8.22.custom.css" rel="stylesheet" />
<script type="text/javascript" src="js/jquery-1.7.2.min.js"></script>
<script type="text/javascript" src="js/
    jquery-ui-1.8.22.custom.min.js"></script>
<script type="text/javascript">
/* <![CDATA[ */
$(document).ready(function(){
    $("#maritalStatus").buttonset();
});
/* ]]> */
</script>
</head>
<body>
<form>
    <div id="maritalStatus">
        <input type="radio" id="maritalStatus1" name="radio" />
            <label for="maritalStatus1">Single</label>
        <input type="radio" id="maritalStatus2" name="radio"
            checked="checked" />
            <label for="maritalStatus2">Married</label>
        <input type="radio" id="maritalStatus3" name="radio" />
            <label for="maritalStatus3">Divorced</label>
        <input type="radio" id="maritalStatus4" name="radio" />
            <label for="maritalStatus4">Separated</label>
        <input type="radio" id="maritalStatus5" name="radio" />
            <label for="maritalStatus5">Widowed</label>
    </div>
</form>
</body>
```

The Datepicker Widget

In your travels across the web, you have undoubtedly come across pop-up calendars from which you can select a date. Calendars are usually created with JavaScript and

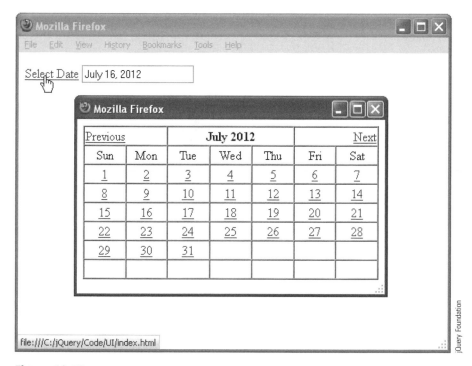

Figure 10.15
Datepicker generated with JavaScript

can be quite involved. For example, the following JavaScript code generates the output shown in Figure 10.15. The code uses the `Date` object to generate the calendar, which pops up when a user clicks the text box, and allows users to scroll back and forth between months. Do *not* spend any time trying to understand this code, because jQuery makes things much easier.

```
<head>
  <meta http-equiv="Content-Type" content="text/html; charset=iso-8859-1" />
  <script type="text/javascript">
    /* <![CDATA[ */
    var dateObject = new Date();
    var month = dateObject.getMonth();
    var monthArray = new Array("January","February"
      ,"March","April","May","June","July","August"
      ,"September","October","November","December");
    function getTodayDate() {
      var dateToday = monthArray[month] + " "
        + dateObject.getDate() + ", "
        + dateObject.getFullYear();
      document.forms[0].reservationDate.value = dateToday;
```

```
  }
  function displayCalendar(whichMonth) {
    calendarWin = window.open("", "CalWindow",
    "status=no,resizable=yes,width=400,height=220, left=200,top=200");
    calendarWin.focus();
    calendarWin.document.write("<!DOCTYPE html PUBLIC '-//W3C//DTD
      XHTML 1.0 Strict//EN' 'http://www.w3.org/TR/xhtml1/DTD/
      xhtml1-strict.dtd'><html xmlns='http://www.w3.org/1999/xhtml'>
      <head><title>Date Picker</title></head><body>");
    calendarWin.document.write("<table cellspacing='0' border='1'
      width='100%'>");
    calendarWin.document.write("<colgroup span='7' width='50' />");
    if (whichMonth == -1)
      dateObject.setMonth(dateObject.getMonth()-1);
    else if (whichMonth == 1)
      dateObject.setMonth(dateObject.getMonth()+1);
    var month = dateObject.getMonth();
    calendarWin.document.write("<tr><td colspan='2'>
      <a href='' onclick='self.opener.displayCalendar(-1);
        return false'>Previous</a></td><td colspan='3'
        align='center'><strong>" + monthArray[month] + " "
        + dateObject.getFullYear() + "</strong></td><td colspan='2'
        align='right'><a href='' onclick='self.opener.displayCalendar(1);
        return false'>Next</a></td></tr>");
    calendarWin.document.write("<tr align='center'>
      <td>Sun</td><td>Mon</td><td>Tue</td><td>Wed</td>
      <td>Thu</td><td>Fri</td><td>Sat</td></tr>");
    calendarWin.document.write("<tr align='center'>");
    dateObject.setDate(1);
    var dayOfWeek = dateObject.getDay();
    for (var i=0; i<dayOfWeek; ++i) {
      calendarWin.document.write("<td> </td>");
    }
    var daysWithDates = 7 - dayOfWeek;
    var dateCounter = 1;
    for(var i=0; i<daysWithDates; ++i) {
      var curDate = monthArray[month] + " "
        + dateCounter + ", "
        + dateObject.getFullYear();
      calendarWin.document.write(
        "<td><a href='' onclick='self.opener.document
        .reservationDate.value=\"" + curDate + "\";self.close()'>"
        + dateCounter + "</a></td>");
        ++dateCounter;
```

```
          }
        var numDays = 0;
        // January, March, May, July, August, October, December
        if (month == 0 || month == 2 || month == 4
          || month == 6 || month == 7 || month == 9
          || month == 11)
          numDays = 31;
        // February
        else if (month == 1)
          numDays = 28;
        // April, June, September, November
        else if (month == 3 || month == 5 || month == 8
          || month == 10)
          numDays = 30;
        for (var rowCounter = 0; rowCounter < 5; ++rowCounter) {
          var weekDayCounter = 0;
          calendarWin.document.write("<tr align='center'>");
          while (weekDayCounter < 7) {
            var curDate = monthArray[month] + " "
            + dateCounter + ", "
            + dateObject.getFullYear();
            if (dateCounter <= numDays)
            calendarWin.document.write("<td><a href=''
              onclick='self.opener.document.getElementById(
              \"reservationDate\").value=\"" + curDate
              + "\";self.close()'>" + dateCounter + "</a></td>");
            else
            calendarWin.document.write("<td>  </td>");
            ++weekDayCounter;
            ++dateCounter;
          }
          calendarWin.document.write("</tr>");
        }
        calendarWin.document.write("</table></body></html>");
        calendarWin.document.close();
      }
/* ]]> */
  </script>
</head>
<body onload="getTodayDate()">
<p>Select Date</a> <input type="text"
        id="reservationDate" onclick="displayCalendar()" /></p>
</body>
```

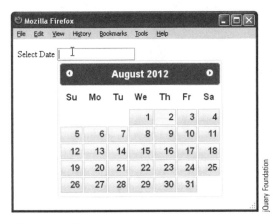

Figure 10.16
Datepicker generated with jQuery UI Datepicker widget

The jQuery UI Datepicker widget contains all of the calendar function created for you, with far more functionality than is available with the preceding example. The following code demonstrates how to generate the calendar, formatted with the Blitzer theme, shown in Figure 10.16:

```
<head>
<meta http-equiv="Content-Type" content="text/html; charset=iso-8859-1" />
<title></title>
<link href="css/blitzer/jquery-ui-1.8.22.custom.css"
          rel="stylesheet" type="text/css" />
<script src="js/jquery-1.7.2.min.js" type="text/javascript"></script>
<script src="js/jquery-ui-1.8.22.custom.min.js"
          type="text/javascript"></script>
<script type="text/javascript">
/* <![CDATA[ */
$(document).ready(function(){
    $("#datepicker").datepicker();
});
/* ]]> */
</script>
</head>
<body>
<p>Select Date  <input id="datepicker" type="text"></p>
</body>
```

The Dialog Widget

JavaScript's `window.alert()` function generates a basic dialog box that displays information. The jQuery UI's Dialog widget allows you to create dialog boxes with much greater functionality.

To define the content that will appear in a Dialog widget, place it within a container element such as a `<div>` tag pair. Then, you use the `.dialog()` method to control the dialog box. By default, the `.dialog()` method automatically opens the dialog box when the page first loads. The following code automatically opens the dialog box represented by the `<div>` element with an ID of `special` when the page first loads. Several options are passed to the `.dialog()` method, including the `height` and `width` options to control the size of the dialog box and the `modal` option, which disables all other items on the page. The `buttons` option creates a button on the dialog box with a label of `Closed`. Notice that the button closes the dialog box by passing a value of `close` to the `.dialog()` method. Finally, the `show` and `hide` options create animation effects when the dialog box opens and closes. Figure 10.17 shows the dialog box.

```
...
<script type="text/javascript">
/* <![CDATA[ */
$(document).ready(function(){
    $("#special").dialog({
        height: 150,
        width: 250,
        modal: true,
        buttons: {"Close": function() {$(this).dialog("close");}},
        show: "blind",
        hide: "fade"
    });
});
</script>
</head>
<body>
<div id="special" title="Basic dialog">
<strong>Today's special</strong>: buy a large meat lover's pizza
        and receive a free Caesar salad and a two liter bottle
        of Diet Pepsi!
</div>
...
```

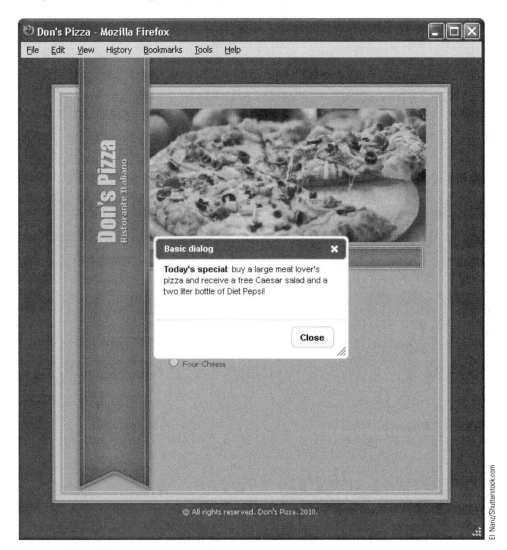

Figure 10.17
The Dialog widget in action

Tip

See http://docs.jquery.com/UI/Effects for a listing of additional animation effects that you can use with the jQuery UI.

The Progressbar Widget

The Progressbar widget is one of the simplest of the jQuery UI widgets; it displays a progress bar representing the completion status of the current task. The only options available to the Progressbar widget are the `disabled` option, which determines whether the widget is enabled, and the `value` option, which is assigned a value between 0 and 100 to identify the completion percentage of the current task. The visual display of the progress bar is determined by the theme you selected when you downloaded the jQuery UI code.

To add a progress bar to your pages, create an empty container element, such as a <div> element, with an ID that jQuery will use to identify the progress bar. Then, pass a value between 0 and 100 to the .progressbar() method to generate a progress bar that visually displays the completion percentage.

For example, the following <script> and <div> elements display a progress bar that is 50 percent complete by using a <div> element with an ID of completion:

```
<script type="text/javascript"
$(document).ready(function(){
    $("#completion").progressbar({value: 50});});
/* ]]> */
</script>
<div id="completion"></div>
```

As a more complex example, consider the following code, which renders the progress bars shown in Figure 10.18. The figure shows three pages, each of which represents a portion of a product registration form. The progress bar is rendered with the jQuery UI Blitzer theme.

```
// Customer Information page
$("#progressbar").progressbar({value: 30});});
// Product Information page 1
$("#progressbar").progressbar({value: 60});});
// Product Information page 2
$("#progressbar").progressbar({value: 90});});
```

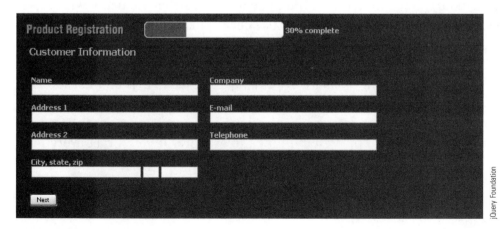

Figure 10.18
A progressbar widget example

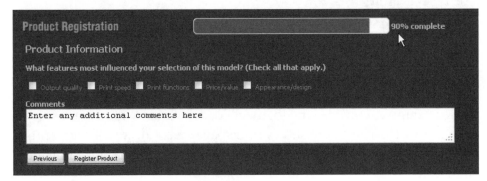

Figure 10.18
A progressbar widget example (continued)

SUMMARY

You can use the jQuery UI library to add far more advanced functionality to your web pages, including dragging and dropping elements, resizing elements with resizable handles, and sorting elements with a mouse click. This chapter—and book—only scratches the surface of what you can accomplish with jQuery. Hopefully, you have learned enough to give you the necessary skills to start working as a JavaScript and jQuery developer, and use your skills as a springboard to launch your web development career. Keep in mind that your goal in the study of JavaScript programming, or any technology subject for that matter, should not be memorizing facts and syntax. Instead, your goal should be to understand how things work. If you forget everything else you learned in this book, remember this: The best programmers in the world do not necessarily know all the answers. Rather, they know where to find the answers. Build yourself a library of reference books that you can use to find the answers you need. Best of luck in your career!

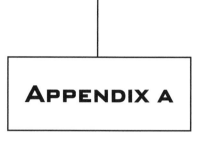

APPENDIX A

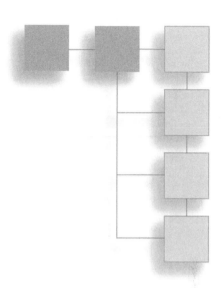

jQuery API

SELECTING AND FILTERING

Basic Selectors

Selector	Selects
All ("*")	All elements.
Element ("*element*")	All elements that match the specified element name.
ID ("#*id*")	The first element that matches the specified id attribute.
Multiple ("*selector1, selector2, …*")	All elements that match the results of one or more specified selectors.

Hierarchical Selectors

Selector	Selects
Child ("*parent* > *child*")	All specified child elements of a specified parent element.
Descendant ("*ancestor descendant*")	All specified descendant elements of a specified ancestor.
Next Adjacent ("*prev + next*")	All specified sibling elements that immediately follow a specified previous sibling element.
Next Siblings ("*prev ~ siblings*")	All specified sibling elements that follow the specified element, regardless of hierarchy.

Basic and Hierarchical Filters

Selector	Selects
:animated()	All elements currently running an animation.
:eq()	An element according to a specified index.
:even	All even elements.
:first	The first element.
:first-child	The first child element.
:gt()	All elements greater than a specified index.
:header	All heading-level elements, <h1> through <h6>.
:last	The last element.
:last-child	The last child element.
:lt()	All elements less than a specified index.
:not()	All elements that do not matching a specified selector.
:nth-child()	All elements that are the *n*th child of a specified selector.
:odd	All odd elements.
:only-child	All odd child elements.

Form Filters

Filter	Returns
:button	All `<button>` elements.
:checkbox	All `<input>` elements with a `type` attribute of `checkbox`.
:checked	All checked input fields.
:disabled	All disabled input fields.
:enabled	All enabled input fields.
:file	All `<file>` elements.
:focus	The element with the current focus.
:hidden	All hidden elements.
:image	All `<image>` elements.
:input	All `<input>` elements
:password	All `<input>` elements with a `type` attribute of `password`.
:radio	All `<input>` elements with a `type` attribute of `radio`.
:reset	All `<reset>` elements.
:selected	All selected elements.
:submit	All `<submit>` elements.
:text	All `<input>` elements with a `type` attribute of `text`.
:visible	All visible elements.

Attribute Selectors

Selector	Selects
Attribute Contains Prefix Selector [*name*|=*"value"*]	Elements with the specified attribute and value or with a value that begins with the specified value followed by a hyphen (-).
Attribute Contains Selector [*name**=*"value"*]	Elements with the specified attribute with a value containing the specified string.
Attribute Contains Word Selector [*name*~=*"value"*]	Elements with the specified attribute with a value containing the specified word.

Selector	Selects
Attribute Ends With Selector [*name$="value"*]	Elements with the specified attribute with a value ending with the specified string.
Attribute Equals Selector [*name="value"*]	Elements with the specified attribute name and value.
Attribute Not Equal Selector [*name!="value"*]	Elements that either do not include the specified attribute or that include the specified attribute with a value that does not match the specified string.
Attribute Starts With Selector [*name^="value"*]	Elements with the specified attribute with a value beginning with the specified string.
Has Attribute Selector [*name*]	Elements that include the specified attribute regardless of the assigned value.
Multiple Attribute Selector [*name="value"*][*name2="value2"*]	Elements that match all of the specified attribute names and values.

Attribute Methods

Method	Description
.attr()	Accessor method that gets the attribute value from the first element in a set of matching elements or sets the attribute value for all matching elements.
.html()	Accessor method that gets the content from the first element in a set of matching elements or sets the content for all matching elements.
.removeAttr()	Removes a specified attribute from a set of matching elements.
.val()	Accessor method that gets the attribute value from the first input field in a set of matching elements or sets the attribute value for all matching input fields.

EVENTS

Methods

Method	Description
bind(*event, data, function*)	The bind() method accepts an optional *data* argument. The *data* argument is an object that is passed to the *event* object of the attached function as *event.data*.
bind(*event, function*)	Attaches a function that is executed when the event occurs. Multiple events can be specified in the event argument; if you specify multiple events, each event must be separated with a single space.
blur()	Triggers the blur event of each selected element.
blur(*function*)	Attaches a function to the blur event of each selected element.
change()	Triggers the change event of each selected element.
change(*function*)	Attaches a function to the change event of each selected element.
click()	Triggers the click event of each selected element.
click(*function*)	Attaches a function to the click event of each selected element.
dblclick()	Triggers the dblclick (double-click) event of each selected element.
dblclick(*function*)	Attaches a function to the dblclick event of each selected element.
error()	Triggers the error event of each selected element.
error(*function*)	Attaches a function to the error event of each selected element.
focus()	Triggers the focus event of each selected element.
focus(*function*)	Attaches a function to the focus event of each selected element.
hover(*mouseover, mouseout*)	Attaches a function for mouseover, and a function for mouseout to the same element.
keydown()	Triggers the keydown event of each selected element.
keydown(*function*)	Attaches a function to the keydown event of each selected element.
keyup()	Triggers the keyup event of each selected element.

Method	Description
keyup(*function*)	Attaches a function to the keyup event of each selected element.
load(*function*)	Attaches a function to the load event of each selected element.
mousedown(*function*)	Attaches a function to the mousedown event of each selected element.
mousemove(*function*)	Attaches a function to the mousemove event of each selected element.
mouseout(*function*)	Attaches a function to the mouseout event of each selected element.
mouseover(*function*)	Attaches a function to the mouseover event of each selected element.
mouseup(*function*)	Attaches a function to the mouseup event of each selected element.
one(*event, data, function*)	The one() method accepts an optional *data* argument. The *data* argument is an object that is passed to the event object of the attached function as *event.data*.
one(*event, function*)	Attaches a function to be fired for the specified event. The function is only executed once. Subsequent events will not execute the specified function.
ready(*function*)	Attaches a function that is executed when the DOM is completely loaded, that is, all markup, CSS, and JavaScript are loaded, but not necessarily images.
resize(*function*)	Attaches a function to the resize event of each selected element.
scroll(*function*)	Attaches a function to the scroll event of each selected element.
select()	Triggers the select event of each selected element.
select(*function*)	Attaches a function to the select event of each selected element.
submit()	Triggers the submit event of each selected element.
submit(*function*)	Attaches a function to the submit event of each selected element.
toggle(*function1, function2, function3…*)	Upon first click, the first function is executed; upon second click, the second function is executed; upon third click, the third function is executed, and so on. A minimum of two functions must be specified; an unlimited number of total functions may be specified.

Method	Description
`trigger(event)`	Triggers the specified event on matched elements.
`trigger(event, data)`	The `trigger()` method accepts an optional *data* argument. The *data* argument is an object that is passed to *event* object functions being triggered as *event.data*.
`triggerHandler(event)`	Triggers the specified event on matched elements while canceling the browser's default action for any given event.
`triggerHandler(event, data)`	The `triggerHandler()` method accepts an optional *data* argument. The *data* argument is an object that is passed to *event* object functions being triggered as *event.data*.
`unbind(event, function)`	Removes the event and function.
`unload(function)`	Attaches a function to the `unload` event of each selected element.

Object Normalization

Method/Property	Description
`event.type`	Provides the type of event, for example, click, mouseover, keyup, and so on.
`event.target`	The DOM element that triggered the event.
`event.pageX, event.pageY`	The mouse coordinates relative to the document.
`event.preventDefault()`	Prevents the browser's default action for a given event, for example, submitting a form, or navigating to the `href` attribute of an `<a>` element.
`event.stopPropagation()`	Stops the propagation of an event from a child or descendant element to its parent or ancestor elements, which prevents the same event from running on the later ancestor elements.
`event.data`	An object passed to the function acting as an event handler. See the data argument specified for various methods under "Event Handling" in the previous table.

MANIPULATING ATTRIBUTES AND DATA CACHING

Methods and Properties

Method/Property	Description
addClass(*class*)	Adds the specified class name to each selected element. Elements can have one or more class names.
attr(*key*, *function*)	Sets an attribute's value depending on the return value of the callback function that you specify. The callback function is executed within the context of each selected element, where each selected element can be accessed within the function via this.
attr(*key*, *value*)	Allows you to specify an attribute by providing the name of the attribute in the key argument and its value in the value argument.
attr(*name*)	Returns the attribute value for the specified attribute from the first element present in a selection. If no element is present, the method returns "undefined."

attr(*properties*)	Allows you to set attributes via the specification of key=value pairs. For example:
	
	`attr({`
	`    id: 'someIDName',`
	`    href: '/example.html',`
	`    title: 'Some tooltip text.'`
	`});`

data(*name*)	Returns data stored for an element by the specified name for the selected elements.
data(*name*, *value*)	Stores data by the specified name with the selected elements, and also returns the value.
hasClass(*class*)	Returns true if the specified class name is present on at least one of the selected elements.

Method/Property	Description
`html()`	Returns the HTML contents, or `innerHTML`, of the first element of the selection. This method does not work on XML documents, but does work on XHTML documents.
`html(value)`	Sets the HTML contents of every selected element. This method does not work on XML documents, but does work on XHTML documents.
`removeAttr(name)`	Removes the specified attribute from the element(s).
`removeClass(class)`	Removes the specified class name from each selected element.
`removeData(name)`	Removes the data by the specified name from the selected elements.
`text()`	Returns the text content of each selected element.
`text(value)`	Sets the text content of each selected element. HTML source code will not be rendered.
`toggleClass(class)`	Adds the specified class name if it is not present, and removes the specified class name if it is present.
`val()`	Returns the contents of the value attribute for the first element of the selection. For `<select>` elements with attribute `multiple="multiple"`, an array of selected values is returned.
`val(value)`	When providing a single value, this method sets the contents of the value attribute for each selected element.
`val(values)`	When providing multiple values, this method checks or selects radio buttons, checkboxes, or select options that match the set of values.

Manipulating Content

Methods and Properties

Method/Property	Description
after(*content*)	Inserts the specified content after each selected element.
append(*content*)	Appends the specified content to the inside of every selected element.
appendTo(*selector*)	Appends all of the selected elements to the elements specified by the selector argument.
before(*content*)	Inserts the specified content before each selected element.
Clone()	Clones the selected elements; returns the jQuery object including the clones you created.
Clone(*true*)	Clones the selected elements and their event handlers; returns the jQuery object including the clones you created.
empty()	Removes all child nodes from the selected elements.
html()	Returns the HTML contents, or innerHTML, of the first element of the selection. This method does not work on XML documents, but does work on XHTML documents.
html(*value*)	Sets the HTML contents of every selected element. This method does not work on XML documents, but does work on XHTML documents.
insertAfter(*selector*)	Inserts the selected elements after the elements specified by the selector argument.
insertBefore(*selector*)	Inserts the selected elements before the selectors specified by the selector argument.

Method/Property	Description
prepend(*content*)	Prepends the specified content to the inside of each selected element.
prependTo(*selector*)	Prepends all of the selected elements to the elements specified by the selector argument.
remove(*selector*)	Removes the selected elements from the DOM.
replaceAll(*selector*)	Replaces the elements specified in the selector argument with the selected elements.
replaceWith(*content*)	Replaces each selected element with the specified HTML or DOM elements. This method returns the jQuery object including the element that was replaced.
text()	Returns the text content of each selected element.
text(*value*)	Sets the text content of each selected element. HTML source code will not be rendered.
wrap(*element*)	Wraps each selected element with the specified element from the DOM.
wrap(*html*)	Wraps each selected element with the specified HTML content.
wrapAll(*element*)	Wraps all of the selected elements with the specified element from the DOM.
wrapAll(*html*)	Wraps all of the selected elements with a single wrapper specified as HTML.
wrapInner(*element*)	Wraps the inner contents of each selected element with the specified element from the DOM.
wrapInner(*html*)	Wraps the inner contents of each selected element with the specified HTML.

AJAX

Methods

Method	Description
ajaxComplete(*function*)	Attaches a function to be executed when an AJAX request is completed.
ajaxError(*function*)	Attaches a function to be executed when an AJAX request fails.
ajaxSend(*function*)	Attaches a function to be executed before an AJAX request is sent.
ajaxStart(*function*)	Attaches a function to be executed when an AJAX request begins (if not already active).
ajaxStop(*function*)	Attaches a function to be executed when an AJAX request ends.
ajaxSuccess(*function*)	Attaches a function to be executed when an AJAX request has completed successfully.
jQuery.ajax(*options*) $.ajax(*options*)	Allows you to pass an object literal specifying various options in key=value pairs. For the complete list of options, see the "Options" section. This method is used by jQuery's other AJAX methods to make AJAX requests. You should use this method only if you require finer-grained control over an AJAX request than is possible with jQuery's other methods.
jQuery.ajaxSetup(*options*) $.ajaxSetup(*options*)	Configures the default options for AJAX requests. The option argument is passed as an object literal, in key=value pairs. See the "Options" section.
jQuery.get(*url*, [*data*], [*function*], [*type*]) $.get(*url*, [*data*], [*function*], [*type*]))	Initiates an HTTP request using the GET method.

Method	Description
`jQuery.getJSON(url, [data], [function])` `$.getJSON(url, [data], [function])`	Initiates an HTTP request using the GET method, in which the response will be JSON-formatted data.
`jQuery.getScript(url, [function])` `$.getScript(url, [function])`	Loads and executes a new JavaScript file via the GET method asynchronously.
`jQuery.post(url, [data], [function], [type])` `$.post(url, [data], [function], [type])`	Initiates an HTTP request using the POST method.
`load(url, [data], [function])`	Loads HTML from a remote file and inserts the HTML inside of the selected elements. The data argument (optional) is specified as an object literal, defining the data you want to pass to the server in key=value pairs. The function argument (also optional) is the callback method that will handle the data once it is returned from the server.
`serialize()`	Serializes a set of input elements into a string of data.
`serializeArray()`	Serializes all forms and form elements into a JSON structure.

Options

Option	Description
`async`	By default, jQuery sends all AJAX requests asynchronously. To send a synchronous request, set this property to `false`.
`beforeSend`	The function you specify for this option is executed before the AJAX request is sent.
`cache`	Whether or not the AJAX request should be cached. The default is `true`, `false` for `dataType` script.
`complete`	This option allows you to specify a function that is executed when the AJAX request has completed.
`contentType`	The MIME type of data being sent to the server. The default is application/x-www-form-urlencoded.
`data`	The data to be sent to the server with a `GET` or `POST` request. Can be specified as either a string of ampersand-delimited arguments or as an object literal in key=value pairs.

`dataFilter`	A function to be used to handle the raw response data of `XMLHttpRequest`. This is a pre-filtering function to sanitize the response. You should return the sanitized data. The function has two arguments: the raw data returned from the server and the type parameter (see `dataType`):
	
	```function (data, type) {```
	``` // do something```
	``` // return the sanitized data```
	``` return data;```
	```}```

`dataType`	The type of data that you expect to receive in your response from the server. jQuery automatically determines whether to pass `responseText` or `responseXML` to the callback function handling the response, depending on the MIME type of the data returned by the server. See the "Types" section for a list of allowed data types.
`error`	A function that is executed if the AJAX request fails.
`global`	Whether or not to trigger the global AJAX event handlers for the request, for example, the handlers set by the various AJAX Event methods. The default is `true`.

Option	Description
ifModified	Allows the request to be successful only if the request has been modified since the last request. This is determined by checking the time specified in the Last-Modified HTTP header. The default is false (ignore the Last-Modified header).
jsonp	Overrides the callback function name in a jsonp request. This value will be used instead of callback in the callback=? part of the query string in the URL for a GET or the data for a POST. So {jsonp:'onJsonPLoad'} would result in onJsonPLoad=? passed to the server.
password	A password to use in response to an HTTP access authentication request.
processData	By default, data passed in to the data option will be processed and transformed into a query string, fitting to the default content-type application/x-www-form-urlencoded. If you want to send DOMDocuments or other non-processed data, set this option to false. The default is true.
scriptCharset	For GET requests where the dataType is set to script or jsonp. Forces the request to be interpreted with the specified charset. This is needed only if the charset of local content is different from the remote content being loaded.
success	A function that is executed upon success of the AJAX request.
timeout	Sets the amount of time in milliseconds (ms) to allow before a time-out will occur.
type	The type of HTTP request, one of GET or POST. You can also specify PUT or DELETE. However, those methods are not supported by all browsers.
url	The URL to request.
username	A username to specify in response to an HTTP authentication required request.
xhr	Callback for creating the XMLHttpRequest object. Defaults to the ActiveXObject when available (IE), the XMLHttpRequest otherwise. Override to provide your own implementation for XMLHttpRequest or enhancements to the factory.

Types

Allowed for the `dataType` option, or `type` argument.

Type	Description
html	Returns HTML as plain text. `<script>` elements are evaluated upon inserting into the DOM.
json	Evaluates the response as JSON and returns a JavaScript object.
jsonp	Loads in a JSON block using JSONP. Will add an extra `?callback=?` to the end of your URL to specify the callback.
script	Evaluates the response as JavaScript and returns the script as plain text to the callback function. Disables caching unless the cache option is used. Note: This type of request will make `POST` requests into `GET` requests.
text	Returns the server response as a plain text string.
xml	Returns an XML document that can be processed with jQuery.

CSS

Methods

Method	Description

css(*properties*)	Sets the specified CSS properties. The *properties* argument is defined as an object literal of key=value pairs, for example:
	
	`$('div').css({`
	
	  `backgroundColor: 'red',`
	
	  `marginLeft: '10px'`
	
	`});`

css(*property*)	Returns the specified CSS property value from the first selected element, for example: `$('div').css('background-color')`

Method	Description
css(*property*, *value*)	Sets the specified CSS property value, for example: `$('div').css('background', 'red');`
height()	Returns the pixel height (CSS height, excluding borders and padding) of the first selected element.
height(*value*)	Sets the pixel height (CSS height) of the first selected element. If no unit of measurement is provided, px (pixels) is used.
offset()	Returns the offset position of the first selected element relative to the viewport. `var $offset = $('div').offset();` `alert('Left: ' + $offset.left);` `alert('Top: ' + $offset.top);`
outerHeight(*options*)	Returns the offsetHeight (includes the pixel height, borders, and padding) of the first selected element. The *options* argument is a JavaScript object literal of options. See the "Options" section for more information.
outerWidth(*options*)	Returns the offsetWidth (includes the pixel width, borders, and padding) of the first selected element. The *options* argument is a JavaScript object literal of options. See the "Options" section for more information.
width()	Returns the pixel width (CSS width, excluding borders and padding) of the first selected element.
width(*value*)	Sets the pixel width (CSS width) of the first selected element. If no unit of measurement is provided, px (pixels) is used.

Option

Option	Description
margin	When set to true, the margin will be included in the calculation for offsetWidth or offsetHeight.

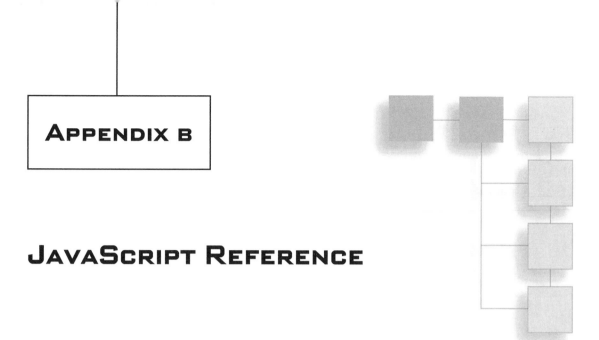

APPENDIX B

JavaScript Reference

Comment Types

Line Comments

```
<script type="text/javascript">
// Line comments are preceded by two slashes.
</script>
```

Block Comments

```
<script type="text/javascript">
/*
This line is part of the block comment.
This line is also part of the block comment.
*/
/* This is another way of creating a block comment. */
</script>
```

JavaScript Reserved Words

abstract	else	instanceof	switch
boolean	enum	int	synchronized
break	export	interface	this
byte	extends	long	throw
case	false	native	throws
catch	final	new	transient
char	finally	null	true
class	float	package	try
const	for	private	typeof
continue	function	protected	var
debugger	goto	public	void
default	if	return	volatile
delete	implements	short	while
do	import	static	with
double	in	super	

Events

JavaScript Events

Event	Triggered When
abort	The loading of an image is interrupted.
blur	An element, such as a radio button, becomes inactive.
click	The user clicks an element once.
change	The value of an element, such as text box, changes.
error	A document or image is being loaded.
focus	An element, such as a command button, becomes active.
load	A document or image loads.

Event	Triggered When
mouseout	The mouse moves off an element.
mouseover	The mouse moves over an element.
reset	A form's fields are reset to its default values.
select	A user selects a field in a form.
submit	A user submits a form.
unload	A document unloads.

Elements and Associated Events

Element	Description	Event
`<a>`	Anchor	onfocus, onblur, onclick, ondblclick, onmousedown, onmouseup, onmouseover, onmousemove, onmouseout, onkeypress, onkeydown, onkeyup
`<img>`	Image	onclick, ondblclick, onmousedown, onmouseup, onmouseover, onmousemove, onmouseout, onkeypress, onkeydown, onkeyup
`<body>`	Document body	onload, onunload, onclick, ondblclick, onmousedown, onmouseup, onmouseover, onmousemove, onmouseout, onkeypress, onkeydown, onkeyup
`<form>`	Form	onsubmit, onreset, onclick, ondblclick, onmousedown, onmouseup, onmouseover, onmousemove, onmouseout, onkeypress, onkeydown, onkeyup
`<input>`	Form control	tabindex, accesskey, onfocus, onblur, onselect, onchange, onclick, ondblclick, onmousedown, onmouseup, onmouseover, onmousemove, onmouseout, onkeypress, onkeydown, onkeyup
`<textarea>`	Text area	onfocus, onblur, onselect, onchange, onclick, ondblclick, onmousedown, onmouseup, onmouseover, onmousemove, onmouseout, onkeypress, onkeydown, onkeyup
`<select>`	Selection	onfocus, onblur, onchange

Primitive Data Types

Data Type	Description
Integer numbers	Positive or negative numbers with no decimal places.
Floating-point numbers	Positive or negative numbers with decimal places or numbers written using exponential notation.
Boolean	A logical value of `true` or `false`.
String	Text such as "Hello World".
Undefined	A variable that has never had a value assigned to it, has not been declared, or does not exist.
Null	An empty value.

JavaScript Escape Sequences

Escape Sequence	Character
`\\`	Backslash
`\b`	Backspace
`\r`	Carriage return
`\"`	Double quotation mark
`\f`	Form feed
`\t`	Horizontal tab
`\n`	New line
`\0`	Null character
`\'`	Single quotation mark
`\v`	Vertical tab
`\x XX`	Latin-1 character specified by the *XX* characters, which represent two hexadecimal digits
`\x XXXX`	Unicode character specified by the *XXXX* characters, which represent four hexadecimal digits

OPERATORS

JavaScript Operator Types

Operator Type	Description
Arithmetic	Used for performing mathematical calculations.
Assignment	Assigns values to variables.
Comparison	Compares operands and returns a Boolean value.
Logical	Used for performing Boolean operations on Boolean operands.
String	Performs operations on strings.
Special	Used for various purposes and do not fit within other operator categories.

Arithmetic Binary Operators

Operator	Name	Description
+	Addition	Adds two operands.
−	Subtraction	Subtracts one operand from another operand.
*	Multiplication	Multiplies one operand by another operand.
/	Division	Divides one operand by another operand.
%	Modulus	Divides one operand by another operand and returns the remainder.

Arithmetic Unary Operators

Operator	Name	Description
++	Increment	Increases an operand by a value of one.
––	Decrement	Decreases an operand by a value of one.
–	Negation	Returns the opposite value (negative or positive) of an operand.

Assignment Operators

Operator	Name	Description
=	Assignment	Assigns the value of the right operand to the left operand.
+=	Compound addition assignment	Combines the value of the right operand with the value of the left operand or adds the value of the right operand to the value of the left operand and assigns the new value to the left operand.
-=	Compound subtraction assignment	Subtracts the value of the right operand from the value of the left operand and assigns the new value to the left operand.
*=	Compound multiplication assignment	Multiplies the value of the right operand by the value of the left operand and assigns the new value to the left operand.
/=	Compound division assignment	Divides the value of the left operand by the value of the right operand and assigns the new value to the left operand.
%=	Compound modulus assignment	Divides the value of the left operand by the value of the right operand and assigns the remainder to the left operand (modulus).

Comparison Operators

Operator	Name	Description
==	Equal	Returns `true` if the operands are equal.
===	Strict equal	Returns `true` if the operands are equal and of the same type.
!=	Not equal	Returns `true` if the operands are not equal.
!==	Strict not equal	Returns `true` if the operands are not equal or not of the same type.
>	Greater than	Returns `true` if the left operand is greater than the right operand.
<	Less than	Returns `true` if the left operand is less than the right operand.
>=	Greater than or equal	Returns `true` if the left operand is greater than or equal to the right operand.
<=	Less than or equal	Returns `true` if the left operand is less than or equal to the right operand.

Logical Operators

Operator	Name	Description
&&	And	Returns `true` if both the left operand and right operand return a value of `true`; otherwise, it returns a value of `false`.
||	Or	Returns `true` if the left operand or right operand returns a value of `true`. If neither operand returns a value of `true`, the expression containing the || operator returns a value of `false`.
!	Not	Returns `true` if an expression is `false` and returns `false` if an expression is `true`.

Operator Precedence

Operators	Description	Associativity
.	Objects—highest precedence	Left to right
[]	Array elements—highest precedence	Left to right
()	Functions/evaluation—highest precedence	Left to right
new	New object—highest precedence	Right to left
!	Not	Right to left
-	Unary negation	Right to left
++	Increment	Right to left
--	Decrement	Right to left
typeof	Data type	Right to left
void	Void	Right to left
delete	Delete object	Right to left
* / %	Multiplication/division/modulus	Left to right
+ -	Addition/subtraction/concatenation	Left to right
< <= > >=	Comparison	Left to right
instanceof	Object type	Left to right
in	Object property	Left to right
== != === !==	Equality	Left to right
&&	Logical and	Left to right
||	Logical or	Left to right
?:	Conditional	Right to left
= += -= *= /= %=	Compound assignment	Right to left
,	Comma—lowest precedence	Left to right

CONTROL STRUCTURES AND STATEMENTS

if Statements

The `if` statement is used to execute specific programming code if the evaluation of a conditional expression returns a value of `true`. The syntax for a simple `if` statement is as follows:

```
if (conditional expression) {
    statement(s);
}
```

if...else Statements

An `if` statement that includes an else clause is called an `if...else` statement. You can think of an else clause as being a backup plan that is implemented when the condition returns a value of `false`. The syntax for an `if...else` statement is as follows:

```
if (conditional expression) {
    statement(s);
}
else {
    statement(s);
}
```

switch Statements

The `switch` statement controls program flow by executing a specific set of statements, depending on the value of an expression. The `switch` statement compares the value of an expression to a value contained within a special statement called a `case` label. A `case` label in a `switch` statement represents a specific value and contains one or more statements that execute if the value of the case label matches the value of the `switch` statement's expression. For example, your script for an insurance company might include a variable named `customerAge`. A `switch` statement can evaluate the variable and compare it to a case label within the `switch` construct. The `switch` statement might contain several case labels for different age groups that calculate insurance rates based on a customer's age. If the `customerAge` variable is equal to 25, the statements that are part of the "25" case label execute and calculate insurance rates for customers who are 25 or older. Although you could accomplish the same task using `if` or `if...else` statements, a `switch` statement makes it easier to organize the different branches of code that can be executed. The syntax for the `switch` statement is as follows:

```
switch (expression) {
    case label:
        statement(s);
        break;
    case label:
        statement(s);
        break;
    ...
    default:
        statement(s);
}
```

while Statements

The while statement, which repeats a statement or series of statements as long as a given conditional expression evaluates to true. The syntax for the while statement is as follows:

```
while (conditional expression) {
    statement(s);
}
```

do...while Statements

The do...while statement executes a statement or statements once, then repeats the execution as long as a given conditional expression evaluates to true. The syntax for the do...while statement is as follows:

```
do {
    statement(s);
} while (conditional expression);
```

for Statements

The for statement is used for repeating a statement or series of statements as long as a given conditional expression evaluates to true. The for statement performs essentially the same function as the while statement: if a conditional expression within the for statement evaluates to true, then the for statement executes and will continue to execute repeatedly until the conditional expression evaluates to false. The syntax of the for statement is as follows:

```
for (initialization expression; condition; update statement) {
    statement(s);
}
```

for...in Statements

To execute the same statement or command block for all the properties within a custom object, you can use the for...in statement, which is a looping statement similar to the for statement. The syntax of the for...in statement is as follows:

```
for (variable in object) {
    statement(s);
}
```

with Statements

The with statement eliminates the need to retype the name of an object when properties of the same object are being referenced in a series. To use the with statement, you create a structure similar to an if statement and pass the name of the object as a conditional expression. You can then refer to all of the object properties without referring to the object itself. The syntax of the with statement is as follows:

```
with (object) {
    statement(s);
}
```

break Statements

A break statement is used to exit switch statements and other program control statements such as the while, do...while, for, and for...in looping statements. To end a switch statement once it performs its required task, you should include a break statement within each case label.

The following code shows a switch statement contained within a function. When the function is called, it is passed an argument named americanCity. The switch statement compares the contents of the americanCity argument to the case labels. If a match is found, the city's state is returned and a break statement ends the switch statement. If a match is not found, the value "United States" is returned from the default label.

```
function city_location(americanCity) {
    switch (americanCity) {
        case "Boston":
            return "Massachusetts";
            break;
        case "Chicago":
            return "Illinois";
            break;
```

```
            case "Los Angeles":
                return "California";
                break;
            case "Miami":
                return "Florida";
                break;
            case "New York":
                return "New York";
                break;
            default:
                return "United States";
    }
}
document.write("<p>" + city_location("Boston") + "</p>");
```

continue Statements

The `continue` statement halts a looping statement and restarts the loop with a new iteration. You use the `continue` statement when you want to stop the loop for the current iteration, but want the loop to continue with a new iteration. In the following code, when the `count` variable equals 3, the `continue` statement stops the current iteration of the `for` loop, and the script skips printing the number 3. However, the loop continues to iterate until the conditional expression `count <= 5` is `false`.

```
for (var count = 1; count < stockArray.length; ++count) {
    if (count == 3)
        continue;
    document.write("<p>" + count + "</p>");
}
```

BUILT-IN JAVASCRIPT FUNCTIONS

Function	Description
eval()	Evaluates expressions contained within strings.
isFinite()	Determines whether a number is finite.
isNaN()	Determines whether a value is the special value NaN (not a number).
parseInt()	Converts string literals to integers.
parseFloat()	Converts string literals to floating-point numbers.

Function	Description
encodeURI()	Encodes a text string so that it becomes a valid URI.
encodeURIComponent()	Encodes a text string so that it becomes a valid URI component.
decodeURI()	Decodes text strings encoded with encodeURI().
decodeURIComponent()	Decodes text strings encoded with encodeURIComponent().

BUILT-IN JAVASCRIPT CLASSES

Array Class

Methods

Method	Description
Array()	Array object constructor.
concat()	Combines two arrays into a single array.
join()	Combines all elements of an array into a string.
pop()	Removes and returns the last element from an array.
push()	Adds and returns a new array element.
reverse()	Transposes elements of an array.
shift()	Removes and returns the first element from an array.
slice()	Creates a new array from a section of an existing array.
splice()	Adds or removes array elements.
sort()	Sorts elements of an array.
unshift()	Adds new elements to the start of an array and returns the new array length.

Properties

Property	Description
length	Returns the number of elements in an array.

Date Class

Methods

Method	Description
Date()	Date object constructor.
getDate()	Returns the date of a Date object.
getDay()	Returns the day of a Date object.
getFullYear()	Returns the year of a Date object in a four-digit format.
getHours()	Returns the hour of a Date object.
getMilliseconds()	Returns the milliseconds of a Date object.
getMinutes()	Returns the minutes of a Date object.
getMonth()	Returns the month of a Date object.
getSeconds()	Returns the seconds of a Date object.
getTime()	Returns the time of a Date object.
getTimezoneOffset()	Returns the time difference between the user's computer and GMT.
getUTCDate()	Returns the date of a Date object in universal time.
getUTCDay()	Returns the day of a Date object in universal time.
getUTCFullYear()	Returns the four-digit year of a Date object in universal time.
getUTCHours()	Returns the hours of a Date object in universal time.
getUTCMilliseconds()	Returns the milliseconds of a Date object in universal time.
getUTCMinutes()	Returns the minutes of a Date object in universal time.
getUTCMonth()	Returns the month of a Date object in universal time.
getUTCSeconds()	Returns the seconds of a Date object in universal time.
getYear()	Returns the year of a Date object.
parse()	Returns a string containing the number of milliseconds since January 1, 1970.
setDate()	Sets the date of a Date object.
setFullYear()	Sets the four-digit year of a Date object.
setHours()	Sets the hours of a Date object.
setMilliseconds()	Sets the milliseconds of a Date object.

Method	Description
setMinutes()	Sets the minutes of a Date object.
setMonth()	Sets the month of a Date object.
setSeconds()	Sets the seconds of a Date object.
setTime()	Sets the time of a Date object.
setUTCDate()	Sets the date of a Date object in universal time.
setUTCDay()	Sets the day of a Date object in universal time.
setUTCFullYear()	Sets the four-digit year of a Date object in universal time.
setUTCHours()	Sets the hours of a Date object in universal time.
setUTCMilliseconds()	Sets the milliseconds of a Date object in universal time.
setUTCMinutes()	Sets the minutes of a Date object in universal time.
setUTCMonth()	Sets the month of a Date object in universal time.
setUTCSeconds()	Sets the seconds of a Date object in universal time.
setYear()	Sets the two-digit year of a Date object.
toGMTString()	Converts a Date object to a string in GMT timezone format.
toLocaleString()	Converts a Date object to a string and sets it to the current timezone.
toString()	Converts a Date object to a string.

Math Class
Methods

Method	Description
abs(x)	Returns the absolute value of x.
acos(x)	Returns the arc cosine of x.
asin(x)	Returns the arc sine of x.
atan(x)	Returns the arc tangent of x.
atan2(x,y)	Returns the angle from the x-axis.
ceil(x)	Returns the value of x rounded to the next highest integer.
cos(x)	Returns the cosine of x.

Method	Description
exp(x)	Returns the exponent of x.
floor(x)	Returns the value of x rounded to the next lowest integer.
log(x)	Returns the natural logarithm of x.
max(x,y)	Returns the larger of the two numbers.
min(x,y)	Returns the smaller of the two numbers.
pow(x,y)	Returns the value of x raised to the y power.
random()	Returns a random number.
round(x)	Returns the value of x rounded to the nearest integer.
sin(x)	Returns the sine of x.
sqrt(x)	Returns the square root of x.
tan(x)	Returns the tangent of x.

Properties

Property	Description
E	Euler's constant e, which is the base of a natural logarithm; this value is approximately 2.7182818284590452354.
LN10	The natural logarithm of 10, which is approximately 2.302585092994046.
LN2	The natural logarithm of 2, which is approximately 0.6931471805599453.
LOG10E	The base-10 logarithm of e, the base of the natural logarithms; this value is approximately 0.4342944819032518.
LOG2E	The base-2 logarithm of e, the base of the natural logarithms; this value is approximately 1.4426950408889634.
PI	A constant representing the ratio of the circumference of a circle to its diameter, which is approximately 3.1415926535897932.
SQRT1_2	The square root of 1/2, which is approximately 0.7071067811865476.
SQRT2	The square root of 2, which is approximately 1.4142135623730951.

Number Class

Methods

Method	Description
Number()	Number object constructor.
toExponential()	Converts a number to a string in exponential notation using a specified number of decimal places.
toFixed()	Converts a number to a string with a specified number of decimal places.
toLocaleString()	Converts a number to a string that is formatted with local numeric formatting conventions.
toPrecision()	Converts a number to a string with a specific number of decimal places, either in exponential notation or in fixed notation.
toString()	Converts a number to a string using a specified radix.

Properties

Property	Description
MAX_VALUE	The largest positive number that can be used in JavaScript.
MIN_VALUE	The smallest positive number that can be used in JavaScript.
NaN	The value NaN, which stands for "not a number".
NEGATIVE_INFINITY	The value of negative infinity.
POSITIVE_INFINITY	The value of positive infinity.

String Class
Methods

Method	Description
charAt(*index*)	Returns the character at the specified position in a text string. Returns an empty string if the specified position is greater than the length of the string.
charCodeAt(*index*)	Returns the Unicode character at the specified position in a text string. Returns NaN if the specified position is greater than the length of the string.
concat(*value1*, *value2*, ...)	Creates a new string by combining the *value* arguments.
indexOf(*text*, *index*)	Returns the position number in a string of the first character in the *text* argument. If the *index* argument is included, the indexOf() method starts searching at that position within the string. Returns -1 if the text is not found.
lastIndexOf(*text*, *index*)	Returns the position number in a string of the last instance of the first character in the *text* argument. If the *index* argument is included, the lastIndexOf() method starts searching at that position within the string. Returns -1 if the character or string is not found.
match()	Returns an array containing the results that match the *pattern* argument.
replace(*text*, *pattern*)	Creates a new string with all instances of the *text* argument replaced with the value of the *pattern* argument.
search(*pattern*)	Returns the position number in a string of the first instance of the first character in the *text* argument.
slice(*starting index*, *ending index*)	Extracts text from a string starting with the position number in the string of the *starting index* argument and ending with the position number of the *ending index* argument. Allows negative argument values.
split(*text*, *limit*)	Separates a string into an array at the character or characters specified by the *text* argument. The *limit* argument determines the maximum length of the array.

Method	Description
substring(*starting index*, *ending index*)	Extracts text from a string starting with the position number in the string of the *starting index* argument and ending with the position number of the *ending index* argument. Does not allow negative argument values.
toLowerCase()	Converts a text string to lowercase.
toString()	Converts a number to a string.
toUpperCase()	Converts a text string to uppercase.
valueOf()	Returns the primitive value of a string.

Properties

Method	Description
length	Returns the number of characters in a string.

OBJECTS OF THE BROWSER OBJECT MODEL

Document Object
Methods

Method	Description
close()	Closes a new document that was created with the open() method.
getElementById(*ID*)	Returns the element represented by *ID*.
getElementsByName(*name*)	Returns a collection of elements represented by *name*.
open()	Opens a new document in a window or frame.
write(text)	Writes new text to a document.
writeln(text)	Writes new text to a document, followed by a line break.

Properties

Property	Description
anchors	Returns a collection of the document's anchor elements.
applets	Returns a collection of the document's applets.
body	Returns the document's `<body>` or `<frameset>` element.
cookie	Returns the current document's cookie string, which contains small pieces of information about a user that are stored by a web server in text files on the user's computer.
domain	Returns the domain name of the server where the current document is located.
forms	Returns a collection of the document's forms.
images	Returns a collection of the document's images.
links	Returns a collection of a document's links.
referrer	Returns the Uniform Resource Locator (URL) of the document that provided a link to the current document.
title	Returns or sets the title of the document as specified by the `<title>` element in the document `<head>` section.
URL	Returns the URL of the current document.

History Object

Methods

Method	Description
back()	Produces same result as clicking a web browser's Back button.
forward()	Produces same result as clicking a web browser's Forward button.
go()	Opens a specific document in the history list.

Properties

Property	Description
length	Contains the specific number of documents that have been opened during the current browser session.

Location Object
Methods

Method	Description
assign()	Loads a new web page.
reload()	Causes the page that currently appears in the web browser to open again.
replace()	Replaces the currently loaded URL with a different one.

Properties

Property	Description
assign()	Loads a new web page.
hash	A URL's anchor.
host	The host and domain name (or IP address) of a network host.
hostname	A combination of the URL's hostname and port sections.
href	The full URL address.
pathname	The URL's path.
port	The URL's port.
protocol	The URL's protocol.
search	A URL's search or query portion.

Navigator Object
Properties

Properties	Description
appCodeName	The web browser code name.
appName	The web browser name.
appVersion	The web browser version.
platform	The operating system in use on the client computer.
userAgent	The string stored in the HTTP user-agent request header, which contains information about the browser, the platform name, and compatibility.

Screen Object
Properties

Properties	Description
availHeight	Returns the available height, in pixels, of the screen that displays the web browser.
availWidth	Returns the available width, in pixels, of the screen that displays the web browser.
colorDepth	Returns the number of bits that are used for color on the screen.
height	Returns the total height, in pixels, of the screen that displays the web browser.
width	Returns the total width, in pixels, of the screen that displays the web browser.

Window Object
Methods

Method	Description
`alert()`	Displays a simple message dialog box with an OK button.
`blur()`	Removes focus from a window.
`clearInterval()`	Cancels an interval that was set with `setInterval()`.
`clearTimeout()`	Cancels a timeout that was set with `setTimeout()`.
`close()`	Closes a web browser window.
`Confirm()`	Displays a confirmation dialog box with OK and Cancel buttons.
`focus()`	Makes a `Window` object the active window.
`moveBy()`	Moves the window relative to the current position.
`moveTo()`	Moves the window to an absolute position.
`open()`	Opens a new web browser window.
`print()`	Prints the document displayed in the window or frame.
`prompt()`	Displays a dialog box prompting a user to enter information.
`resizeBy()`	Resizes a window by a specified amount.
`resizeTo()`	Resizes a window to a specified size.
`scrollBy()`	Scrolls the window by a specified amount.
`scrollTo()`	Scrolls the window to a specified position.
`setInterval()`	Repeatedly executes a function after a specified number of milliseconds have elapsed.
`setTimeout()`	Executes a function once after a specified number of milliseconds have elapsed.

Properties

Properties	Description
closed	Returns a Boolean value that indicates whether a window has been closed.
defaultStatus	Sets the default text that is written to the status bar.
document	Returns a reference to the Document object.
frames[]	Returns an array listing the Frame objects in a window.
history	Returns a reference to the History object.
location	Returns a reference to the Location object.
name	Returns the name of the window.
navigator	Returns a reference to the Navigator object.
opener	Refers to the window that opened the current window.
parent	Returns the parent frame that contains the current frame.
self	Returns a self-reference to the Window object; identical to the window property.
status	Specifies temporary text that is written to the status bar.
top	Returns the topmost Window object that contains the current frame.
window	Returns a self-reference to the Window object; identical to the self property.

OBJECTS OF THE DOCUMENT OBJECT MODEL

Form Object
Methods

Method	Description
reset()	Resets a form without the use of a Reset button.
submit()	Submits a form without the use of a Submit button.

Properties

Property	Description
action	Returns the URL to which form data will be submitted.
encoding	Sets and returns a string representing the MIME type of the data being submitted.
length	Returns an integer representing the number of elements in the form.
method	Sets and returns a string representing one of the two options for submitting form data: GET or POST.

Events

Event	Description
reset	Executes when a form's Reset button is clicked.
submit	Executes when a form's Submit button is clicked.

Image Object
Properties

Property	Description
border	A read-only property containing the border width, in pixels, as specified by the border attribute of the <img> element.
complete	A Boolean value that returns true when an image is completely loaded.
height	A read-only property containing the height of the image as specified by the height attribute of the <img> element.
hspace	A read-only property containing the amount of horizontal space, in pixels, to the left and right of the image, as specified by the hspace attribute of the <img> element.
lowsrc	The URL of an alternate, low-resolution image.
name	A name assigned to the element.

Property	Description
src	The URL of the displayed image.
vspace	A read-only property containing the amount of vertical space, in pixels, above and below the image, as specified by the vspace attribute of the <img> element.
width	A read-only property containing the width of the image as specified by the width attribute of the <img> element.

Events

Property	Description
onabort	Executes when the user cancels the loading of an image, usually by clicking the Stop button.
onerror	Executes when an error occurs while an image is loading.
onload	Executes after an image is loaded.

Input Object

Methods and Their Associated Form Controls

Method	Description	Form Controls
blur()	Removes focus from a form control	Buttons, check boxes, radio buttons, Reset buttons, Submit buttons, text boxes, text areas, password boxes, file boxes, and selection lists
click()	Activates a form control's click event	Buttons, check boxes, radio buttons, Reset buttons, Submit buttons, and selection lists
focus()	Changes focus to a form control	Buttons, check boxes, radio buttons, Reset buttons, Submit buttons, text boxes, text areas, password boxes, file boxes, and selection lists
select()	Selects the text in a form control	Text boxes, text areas, password boxes, and file boxes

Properties and Their Associated Form Controls

Property	Description	Form Controls
checked	Sets and returns the checked status of a check box or radio button.	Check boxes and radio buttons
defaultChecked	Determines the control that is checked by default in a check box group or radio button group.	Check boxes and radio buttons
defaultValue	Specifies the default text that will appear in a form control boxes.	Text, text areas, password boxes, and file boxes
form	Returns a reference to the form that contains the control.	Buttons, check boxes, radio buttons, Reset buttons, Submit buttons, text boxes, text areas, password boxes, file boxes, selection lists, and hidden text boxes
length	Returns the number of items within a selection list's options[] array.	Selection lists
name	Returns the value assigned to the element's name attribute submit.	Buttons, check boxes, radio buttons, text boxes, text areas, password boxes, file boxes, selection lists, and hidden text boxes
selectedIndex	Returns an integer that represents the element displayed in a selection list, according to its position.	Selection lists
type	Returns the type of form element: button, checkbox, file, hidden, password, radio, reset, select-one, select-multiple, submit, text, or textarea.	Buttons, check boxes, radio buttons, Reset buttons, Submit buttons, text boxes, text areas, password boxes, file boxes, selection lists, and hidden text boxes
value	Sets and returns the value of form controls.	Buttons, check boxes, radio buttons, Reset buttons, Submit buttons, text boxes, text areas, password boxes, file boxes, and hidden text boxes

Events and Their Associated Form Controls

Event	Description	Form Controls
blur	An element, such as a radio button, becomes inactive.	Buttons, check boxes, radio buttons, Reset buttons, Submit buttons, text boxes, text areas, password boxes, file boxes, and selection lists
change	The value of an element, such as a text box, changes.	Text boxes, text areas, password boxes, file boxes, and selection lists
click	The user clicks an element once.	Buttons, check boxes, radio buttons, Reset buttons, and Submit buttons
focus	An element, such as a command button, becomes active.	Buttons, check boxes, radio buttons, Reset buttons, Submit buttons, text boxes, text areas, password boxes, file boxes, and selection lists

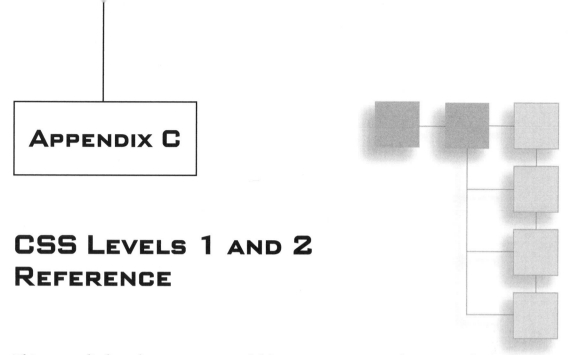

APPENDIX C

CSS LEVELS 1 AND 2 REFERENCE

This appendix lists the properties available to CSS recommendation, Level 1 (CSS1) and CSS recommendation, Level 2 (CSS2). You can find the latest information on CSS at the W3C's website at www.w3.org/Style/CSS/.

BACKGROUND PROPERTIES

Property	Description	Values
background	Sets all the background properties in one declaration.	background-color | background-image | background-repeat | background-attachment | background-position
background-attachment	Determines whether an image specified with background-image will scroll with a web page's content or be in a fixed position.	scroll | fixed
background-color	Sets the background color of an element.	color_name | hex_number | rgb_number | transparent
background-image	Sets the background image of an element.	none | url('url')

Property	Description	Values
background-position	Specifies the initial position of an image specified with background-image.	left top | left center | left bottom | right top | right center | right bottom | center top | center center | center bottom | *x% I%* | *xpos ypos*
background-repeat	Determines how an image specified with background-image is repeated on the page.	repeat | repeat-x | repeat-y | no-repeat

BORDER AND OUTLINE PROPERTIES

Property	Description	Values
border	Sets all the border properties in one declaration.	*border-width* | *border-style* | *border-color*
border-bottom	Sets all of the width, style, and color properties for an element's bottom border in one declaration.	*border-bottom-width* | *border-bottom-style* | *border-bottom-color*
border-bottom-color	Sets the bottom border color of an element.	*color_name* | *hex_number* | *rgb_number* | transparent
border-bottom-style	Sets the bottom border style of an element.	none | hidden | dotted | dashed | solid | double | groove | ridge | inset | outset
border-bottom-width	Sets the bottom border width of an element.	thin | medium | thick | *length*
border-color	Sets the color of an element's four borders.	*color_name* | *hex_number* | *rgb_number* | transparent
border-left	Sets all of the width, style, and color properties for an element's left border in one declaration.	*border-left-width* | *border-left-style* | *border-left-color*
border-left-color	Sets the left border color of an element.	*color_name* | *hex_number* | *rgb_number* | transparent

Property	Description	Values
border-left-style	Sets the left border style of an element.	none | hidden | dotted | dashed | solid | double | groove | ridge | inset | outset
border-left-width	Sets the left border width of an element.	thin | medium | thick | *length*
border-right	Sets all of the width, style, and color properties for an element's right border in one declaration.	*border-right-width* | *border-right-style* | *border-right-color*
border-right-color	Sets the right border color of an element.	*color_name* | *hex_number* | *rgb_number* | transparent
border-right-style	Sets the right border style of an element.	none | hidden | dotted | dashed | solid | double | groove | ridge | inset | outset
border-right-width	Sets the right border width of an element.	thin | medium | thick | *length*
border-style	Sets the style of an element's borders.	none | hidden | dotted | dashed | solid | double | groove | ridge | inset | outset
border-top	Sets all of the width, style, and color properties for an element's top border in one declaration.	*border-top-width* | *border-top-style* | *border-top-color*
border-top-color	Sets the top border color of an element.	*color_name* | *hex_number* | *rgb_number* | transparent
border-top-style	Sets the top border style of an element.	none | hidden | dotted | dashed | solid | double | groove | ridge | inset | outset
border-top-width	Sets the top border width of an element.	thin | medium | thick | *length*
border-width	Sets all of the border properties in one declaration.	thin | medium | thick | *length*
outline	Sets all of the outline properties in one declaration.	*outline-color outline-style outline-width*
outline-color	Sets the outline color of an element or group of elements.	*color_name* | *hex_number* | *rgb_number* | invert

Property	Description	Values
outline-style	Sets the outline style color of an element or group of elements.	none | hidden | dotted | dashed | solid | double | groove | ridge | inset | outset
outline-width	Sets the outline width of an element or group of elements.	thin | medium | thick | *length*

DIMENSION PROPERTIES

Property	Description	Values
height	Determines the height of an element.	auto | *length* | %
max-height	Determines the maximum height of an element.	none | *length* | %
max-width	Determines the maximum width of an element.	none | *length* | %
min-height	Determines the minimum height of an element.	*length* | %
min-width	Determines the minimum width of an element.	*length* | %
width	Determines the width of an element.	auto | *length* | %

FONT PROPERTIES

Property	Description	Values
font	Sets all the font properties in one declaration.	*font-style* | *font-variant* | *font-weight* | *font-size/line-height* | *font-family* | caption | icon | menu | message-box | small-caption | status-bar
font-family	Specifies a list of font names or generic font names.	*family-name* | *generic-family*

Property	Description	Values
font-size	Specifies the size of a font.	xx-small | x-small | small | medium | large | x-large | xx-large | smaller | larger | *length* | *%*
font-style	Sets the style of a font.	normal | italic | oblique
font-variant	Specifies whether the font should appear in small caps.	normal | small-caps
font-weight	Sets the weight of a font.	normal | bold | bolder | lighter | 100 | 200 | 300 | 400 | 500 | 600 | 700 | 800 | 900

LIST PROPERTIES

Property	Description	Values
list-style	Sets all of the list-style-type, list-style-image, and list-style-position properties in one declaration.	*list-style-type* | *list-style-position* | *list-style-image*
list-style-image	Defines an image that will be used as a bullet in an unordered list.	none | url
list-style-position	Determines the indentation for the bullet or number in an unordered or ordered list.	inside | outside
list-style-type	Specifies the bullet or numbering style for an unordered or ordered list.	none | circle | disc | square | armenian | decimal | decimal-leading-zero | georgian | lower-alpha | lower-greek | lower-latin | lower-roman | upper-alpha | upper-latin | upper-roman

MARGIN PROPERTIES

Property	Description	Values
margin	Sets all of the margin properties in one declaration.	auto | *length* | %
margin-bottom	Sets the bottom margin of an element.	auto | *length* | %
margin-left	Sets the left margin of an element.	auto | *length* | %
margin-right	Sets the right margin of an element.	auto | *length* | %
margin-top	Sets the top margin of an element.	auto | *length* | %

PADDING PROPERTIES

Property	Description	Values
padding	Sets all of the padding properties in one declaration.	*padding-top* | *padding-right* | *padding-bottom* | *padding-left*
padding-bottom	Sets the bottom padding of an element.	*length unit* | *percentage unit*
padding-left	Sets the left padding of an element.	*length unit* | *percentage unit*
padding-right	Sets the right padding of an element.	*length unit* | *percentage unit*
padding-top	Sets the top padding of an element.	*length unit* | *percentage unit*

POSITIONING PROPERTIES

Property	Description	Values
bottom	Determines the position of an element's bottom margin in relation to the document window.	auto | *length* | *%*
clip	Determines the region of an element that is displayed.	rect (*top, right, bottom, left*) | auto
display	Specifies whether to display an element.	none | block | inline | inline-block | inline-table | list-item | run-in | table | table-caption | table-cell | table-column | table-column-group | table-footer-group | table-header-group | table-row | table-row-group
left	Determines the position of an element's left margin in relation to the document window.	auto | *length* | *%*
overflow	Determines how to handle an image that is bigger than its assigned space.	visible | hidden | scroll | auto
position	Specifies the type of CSS positioning.	absolute | fixed | relative | static
right	Determines the position of an element's right margin in relation to the document window.	auto | *length* | *%*
top	Determines the position of an element's top margin in relation to the document window.	auto | *length* | *%*
visibility	Specifies whether an element is visible.	visible | hidden | collapse
z-index	Determines the order in which dynamically positioned elements are layered.	auto | *number*

PRINT PROPERTIES

Property	Description	Values
orphans	Specifies the minimum number of lines in a block element that must be left at the bottom of a page.	*integer*
page-break-after	Determines how the page will break after an element.	auto | always | avoid | left | right
page-break-before	Determines how the page will break before an element.	auto | always | avoid | left | right
page-break-inside	Determines how the page will break inside an element.	auto | avoid |
widows	Specifies the minimum number of lines in a block element that must be left at the top of a page.	*integer*

TEXT PROPERTIES

Property	Description	Values
color	Specifies the text color.	*color_name* | *hex_number* | *rgb_number*
direction	Determines the text direction of the writing system.	ltr | rtl
letter-spacing	Adjusts the spacing between letters.	normal | *length*
line-height	Determines the line height of an element's text.	normal | *number* | *length* | *%*
text-align	Determines the horizontal alignment of an element's text.	left | right | center | justify
text-decoration	Adds decorations to an element's text.	none | underline | overline | line-through | blink

Property	Description	Values
text-indent	Specifies the indentation of an element's text.	*length* | *%*
text-transform	Determines the capitalization of an element's text.	none | capitalize | uppercase | lowercase
vertical-align	Determines the vertical positioning of an element.	*length* | *%* | baseline | sub | super | top | text-top | middle | bottom | text-bottom
white-space	Determines how to handle an element's white space.	normal | nowrap | pre | pre-line | pre-wrap
word-spacing	Adjusts spacing between words.	normal | *length*

TABLE PROPERTIES

Property	Description	Values
border-collapse	Determines whether to collapse a table's borders.	collapse | separate
border-spacing	Controls the spacing between the borders of a table's adjacent cells.	*length length*
caption-side	Specifies where to place a table's caption.	top | bottom
empty-cells	Determines whether to display the borders and backgrounds of empty cells.	hide | show
table-layout	Forces the browser to lay the table out based on the width of the table and its columns, not on the contents of its cells.	auto | fixed

INDEX